Advance Praise for *Collapse and Revival*

This book makes a valuable contribution to the literature on business cycles by carefully and systematically documenting patterns of global recessions and recoveries. Kose and Terrones have written a timely and authoritative book that is rich in analytical material, yet clear and cogent enough to be of broad interest. *Collapse and Revival* will become a standard reference in the international business cycle literature and is required reading for academics, policymakers, and students interested in understanding macroeconomic fluctuations both at the national level and in the global economy.

Eswar Prasad
Nandlal P. Tolani Senior Professor of Trade Policy and
Professor of Economics, Cornell University

This important new book is a welcome study of global business cycles—a phenomenon that goes back centuries. It defines these cycles and identifies four of them in recent decades. It analyzes their salient characteristics and their relationship to national business cycles. It is a must-read for macroeconomists and policymakers.

Michael Bordo
Board of Governors Professor of Economics
Rutgers University

This impressive work culminates a research program of central importance—the investigation of the definition and nature of global recessions and recoveries. The authors deploy a comprehensive statistical documentation of global business cycles in an accessible—yet empirically rigorous—fashion, weaving in the most recent thinking on the linkages between financial crises, recessions, and recoveries. *Collapse and Revival* is sure to become the standard reference on this important subject.

Menzie Chinn
Professor of Public Affairs and Economics
University of Wisconsin

Finally, a clear and insightful guide to global recessions and recoveries. And just in time, with the world trying to recover from its worst economic beating since the Great Depression. This book, written by two leading economists operating in the heart of Washington, will become the bible on global growth and collapse.

Nicholas Bloom
Professor of Economics
Stanford University

For those who want to understand the evolving nature of global economic interactions, *Collapse and Revival* is a treasure of insights.

Kemal Dervis
Vice President of Global Economy and Development
The Brookings Institution

Economic cycles had long been the object of economic researchers and policymakers, prompting an entire industry of analysts trying to outdo each other in forecasting the next turn in a cycle. Then came the global financial crisis, which made crystal clear that forecasting economic activity without consideration of financial conditions can produce embarrassing results. This book, written while we are climbing out of a deep recession, is a must-read for any student of economic cycles. A big takeaway from the book is that economic recessions that coincide with financial crises are deeper and last longer. Let's hope this message will not be forgotten the next time financial excesses are building up.

Luc Laeven
Director General of Research
European Central Bank

Business cycles in general are only moderately synchronized across countries, but Kose and Terrones identify four episodes in the past half century that truly qualify as global recessions. The most notable are 1975 (oil prices) and 2009 (financial crisis). The authors perform an enormous social service in collecting a large number of economic indicators for a larger number of countries. An updated Burns-Mitchell "judgmental method" is then used to identify national and global recessions. Kose and Terrones find, among other things, that the 2009 recession was the most synchronized in their sample. Perhaps, they suggest, that accounts for the diverse patterns of recovery. It's a fascinating study, one that rewards a closer look. And they leave us with an uplifting message: We recovered after each one.

David Backus
Heinz Riehl Professor
Stern School of Business, New York University

The economic and financial crisis starting in 2008 has been a reminder of the need to better understand the dynamics of recessions and recoveries, as well as their increasing global nature. *Collapse and Revival* provides the most current analysis of these issues and it is a must-read for anyone who wants to have a good understanding of the current state of knowledge of what we know about economic crises, how they happen, how long it takes to recover from them, and how they spread across borders.

Antonio Fatas
The Portuguese Council Chaired Professor of European Studies and
Professor of Economics, INSEAD

Advance Praise for *Collapse and Revival*

What are global recessions and recoveries? What are their causes and consequences? Why is the Great Recession different from previous episodes? What policies can prevent global recessions or mitigate their effects by kick-starting a recovery? In this important book, Ayhan Kose and Marco Terrones address these difficult questions with rigorous definitions, facts (lots of facts!), clear prose, and boxes for readers who want to know more about the technical details. The authors summarize what we know about these important phenomena and the book will become an essential resource for policymakers and practitioners who want to put in place policies that can protect us from these catastrophic events. Researchers will be interested in Kose and Terrones' careful description of the available data, econometric methodology, and analysis of what we still don't know about the causes and consequences of global recessions. I am sure that *Collapse and Revival* will be an important stepping stone for future research in this field. This is super cool stuff!

Ugo Panizza
Pictet Chair in Finance and Development
The Graduate Institute, Geneva

This book is very timely. Written by two of the best experts in the field, it offers an excellent analysis of the causes of global recessions and recoveries. The authors document their main features and describe the events that take place around these episodes in a very accessible manner. A must-read for academics and policymakers alike.

Jakob de Haan
Head of Research of De Nederlandsche Bank and
Professor of Political Economy, University of Groningen

Kose and Terrones have written an impressive book on global business cycles, which affect the lives of billions of people, and yet so far have been rather understudied and, unfortunately, not so well understood. Using a clear yet rigorous style, they explain what causes a recession and what makes it global, and also what drives the ensuing recovery. An in-depth analysis of four global recessions, and in particular the recent financial crisis, provides useful tools for understanding, anticipating, and mitigating the effects of future episodes.

Massimiliano Marcellino
Scientific Chair of the Euro Area Business Cycle Network and
Professor of Econometrics, Bocconi University

This book is a must-read for all students of business cycles. Thinking about economic fluctuations from a national perspective is clearly yesterday's problem; Kose and Terrones have done an invaluable service to the profession by focusing on global fluctuations. Policymakers and academics alike will learn a lot from the clear vision of Kose and Terrones. Highly recommended!

Andrew Rose
Associate Dean and Chair of the Faculty
Haas School of Business, University of California, Berkeley

Kose and Terrones provide a very useful volume aimed at substantially increasing our understanding of truly global recessions and recoveries. *Collapse and Revival* not only is a source of valuable background material on the four post–World War II global recessions but also carefully examines the technical issues in business cycle dating and analysis. The treatment of these issues is thorough. The lessons drawn for policy are well supported.

Edwin (Ted) M. Truman
Non-Resident Senior Fellow
Peterson Institute for International Economics

Collapse and Revival is a seminal study on how to think about the cycles of the global economy, which is more multipolar and more integrated than in the past. The carefully conducted analysis and very useful insights provide an essential perspective for thinking about the current state of the global economy and the policies that are needed to cope with many economic and financial challenges we are facing. The notion that policymakers need to closely monitor the financial cycles in their macroeconomic surveillance is particularly important as it challenges the prevailing way that policymakers look at economies.

Stephen L. Jen
Managing Partner
SLJ Macro Partners LLP

Collapse and Revival is an excellent book. Kose and Terrones make sense of the 2009 global recession by systematically examining its causes and consequences in the context of other historical world recessions and downturns. To accomplish this task, they provide coherent objective definitions of global recessions and recoveries that are sure to be among the standards going forward. Their results provide evidence that global downturns, which have synchronous adverse implications for citizens across the globe, are not isolated events, but are sufficiently common to warrant continued attention by researchers.

Mark M. Spiegel
Vice President, International Research and Director
Center for Pacific Basin Studies
Federal Reserve Bank of San Francisco

Advance Praise for *Collapse and Revival*

This important and deeply innovative book provides invaluable insights into global recessions and recoveries. Kose and Terrones develop a comprehensive analysis of the main features of the global cycles, study the unique properties of the 2009 global recession and the subsequent recovery based on real-world data, and examine the complex interactions between global and national cycles. Understanding these concepts is extremely important for policy design. *Collapse and Revival* is a major contribution to the business cycle literature and to the current debates on policy design in a complex and rapidly changing world. It also opens new doors for future research in many fields of our discipline.

Ali Bayar
President of EcoMod Network and Research Professor
Deutsches Institut für Wirtschaftsforschung

Ayhan Kose and Marco Terrones are two insightful scholars with plenty of policy experience. We have learned a lot about international macroeconomics and policies from them. Once again, they delight us with this thoughtful and relevant book. They analyze global recessions and recoveries that have taken place since 1960, drawing parallels and differences across them. The rigorous description as well as the discussion of policy implications are very important. Scholars and policymakers will gain a lot reading this book—an original and novel study of the global business cycle.

José De Gregorio
Professor, Universidad de Chile
and Peterson Institute for International Economics.

Finally! A cogent and yet highly accessible book about the "double whammies" of economic collapse and revival from all over the world and through recent history. Kose and Terrones not only deconstruct the antecedents of these boom-bust cycles, but they effectively describe their consequences, including the large and persistent human and social costs. The most important chapters emphasize the out-of-phase global and national business cycles and the worsening divergence across countries' fiscal and monetary policies. Our politicians and policymakers better take heed of these lessons.

Andrew Karolyi
Professor of Finance
Cornell University

During the short-lived era of the Great Moderation, much of the economics profession deluded themselves into thinking that the business cycle had been tamed in the advanced economies. As the Global Financial Crisis proved otherwise, the interest in studying the causes and varieties of economic cycles resurfaced in the United States, Europe, and elsewhere. This book is essential reading for those academics, policymakers, and market participants who are interested in gaining a better understanding of the booms and busts, and their milder counterparts, in the global economy. The study of business cycles has a rich history, famously connected to the pioneering work of Burns and Mitchell on the U.S. economy in the 1940s. However, the study of economic cycles in the developing world, which comprises a rapidly growing share of world GDP, has remained comparatively understudied. These authors importantly fill that gap and offer a comprehensive and insightful analysis of modern business cycles and that is truly global in scope.

Carmen M. Reinhart
Minos A. Zombanakis Professor of the International Financial System
Harvard University

Although the global nature of business cycles has been acknowledged by both academics and policymakers, there has not been a comprehensive analysis of the complex interactions between global and regional business cycles. This book provides a thorough overview of the cause and nature of global business cycles in light of the recent global financial crisis. *Collapse and Revival* is a must-read for policymakers as well as students of business cycles, and I would also put this book at the top of the reading list for my students who take international economics courses.

Sunghyun Henry Kim
Professor, Sungkyunkwan University

This innovative book by Kose and Terrones offers a fresh perspective on international business cycles: rather than analyzing such cycles as shocks originating in a particular economy and transmitted internationally through various mechanisms, they consider the world economy as an integrated whole, treating it effectively as a single closed economy. This new global perspective is motivated by two relatively new features of the international economy: much greater integration, both real and financial, among its constituent parts, and the greater weight within the whole of emerging and developing countries, making such economies full participants in the evolution of international business cycles. This appealing perspective will undoubtedly cause us to reconsider how we think about the world economy, and calls in particular for hard thinking about the design of institutional mechanisms for responding to global shocks. The "stylized facts" about global business cycles documented in this book provide the indispensable background for such thinking.

Peter Montiel
Fairleigh S. Dickinson Jr. '41 Professor of Economics
Williams College

Advance Praise for *Collapse and Revival*

What happens when the global economy falls into recession and how does it recover? Kose and Terrones answer these and many other important questions in this comprehensive empirical study of Global Business Cycles. Their new book will be an indispensable resource for all serious students of the business cycle.

Mark Watson
Howard Harrison and Gabrielle Snyder Beck Professor
of Economics and Public Affairs
Princeton University

The world economy is closely interlinked through trade and financial linkages. The book by Ayhan Kose and Marco Terrones expands our knowledge of global recessions and recoveries, which are critical for understanding fluctuations in national economies. Its discussion on the nature of global business cycles and the role of policy provide an important ingredient for scholars and policymakers to guide nations toward more stable and sustainable economic growth.

Jong-Wha Lee
Professor, Korea University and
Former Chief Economist of the Asian Development Bank

A tour de force! The thorough analysis of dramatic global economic collapses presented in this book helps readers understand how major global downturns begin, evolve and get resolved. A must read for policymakers, academicians and all those interested to learn the lessons from the past that can help predict (and perhaps even avoid?) the next global contraction.

Liliana Rojas-Suarez
Senior Fellow
Center for Global Development

Kose and Terrones masterfully condense their well-known research on international business and financial cycles in a multimedia book containing a wealth of data, analyses, and useful tools. Their book combines deep insight into the notion of a "world" business cycle with careful attention to the historical context, skillful use of state of the art research methods, and new multimedia capabilities. *Collapse and Revival* will be an invaluable resource for teaching MBAs, for practitioners scrutinizing the world economic horizon, and fellow scholars in the field on international business cycle research.

Alessandro Rebucci
Assistant Professor
Johns Hopkins University Carey Business School

Kose and Terrones have written a monumental, pathbreaking, encyclopedic and readable book on global business cycles. It is a must-read for everyone interested in, or affected by, the contemporary business cycle and the global economy.

Allen Sinai
Chief Global Economist and Strategist
Decision Economics

The events since 2007 have once again demonstrated how devastating global recessions could be. It is likely that such events will repeat in the future in a highly integrated world economy. Hence, understanding causes of global recessions and what drives global recoveries is essential. In this remarkable book, Ayhan Kose and Marco Terrones concentrate on these issues. *Collapse and Revival* presents great value to readers since it clearly has a say on these extremely important issues.

Fatih Özatay
Professor of Economics
TOBB University of Economics and Technology
and Economic Policy Research Foundation of Turkey (TEPAV)

Kose and Terrones, in this invaluable new work, aim to finally provide a workable definition of what "global recessions" and "global recoveries" are. They do so by systematically looking at the four episodes of global contraction and recovery since World War II. They include the last one—of which the European Union "Sovereign Debt Crisis" was a part, the most widespread and severe of those, and therefore dully called "Great Recession." Even if global growth has now returned, Kose and Terrones also stress the fundamental lesson that economic cycles will always be with us, and that therefore the actions of policymakers should aim not only to "fight the last war" but also to increase resilience for that next economic crisis, which will inevitably come at some point.

Lucio Vinhas de Souza
Team Leader, Economics Team
European Political Strategy Centre
European Commission

A valuable and timely study...The authors expediently address critical issues that have a lot of relevance to today's economic climate, helping us better understand global recessions, and the policy options available to expedite recoveries. We may know a lot about the individual economies but their intricate interaction at the global level clearly requires such deeper analysis. The plain language of the book makes it an easy and enjoyable read.

Murat Ulgen
Global Head of Emerging Markets Research
HSBC

Advance Praise for *Collapse and Revival*

Kose and Terrones have drawn on their years of experience in the international policy arena to write a book about the global business cycle that is comprehensive, rigorous, and accessible. Their analysis provides a framework for thinking about the Great Recession of 2009 in the context of previous recessions and addresses a number of interesting questions. What defines a global business cycle? In what sense was the most recent recession different from previous cyclical downturns? What factors can explain the depth of the most recent recession and the weakness of the recovery, and how much of that experience can be attributed to increased globalization? These questions are central to academics as well as to policymakers. Any student of business cycles, and any policymaker concerned with managing them, will find this both an instructive and an enjoyable read.

Linda Tesar
Professor of Economics
University of Michigan

Despite the voluminous literature on the Great Recession, there is a dearth of studies that provide a historical perspective on the causes of global (as opposed to national) downturns and subsequent recoveries. Kose and Terrones, with their careful and insightful study of the past four global recessions, admirably fill the lacuna. They have made a wonderful contribution by clarifying the basic concepts relating to global business cycles, and using a comprehensive database and findings from various branches of macroeconomic research, documenting their main features. The study provides a superb analysis of the broader economic and financial effects of global recessions and recoveries, interactions between global and national business cycles, efficacy of macroeconomic policies, and the lessons to be drawn from the different episodes. A must-read for policymakers, market participants, economists, and layman alike, especially given the concerns about a lurch into yet another global downturn. A remarkable, invaluable resource.

Manmohan Singh Kumar
Chief Economist, Global Growth Markets
CDPQ

Since the financial crisis of 2007–09, the global economy has been in an uncharted territory, searching desperately to find its way out. The weak recovery in developed countries is now being threatened by the headwinds from emerging market economies. Considering these developments, this book by two leading researchers in the field is a very timely and important contribution to the literature. The authors provide a comprehensive framework to better understand global recessions and recoveries, especially after financial shocks on a global scale.

Kamil Yilmaz
Professor of Economics
Koc University

The Great Recession, global recessions, global recoveries. How can citizens of the world understand these terms when many, including often economists, just toss them around without defining them carefully? This book addresses this confusion head-on. It is a masterful, lucidly written, and easily accessible introduction to the subject of global recessions and recoveries. It explains how everybody gets affected by them and why citizens, and economists, should care about their definition and measurement. Importantly, it provides crucial lessons on how to reduce the chances of a global economic collapse and how to avoid anemic revivals. A highly recommended read.

Stijn Claessens
Senior Advisor, Federal Reserve Board and
Professor of International Finance Policy, University of Amsterdam

In an age of declining barriers to global interaction, real and financial sectors are becoming increasingly integrated across the world. Economists are generally well equipped to study national business cycles, but what about worldwide trends? In the age of globalization, understanding worldwide developments is extremely important for all stakeholders, from policymakers to businesspeople. This comprehensive, insightful, and rigorous study teaches to track, analyze, and interpret global business cycles. Written by top scholars in the field, *Collapse and Revival* features a rich data review of business-cycle trends at all levels and presents established as well as novel empirical tools, including an interesting way of measuring global business cycles. It is easily accessible to a nontechnical audience and includes rich analysis of a wide variety of relevant topics. It is an excellent resource for economists, policymakers, and professionals working in the risk and finance fields.

Michael G. Plummer
Director, SAIS Europe, and Eni Professor of International Economics
Johns Hopkins University

This lucid and timely book fills important gaps in our thinking about how the global economy and markets really work. It is essential reading for policymakers, business leaders, and economists. In clear and jargon-free language, supported by excellent online and media resources, *Collapse and Revival* is an elegant and sophisticated exploration of how global recessions begin and end, two critical economic questions of our time. The authors, members of a new generation of global macroeconomists working at the frontiers of the profession, have made an outstanding contribution to the field.

Jean Pierre Lacombe
Chief Global Markets
Head of IFC Research

COLLAPSE
AND REVIVAL

COLLAPSE
AND REVIVAL

UNDERSTANDING GLOBAL
RECESSIONS AND RECOVERIES

M. AYHAN KOSE • MARCO E. TERRONES

INTERNATIONAL MONETARY FUND

© 2015 International Monetary Fund

Cataloging-in-Publication Data
Joint Bank-Fund Library

Kose, M. Ayhan.
   Collapse and revival : understanding global recessions and recoveries / by M. Ayhan Kose and
     Marco Terrones. – Washington, D.C. : International Monetary Fund, 2015.
        pages ; cm.

   Includes bibliographical references and index.

   1. Financial crises. 2. Recessions. 3. Business cycles. 4. Global Financial Crisis, 2008–2009.
I. Terrones, Marco. II. International Monetary Fund.

HB3722.K67 2015

Recommended citation: Kose, M. Ayhan, and Marco E. Terrones. 2015. *Collapse and Revival: Understanding Global Recessions and Recoveries*. Washington: International Monetary Fund.

ISBN: 978-1-48437-041-4 (paper)
ISBN: 978-1-51357-002-0 (hardback)
ISBN: 978-1-48439-173-0 (ePub)
ISBN: 978-1-48434-244-2 (Mobi)
ISBN: 978-1-47552-336-2 (PDF)

Information about and access to digital content associated with this book are available at:
www.elibrary.imf.org/CollapseAndRevival

Publication orders may be placed online, by fax, or through the mail:
International Monetary Fund, Publication Services
P.O. Box 92780, Washington, DC 20090, U.S.A.
Telephone: (202) 623-7430 Fax: (202) 623-7201
E-mail: publications@imf.org
www.imfbookstore.org
www.elibrary.imf.org

To Zeynep and Hüseyin

To Maria Teresa, Gianmarco, and Jasmine

Summary of Contents

Contents

All the figures and tables were created by the authors using the data sources outlined in Appendix B.

TABLES

MULTIMEDIA CONTENT

Video

Audio

Timeline

Acknowledgments

At the heart of this book lie interactions with our many excellent coauthors and colleagues who greatly helped us in shaping our research on global recessions and recoveries. We are grateful to Kenneth Rogoff for his constant support of our research agenda. We are thankful to Nicholas Bloom and Prakash Loungani for their contributions to some of the background studies we produced together. We would like to thank Olivier Blanchard, Menzie Chinn, Stijn Claessens, Jörg Decressin, and Thomas Helbling for their detailed comments. We are grateful to Tamim Bayoumi, Charles Calomiris, José de Gregorio, Francis Diebold, Sandra Eickmeier, Alejandro Izquierdo, Massimiliano Marcellino, Enrique Mendoza, Adrian Pagan, Eswar Prasad, Alessandro Rebucci, Liliana Rojas-Suarez, Mark Spiegel, Gustavo Yamada, Kamil Yilmaz, Kei-Mu Yi, and participants at many conferences and seminars for useful suggestions on the preliminary drafts of some chapters. We owe a debt of gratitude to Ezgi Ozturk for outstanding research assistance. Bennet Voorhees provided excellent research support for some of the background studies.

We have been extremely lucky to work with a number of consummate professionals who were involved in the production process. We are thankful to Mark E. Felsenthal, Tracey Lookadoo, and Dana Vorisek for editorial assistance. We are indebted to Jeremy Clift, Gemma Diaz, Joanne Creary Johnson, Linda Griffin Kean, and Patricia C. Loo of the International Monetary Fund's Communications Department for patiently coordinating the production process.

We would also like to thank the Multimedia Services Section of the IMF's Technology and General Services Department, including video producer Dana Schiopu; video/photo project manager Nailah Fields; video editors Gokhan Karahan, Kris Rucinski, Bill Connell, and N'Namdi Washington; and Alex Curro, who handled the video archive. Dana Schiopu and Steve Jaffe were responsible for photography; and Gokhan Karahan, Kris Rucinski, and Alex Silver oversaw the video shoots.

The views expressed in this book are our own and do not necessarily represent the views and policies of the institutions with which we are affiliated.

About the Authors

M. Ayhan Kose is Director of the World Bank Group's Development Prospects Group. He was previously Assistant to the Director of the Research Department at the IMF. He has published extensively in leading academic and policy-oriented outlets. He holds a PhD in economics from the Tippie College of Business of the University of Iowa.

Marco E. Terrones is a Deputy Division Chief in the Research Department of the International Monetary Fund. He has published in top journals, several collected volumes, and the IMF's *World Economic Outlook*. His work has been featured in prominent media outlets. He holds a PhD in economics from the University of Wisconsin at Madison.

Introduction

ABOUT THIS BOOK

Much has been written about economic setbacks at the national level. Yet our understanding of globally destructive economic events remains limited. The events of the past eight years have made this evident: the 2008–09 global financial crisis came largely as a surprise, and there was no clear consensus about the appropriate response to either the painful recession generated by the crisis or the sluggish recovery that followed. This book seeks to fill that unfortunate void.

Recessions can be devastating events and can have protracted effects. The world is still recovering from the most recent one—dubbed the Great Recession because of its scale and global reach. What makes a recession a truly global event? What causes a worldwide downturn? Why was the most recent global recession as severe as it was, and does the increasing interconnectedness of the world economy mean that such synchronized events are more likely in the future? What lessons can guide policymakers and scholars in the future?

Ayhan Kose and Marco Terrones seek to answer these questions. To aid our understanding of globally catastrophic economic events, they first clarify key concepts. They define what makes a recession global and identify four such episodes: 1975, 1982, 1991, and 2009. They track the global business cycle through the collapses associated with these global recessions and back to the global recoveries that ensued.

HOW THIS BOOK IS ORGANIZED

Part I sets the stage by defining critical terms—most important, global recession and recovery—and by outlining the authors' methodology. Part II studies the four worldwide recession episodes, including what lay behind the collapses and how the revivals unfolded. Part III puts the 2009 episode under a microscope to examine why its reverberations were so widely felt and why the recovery has been so anemic. Part IV analyzes global recessions in the context of global business cycles and draws lessons for policymakers and scholars. A series of appendices offer in-depth information on the country-specific effects of global recessions, including a detailed timeline, excerpts taken from the media articles covering these historical events, and summaries of relevant academic studies.

ABOUT THE MULTIMEDIA CONTENT

The digital editions of this book are supplemented by a variety of audiovisual materials that provide real-world examples and background to help readers better understand the full impact of global recessions on people's lives. Access to the digital content is available on the enclosed DVD and on this website: www.elibrary.imf.org/CollapseAndRevival. The supplementary material includes an interactive timeline of the four global recessions, an overview video about the findings of the book, video interviews with the authors, detailed analysis of the impact of global crises in various geographic regions, and video coverage of the 2008–09 global financial crisis. Only by understanding the factors behind global recessions can we forge better tools to predict them, mitigate their adverse effects, and promote healthy recoveries. This innovative and comprehensive book is a fundamental step toward improving our understanding of these devastating events.

Icons Used in This Book

The icons below are used to indicate the availability online or on the enclosed DVD of related audio-visual materials. These are hyperlinked in digital editions of this book.

 VIDEO: Included are video interviews with the authors, detailed analysis of the impact of the crises in various geographic regions, and media coverage and analysis of the global financial crisis sparked by the collapse of U.S. investment bank Lehman Brothers.

 AUDIO: Included are speeches and comments about global crises.

 TIMELINE: An interactive timeline focuses on each specific global recession: 1975, 1982, 1991, and 2009.

Information about and access to digital content associated with this book are available at:
www.elibrary.imf.org/CollapseAndRevival

These icons were created for the Noun Project (thenounproject.com) by Mike Arndt (video icon), Nate Eul (audio icon), and Leinad Lehmko (timeline icon).

The duller textbook definition of a recession is two consecutive quarters of declining output. But recession can also be used to describe any period in which GDP growth falls below an economy's trend growth rate . . . Another complication is the definition of a world recession.

The Economist (1999)

Last September, you pressed me hard on whether the IMF officially viewed the projected downturn as a global recession. My answer was that we did not have an official definition. No one seemed to believe me, though it was true.

Kenneth Rogoff (2002a)

Many economists are now predicting the worst global recession since the 1930s. Such grim warnings discourage spending by households and businesses, depressing output even more. It is unfortunate, therefore, that there is so much confusion about what pundits mean when they talk about a "global recession"... The trouble is that there is no agreed definition of a global recession.

The Economist (2008a)

Leading economic organizations and business leaders are talking about "a global recession." But it is not easy to define. It really depends what you mean. Even for national economies the word "recession" has more than one meaning. But although there is more than one, these definitions are widely used and understood. That is less true of global recessions. I have heard several different thresholds (of global growth)...for judging whether a year counts as a (global) recession. Global output growth below 3, 2.5, and 2 percent have all been suggested.

Andrew Walker (2009)

Watch out. The world is not ready for the next recession... It is only a matter of time before the next recession strikes. The danger is that, having used up their arsenal, governments and central banks will not have the ammunition to fight the next recession. Paradoxically, reducing that risk requires a willingness to keep policy looser for longer today.

The Economist (2015)

CHAPTER 1

Overview

The beginning of a long nightmare . . .

Recessions are devastating events that can wreak havoc on people's lives and cause lingering damage to national economies. The world is still recovering from the most recent global recession—dubbed the Great Recession because of its scale and reach—and the possibility of another downturn persists as the world economy struggles to regain lost ground.

The 2008 bankruptcy of Lehman Brothers, one of the largest U.S. investment banks, sparked turmoil in the world economy and financial system, and the resulting global recession had dire and extreme consequences. What began as loan defaults in the U.S. subprime mortgage market spiraled into a series of events that cut through the international financial system, leading to corporate defaults, slashed stock values, and diminished household wealth. The downturn put millions of people out of work and triggered a huge rise in the debt of nations.

The effects are still with us. Despite tentative signs of a pickup in 2010–11, stimulated by aggressive central bank interventions, the world has since been battered by a series of setbacks that have slowed the recovery. In 2012, the euro area financial crisis frustrated hopes for a rapid rebound. After the turbulence in Europe appeared to be under control, the recovery continued to lag behind expectations in 2014, despite a pickup in growth in advanced economies, as emerging market and developing country economies slowed.

In early 2015, signs of durable growth in the United States stirred optimism about global growth prospects, but significant risks continue to cloud the outlook. The impending normalization of monetary policies in advanced economies poses challenges for the developing world. The fragility of growth in the euro area and Japan causes concern. A synchronized and protracted slowdown in emerging market economies is troubling. Daily headlines bring fresh reminders of worrisome geopolitical risks.

Thus, the possibility of another global recession lingers in light of the persistently weak recovery, even though damage from the previous one has yet to be fully repaired. Economists generally expect economies to bounce back to trend growth after a recession; this time, the pace and strength of the recovery have repeatedly disappointed. Add to that the side effect of continued increases in income inequality, particularly in some advanced economies, where the wealthiest have moved ahead while the fortunes of the middle classes have stagnated since the recession.

03:31

The Turning Point: The collapse of Lehman Brothers was a critical turning point during the last global financial crisis.

. . . that we don't fully understand

What is increasingly clear is that we do not fully understand what causes global recessions and what drives global recoveries. Moreover, despite ubiquitous discussion in the media and in policy circles about recessions on a national and global scale, there are, surprisingly, no commonly accepted definitions of global recession and global recovery.

This book attempts to define the terms "global recession" and "global recovery" and to delve into their causes and consequences. We document their main features and describe the events that take place around these episodes. In light of our findings, we put the latest global recession and ongoing recovery in perspective. In addition, we analyze the interactions between global and national business cycles.

01:00
What is a global recession?

What is a global recession? A recession can be called global when there is a contraction in world real output per capita accompanied by a broad, synchronized decline in various other measures of global economic activity. This has happened four times over the past half century: in 1975, 1982, 1991, and 2009. Although each episode had its own unique features, there are many similarities.

A global recession corresponds to a contraction in world real output per capita accompanied by a broad, synchronized decline in various other measures of global economic activity.

The world economy also experienced two periods—in 1998 and 2001—when growth slowed significantly without tipping into outright recession. The four global recessions and two slowdowns we identify during 1960–2014 together imply that the world economy comes to the verge of a recession or a near-stall every nine years, with a 7 percent chance of a global recession in any given year.

What is a global recovery? A recovery can be defined as global when there is a broad rebound in worldwide activity one to three years following a global recession. Historically, the world economy has been able to return to its pre-recession level of output within a year after a recession.

01:01
What is a global recovery?

What happens during global recessions and recoveries? During a global recession, the average annual decline in world output per capita is about 0.7 percent—roughly 3 percentage points lower than the global average rate of growth. In addition, a wide range of macroeconomic and financial variables decline across the board during global recessions. Global recoveries are characterized by a synchronized pickup in worldwide consumption, investment, and trade. The average growth of world output per capita is 2.3 percent during a global recovery. Credit and asset prices fluctuate sharply around the occurrence of global recessions and recoveries.

A global recovery is a broad rebound in worldwide activity in one to three years following a global recession.

What is unique about the latest recession and subsequent recovery? The 2009 episode was the most severe of the four global recessions of the past half century and the only one during which world output contracted outright—truly deserving of the "Great Recession" label. The recovery, on the other hand, has played out along significantly different trajectories for advanced versus emerging market economies. For advanced economies, it has been the weakest recovery among the four episodes; for emerging market economies—at least until 2014—it has been the strongest.

What explains the depth of the 2009 global recession and the weakness of the recovery in advanced economies? Four principal factors appear to be at work: the highly synchronized nature of the recession, the severity of financial disruption preceding the recession, unusually high levels of macroeconomic and policy uncertainty during the recovery, and the divergent paths of fiscal and monetary policies and the unevenness of their relative effectiveness after 2010. While each of these factors has played a special role, their unfortunate coincidence appears to have led to an unusually damaging episode.

The 2009 global recession was the most synchronized of the four episodes, with almost all advanced economies and a large number of emerging market and developing economies simultaneously experiencing recessions. This is important because historical evidence suggests that highly synchronized recessions tend to be deeper and longer. Moreover, recoveries that follow synchronized recessions are often slower.

The recent global recession also coincided with the most severe financial crisis since the Great Depression. Recessions accompanied by serious financial market turmoil often lead to larger contractions in output and last longer than other downturns. Recoveries following such recessions tend to be weaker and more protracted. For advanced economies, the 2009 global recession was a textbook example of these effects.

Furthermore, macroeconomic and policy uncertainty have remained unusually high during the latest recovery. This has contributed to the dismal performance of labor markets—in the form of persistently high unemployment and flat wages—and stagnant investment growth in advanced economies. Indeed, evidence suggests that periods of elevated uncertainty coincide with lower growth. Recessions accompanied by high uncertainty are often deeper, and recoveries coinciding with excessive macroeconomic and policy uncertainty are generally weaker.

In addition, fiscal and monetary policies in advanced economies appear to play a major role in explaining the dynamics of recession and recovery. Sizable and internationally coordinated fiscal and monetary stimulus programs were instrumental in supporting aggregate demand during the worst of the global financial crisis in 2008–09. However, market pressures and political constraints forced some advanced economies to withdraw fiscal support in 2010 and others to actively pursue fiscal austerity. Some, notably the United States, also introduced extraordinarily loose monetary policies to boost demand and reduce unemployment.

The cutoff of fiscal stimulus made the paths of government spending in these economies quite different than during past recoveries, when fiscal policy was decisively expansionary. Monetary policy has stayed highly accommodative since 2008, but its effectiveness has been hampered by the zero lower bound in

01:16
Former U.K. Prime Minister Gordon Brown recalls the aftermath of the Lehman Brothers failure.

interest rates and the severity of the disruption to financial markets. The divergence between fiscal and monetary policies during the recent recovery has become increasingly pronounced and has led to a difference in the effectiveness of policies as well, reflected by divergent growth paths among recovering economies. Notably, growth in the United States—where monetary policy was aggressively loose—began to improve in 2014, whereas growth has remained weak in Europe, where the central bank was more cautious and policymakers in many countries stayed committed to fiscal austerity for an extended period.

How does global growth interact with domestic growth during global recessions and recoveries? In a highly integrated world economy, national business cycles have become more tightly linked to the global business cycle. The link is even stronger during global recessions. Worldwide downturns tend to have a larger impact on advanced economies than on developing economies. Moreover, countries are often more sensitive to the global cycle the more integrated they are into the global economy.

"Collapse and Revival"

The title of our book aims to describe the evolution of global activity during periods of global recession and recovery. In each of the four global recession episodes we examine, the average world citizen's income declined. Moreover, these episodes led to enormous and long-lasting human and social costs—millions of people lost their jobs, their homes, or both; businesses closed; financial markets plunged; and income inequality widened. In other words, the world economy experienced a period of *collapse* during each global recession, stoking fears of economic apocalypse. After each global recession, however, the world economy was able to go through a period of *revival*.

Collapse and revival are unavoidable features of the global business cycle.

Accepting the endurance of the global cycle

Despite persistent declarations to the contrary, history shows that the global business cycle is alive and well. Therein lies the simple message of our book: collapses and revivals are regular features of the global business cycle. Any prediction that there will be no "next" collapse should thus be met with extreme caution. At the same time, we must be ambitious in our search for better policy prescriptions to mitigate the massive costs associated with collapses while seeking ways to accelerate revivals.

PART I

Setting the Stage

The Rediscovery of the Business Cycle is a sign of the times. Not much more than a decade ago, in what now seems a more innocent age, the "New Economics" had become orthodoxy. Its basic tenet, repeated in similar words was . . . "the conviction that business cycles were not inevitable" . . . [I]t was not until the events of 1974 and 1975, when a recession sprung on an unsuspecting world with an intensity unmatched in the post–World War II period, that the lessons of the "New Economics" were seriously challenged.

Paul A. Volcker (1978)

The most important point to remember is that the business cycle will never be eliminated; it is part of human nature. Indeed, once people think that the cycle has become a thing of the past, they act in ways that sow the seeds of the next recession. If central banks succeed in postponing a recession, they will simply encourage more reckless behavior, making the next downturn worse.

The Economist (2002)

CHAPTER 2

Global Cycles: Toward a Better Understanding

The U.S. baseball season culminates in a championship called the World Series, reflecting a time when the United States was the world when it came to baseball. Likewise, in the 1960s, a recession in the United States could just as well have been called a global recession. The United States accounted for a large share of world output, and cyclical activity in much of the rest of the world was dependent on U.S. conditions. What constitutes a global recession today? What is a global recovery? And what really happens during these episodes? This chapter introduces the conceptual framework we use to study these questions, explains how the rise of emerging market economies changed the global business cycle, and presents a road map for our journey toward a better understanding of global recessions and recoveries.

FUNDAMENTAL QUESTIONS IN SEARCH OF ANSWERS

04:10

Global Cycles:
Toward a better understanding of global business cycles

The depth and breadth of the worldwide recession associated with the 2007–09 financial crisis fueled intensive debate about global business cycles, and the ensuing recovery has added a new twist to these discussions. Three fundamental questions have anchored the debates: What is a global recession? What do we mean by a global recovery? And what really happens during these episodes? Although these issues have taken center stage, our understanding of them is surprisingly limited, primarily reflecting widespread confusion about the very definitions of the underlying concepts.

What is behind this confusion? A recession, by definition, implies a contraction in national gross domestic product (GDP).[1] But the global economy rarely contracts because countries that experience recessions seldom do so in a way that is synchronized enough to translate into an outright decline in world GDP. This difficulty in describing a global recession, in turn, makes it challenging to concretely define a global recovery. Although there are simple rules of thumb to describe a national recession, such as two consecutive quarters of decline in national output, it is not easy to map such rules in a global context. For example, it is difficult to create quarterly GDP series for the world economy because most countries do not have reliable quarterly series over extended periods.

Why Do We Care?

01:22

Why Collapse and Revival? The authors outline the purpose of this book.

Why is it important to have a good understanding of global recessions and recoveries? There are at least three main reasons.

First, as we extensively document in this book, global recessions are highly synchronized and costly events. When a country faces an isolated recession, this probably reflects domestic problems. The country can then employ a wide range of policy tools (if it has the policy space) to cope with a national recession. A global recession, however, often means that a number of countries are subject to a global shock or simultaneously suffer from various domestic economic problems. This might require international coordination of policies to dampen the impact of the global recession on national economies. A solid understanding of the main features of global recessions provides a wealth of lessons that can help mobilize such coordination efforts.

Second, understanding the nature of events surrounding global recessions is critical for effective monitoring of the evolution of national cycles. This is one of the major elements of economic surveillance at the national, regional, and global levels. As we discuss, there are complex linkages between global and national cycles, and the nature of these linkages is very much influenced by the state of the global cycle. For example, the impact of global growth on national growth is much greater during global recessions. Understanding such intricate linkages is vital if we are to better monitor economic activity.

Finally, a good grasp of the concepts of global recession and recovery is obviously necessary to develop analytical models of the global business cycle. Among their many purposes, such models can be used to study the sources of the global cycle, to study the nature of global shocks and their transmission mechanisms across borders, and to forecast fluctuations in world output.

What Does This Book Do?

We provide a comprehensive analysis of global recessions and recoveries. Specifically, we define global recessions and recoveries, document their main features, describe the events surrounding these episodes, put the latest global recession and ongoing recovery in perspective, and analyze the interactions between the global cycle and national business cycles.

We present a careful study of the evolution of global activity during global recessions and recoveries. Global recessions have been periods of collapse, with devastating human and social costs that lead to fears of economic apocalypse. A period of revival has followed each of them, but recovery has often been a long and painful process for some countries, including for many advanced economies during the last episode.

Global recessions have been periods of collapse, with devastating human and social costs that lead to fears of economic apocalypse.

Yet, our message is simple: collapse and revival are unavoidable phases of the global business cycle. This makes it all the more important to improve our understanding of global recessions and recoveries. We ultimately need to develop better policies in order to mitigate the costs associated with collapses while simultaneously accelerating revivals.

How Do We Do It?

A comprehensive book on global recessions and recoveries necessarily includes a healthy combination of the basic findings from academic research and insights from media articles describing the key events at the time of these episodes. The core of this book is based on a research program on global and national business cycles, and we also make extensive use of analytical findings from other branches of macroeconomic research, including research on fiscal and monetary policies, financial crises and cycles, labor markets, and uncertainty. For a better grasp of the key events surrounding global recessions and recoveries, we also conducted a detailed search of media articles around these episodes.

For readers interested in the background academic research, we provide short surveys of the relevant work in FOCUS boxes at the end of some chapters, and cite a number of related studies in notes at the end of the book. In addition, we provide a rich set of excerpts taken from the media articles published at the time of the episodes. These are particularly useful for readers interested in historical anecdotes and seeking a better sense of the prevailing public narrative.

CHANGING NATURE OF THE GLOBAL BUSINESS CYCLE

Before defining global recession and recovery, we need to define the global business cycle. Our definition is quite simple, drawing a parallel to the traditional characterization of a national business cycle[2]—global business cycles are a type of fluctuation found in worldwide economic activity: a global cycle consists of expansions occurring at about the same time in many indicators of global economic activity, followed by similarly global recessions and recoveries which merge into the expansion phase of the next global cycle.[3] A FOCUS box at the end of this chapter briefly introduces the research on global business cycles.

Our understanding of the global business cycle has evolved over time: in the 1960s, it was sufficient to look at cyclical fluctuations in activity in advanced economies, the United States in particular, to have a good sense of it. These countries accounted for the lion's share of world output, nearly 70 percent in the 1960s. Moreover, cyclical activity in much of the rest of the world was largely dependent on conditions in these economies, as they accounted for close to 70 percent of global growth (Figure 2.1).

With the share of advanced economies in world output down to less than 60 percent over the past 10 years, and their contribution to world growth at

FIGURE 2.1
Distribution of World Output and Growth

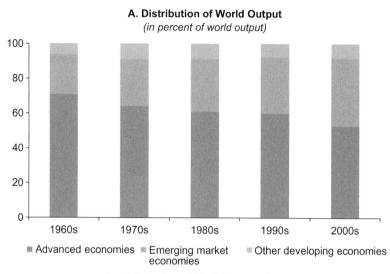

A. Distribution of World Output
(in percent of world output)

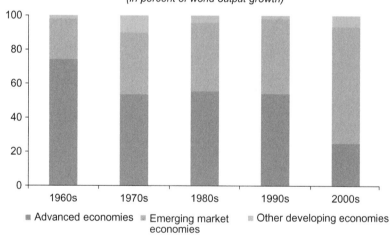

B. Distribution of World Output Growth
(in percent of world output growth)

Note: Each bar in the upper panel corresponds to the average distribution of world output among country groups in the respective decade (computed using purchasing-power-parity exchange rates). Each bar in the lower panel corresponds to the average of each country group's contribution to growth in world gross domestic product in the respective decade. The 2000s period includes 2000–12.

about 20 percent, the coincidence between business cycles in advanced economies and global business cycles can no longer be taken for granted. Indeed, in 2007, at the start of the slowdown in economic activity in the United States and other advanced economies, the hope was that emerging market and developing economies would be somewhat insulated from these developments by the size and strength of their domestic demand and the increased importance of trade among themselves.[4]

FIGURE 2.2
World Trade and Financial Integration

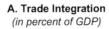

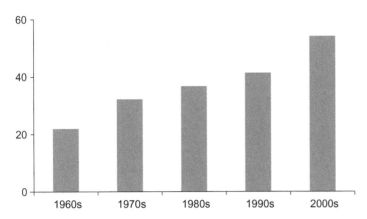

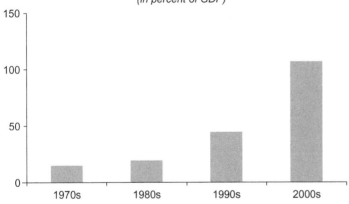

Note: Trade integration is the ratio of total exports and imports to world gross domestic product (GDP). Financial integration is the ratio of total inflows and outflows to world GDP. Each bar corresponds to the average of the indicated measure in the respective decade. The 2000s period includes 2000–12.

At the same time, however, economies are more integrated today through trade and financial flows than in the 1960s, creating greater potential for international spillovers and contagion effects (Figure 2.2). The higher degree of integration increases the feedback, in both directions, between business cycle developments in advanced economies and those in emerging market and developing economies. This raises the odds of more pronounced global business cycles. The implication is that we need a measure of the global business cycle that can account for these evolving changes in the world economy.

Economies are more integrated today through trade and financial flows than in the 1960s, creating greater potential for international spillovers and contagion effects.

MEASURING THE GLOBAL BUSINESS CYCLE

Our measure of the global business cycle tracks yearly movements in world real GDP per capita. This corresponds to the difference between the weighted rate of growth in real GDP of the large number of countries in our data sample and the rate of growth of their populations. We employ a per capita measure as this takes into account the heterogeneity in population growth rates across countries—in particular, emerging market and developing economies tend to have both faster GDP growth than advanced economies and higher rates of population growth.

IDENTIFYING THE TURNING POINTS

To determine the turning points of global business cycles, we employ both a statistical and a judgmental method. These are standard methods used for identifying peaks and troughs in national business cycles. The statistical method identifies local maximum and minimum values of the global GDP per capita series over a given period. The method simply implies that a global recession takes place when the growth rate of these series is negative.

The judgmental method follows the spirit of the approach used by the National Bureau of Economic Research to identify recessions in the United States and the Centre for Economic Policy Research in the euro area. We apply this method at the global level by looking at several indicators of global activity: real GDP per capita, industrial production, unemployment, trade and capital flows, and energy consumption.

The two complementary methods provide an intuitively appealing characterization of the turning points in the global business cycle and translate into a concrete definition of a global recession. Specifically, we define a global recession as a contraction in world real GDP per capita accompanied by a broad decline in various other measures of global economic activity. Because we use annual data, a global recession lasts at least one year. Our definition of a global recovery also closely follows the standard definition used in the context of national business cycles. The recovery phase is associated with a broad rebound in activity during the first year following the trough of the global business cycle. In addition, we examine the evolution of global activity in the first three years after a global recession, recognizing that a global recovery can take longer than a year.

A global recession is a contraction in world real GDP per capita accompanied by a broad decline in various other measures of global economic activity.

A ROAD MAP

Here is a brief road map for our journey toward a better understanding of global recessions and recoveries.

In Chapter 3, we introduce our methodology. We construct a comprehensive database that includes a large number of countries and covers 1960–2012 (we extend our sample using forecast values whenever possible). The database allows us to examine fluctuations in the real economy and the financial sector because it includes a wide range of macroeconomic and financial variables. We then present our approach to defining global recession and recovery and discuss the identification of the turning points in the global business cycle. Readers mainly interested in the properties of global recessions and recoveries can skip Chapter 3 and move directly to Part II.

In Chapter 4, we identify the four global recessions since 1960: 1975, 1982, 1991, and 2009. We present a brief narrative of the key events surrounding each episode and analyze the factors that led to a contraction in global GDP per capita.

In Chapters 5 and 6, we document the main features of global recessions and recoveries. In other words, we analyze what really happens during periods of collapse and revival of the world economy. We study the behavior of macroeconomic and financial variables and investigate how the world economy and different groups of countries perform during global recessions and recoveries. We also examine the similarities and differences across the four episodes. The 2009 global recession is particularly interesting as it coincided with the most severe global financial crisis since the Great Depression.[5] We focus on how that recession and the ensuing recovery compare with previous episodes. In addition, we analyze the two global downturns (1998 and 2001), during which the world economy slowed significantly but was able to escape an outright recession.

The depth of the 2009 global recession and the sluggish recovery in advanced economies have been topics of intense discussion. In Part III, we analyze the main factors that explain the severity of the 2009 recession and the weak and protracted nature of the recovery. Specifically, we consider the roles of four factors: the highly synchronized nature of the global recession; the severity of financial disruption during 2007–09; the unusually high levels of macroeconomic and policy uncertainty during the recovery; and the surprising divergence of macroeconomic policies and their effectiveness after 2010.

In Chapter 7, we study the extent and implications of the synchronization of national business cycles during global recessions. The 2009 global recession was unique in its unprecedented reach, with almost all advanced economies and a large number of emerging market and developing economies experiencing synchronized contractions in activity. We also analyze how the real economy and financial markets exhibit highly synchronized behavior during global recessions. We then examine the implications of highly synchronized recessions for the depth and duration of these episodes and subsequent recoveries. In addition, we review the literature on the impact of the forces of globalization on the degree of business cycle synchronization.

In Chapter 8, we turn to the more controversial question of how financial crises affect the nature of recessions and recoveries. A number of commentators argue that recessions with financial market problems often lead to larger contractions in output and last longer and that recoveries from such recessions tend to be weaker and slower. In contrast, some others claim that such recoveries are no different than others. We carefully analyze the implications of financial disruptions for the real economy and examine the behavior of a wide range of macroeconomic and financial variables during recessions and recoveries associated with such disruptions. We also summarize the literature on the implications of financial crises for recessions and recoveries.

The role of macroeconomic and policy uncertainty has been in the forefront of many discussions about the nature of the latest recovery. This is easy to understand since the ongoing recovery has seen bouts of elevated uncertainty. In Chapter 9, we study the main features of various measures of uncertainty and their association with growth and business cycles in advanced economies, and we interpret the evidence in light of findings from recent research.

Another major debate since 2008 has revolved around the design and use of fiscal and monetary policies. Unlike during the previous episodes, the response to the latest global recovery has featured substantially different paths for fiscal and monetary policies, mainly in advanced economies. In Chapter 10, we examine how these policies have evolved in different groups of countries. In addition, we summarize the literature on the effectiveness of fiscal and monetary policies in mitigating the adverse effects of recessions.

In Part IV, we turn back to the global business cycle. We study the linkages between the global cycle and national cycles in Chapter 11. These manifested themselves in surprisingly different ways during the 2009 global recession and the ensuing recovery, as growth performance varied significantly across different groups of countries. We examine how the sensitivity of national growth to global growth changes over the global business cycle and varies by country. The chapter also includes a brief discussion of the literature on the channels of business cycle transmission from advanced economies to emerging market and developing economies.

We conclude in Chapter 12 with a summary of lessons from our findings and a discussion of their implications for policy design. We also consider areas for future work that could enrich our understanding of global recessions and recoveries.

FOCUS

IS THERE A GLOBAL BUSINESS CYCLE?

Several studies offer extensive evidence for cross-country linkages in business cycle fluctuations, strongly supporting the existence of a global business cycle.[6] Some of these studies focus on the importance of global, regional, and group- and country-specific factors in accounting for fluctuations in the output, consumption, and investment of a large number of countries.

Global Business Cycles

Global (common) factors explain a significant proportion of business cycle fluctuations over the past 50 years, implying that there is a sizable global business cycle.[7] In a recent paper, Hirata, Kose, and Otrok (2013) analyze the importance of global and regional factors in explaining business cycles in a sample of 106 countries, including advanced, emerging market, and other developing economies, during 1960–2010. They report that the global factor accounts on average for 10 percent of the variation in output growth among all countries in their sample. The factor also explains roughly 9 percent of the volatility of the growth rate of consumption and 5 percent of investment. Although the variance shares attributed to the global factor may appear small, they are sizable numbers given that the global factor across the three macroeconomic aggregates is estimated for a very large and diverse set of countries.

The global factor tends to be important in each region, but on average it plays a more dominant role in explaining business cycles in advanced economy regions (North America and Europe), which have stronger intraregional trade and financial linkages than emerging market and developing economy regions (Asia, Latin America and the Caribbean, sub-Saharan Africa, and the Middle East and North Africa). The global factor on average explains about 17 percent of output fluctuations in North America and 27 percent in Europe. In contrast, in the latter group of regions, the global factor explains between 5 percent (in sub-Saharan Africa) and 9 percent (in Asia) of output fluctuations. The global factor is also associated with a substantial share of the variance in consumption and investment growth among the advanced economy regions, accounting on average for about 25 percent and 12 percent of the total variance of these variables, respectively.

Several other studies that examine cross-country correlations also find that business cycles in major advanced economies tend to move together. For example, Hirata and others (2012) report that the average pairwise correlation across advanced economies has been about 0.5 since the mid-1980s, indicating the presence of strong global business cycle linkages. Other studies employing different methodologies reach similar conclusions.[8]

Regional Business Cycles

Are there regional cycles as well? There has been an explosion of research aimed at better understanding regional cycles. Although the evidence of their existence has been mixed, recent studies report that regional cycles have become increasingly pronounced. In particular, some report that, since the mid-1980s, regional factors have become markedly more important in explaining business cycles, especially in regions that have experienced sharp growth in intraregional trade and financial flows. These patterns are particularly strong in North America, Europe, Oceania, and Asia.[9]

To determine the cyclical behavior . . . of different economic activities, we should have a method that yields comparable results when applied to a wide variety of time series. If possible, the results should be in quantitative form, that is, we should measure *the cyclical behavior of economic activities . . . We need to know how the specific cycles of different activities are related to one another in direction of movement, in the timing of their peaks and troughs, and in the duration of their expansions and contractions . . . If there is [consensus among these movements], the dates of specific-cycle troughs of individual activities must be concentrated around certain points of time, and the like must be true of specific-cycle peaks. We can then proceed to identify business cycles . . . assign approximate dates to their troughs and peaks, and plunge into a study of behavior of different economic activities within the periods thus marked off.*

Arthur F. Burns and Wesley C. Mitchell (1947)

CHAPTER 3

Tools of the Trade

What tools do we need to study the features of global recessions and recoveries? The answer is straightforward: we need to construct a comprehensive database and employ robust methodologies widely accepted by the economics profession. This chapter introduces our global database, which includes a wide range of macroeconomic and financial indicators for a large number of countries and describes the two complementary methods we use to identify the dates of global recessions and recoveries.

A GLOBAL DATABASE

02:40

What is a recession? How we can gauge when an economy has slipped into recession.

Our extensive database uses annual series of wide-ranging indicators of economic activity for a large number of countries.[1] Some of these are the components of national income accounts, including gross domestic product (GDP), consumption, and investment. Others are used to track additional measures of activity and prices, such as industrial production, international trade, unemployment, inflation, and commodity prices. The database also includes various measures that capture fluctuations in financial markets: international capital flows, interest rates, credit, and equity and house prices.

Over what period is it best to study global recessions and recoveries? It would be possible to construct a measure of the global business cycle using more than a century of annual data if we focused on a small set of countries and employed a narrow set of activity indicators. For example, using small data sets, the 2009 global recession has often been compared with the Great Depression of the early 1930s.[2]

Our objective here is to provide a systematic analysis of "modern" global recessions and recoveries using multiple measures of global activity and a sample that truly represents the world economy. Our database of annual series therefore covers 163 countries during 1960–2012. We rely mainly on well-known data sets, but we also use other sources. We study the ongoing recovery using the GDP forecasts of the IMF *World Economic Outlook* for 2013 (we provide additional information about the country coverage, variables in the database, and their sources in Appendix B).

We divide the countries in our sample into three functional groups: advanced economies (24), emerging market economies (30), and other developing economies (109). The main distinction between the emerging market and other developing economies is that the former have attained a much higher level of integration into global trade and finance.[3] For instance, since the mid-1980s the average growth rate of total trade (exports plus imports) has been more than twice the growth rate of GDP for the emerging market economies; the corresponding figure for the other developing economies is much lower. Emerging market economies have also received the bulk of private capital flows going from advanced economies to the rest of the world over the past quarter century.

Our regional country samples closely follow the standard geographical groupings, but we also examine groups of emerging market and developing economies in different regions. In addition, we sometimes consider well-known country groups, such as the euro area (Appendices B.2 to B.4 list countries included in each group).

Depending on our objective and data availability, the coverage of our database differs in some chapters. For a smaller group of advanced and emerging market economies, for example, we use higher-frequency, quarterly macroeconomic and financial time series in a few chapters when we analyze the implications of recessions and recoveries accompanied by periods of financial disruptions and uncertainty. In Chapter 11, we use a smaller sample of countries because we include only those with sufficient data coverage to conduct our empirical exercise. We provide the details of these changes in the relevant chapters.

METHODOLOGY: LET'S DATE

Our measure of the global business cycle is the annual growth rate of real world GDP per capita. This is the difference between the weighted real GDP growth of countries in our sample and world population growth.[4] A per capita measure is useful because it accounts for the variation in population growth rates over time and across countries. It also partly dampens the impact on the global business cycle of the significant differential between trend growth rates of advanced economies and emerging market and developing economies. In addition, real world GDP per capita is a primary measure of the overall well-being and living standard of a typical world citizen.

Real world GDP growth per capita is a primary measure of the well-being of the typical world citizen.

We consider two types of weights in computing the growth rate of global GDP: purchasing-power-parity weights and market weights. Purchasing power parity calculates the rate at which the currency of one country would have to be converted into another to buy the same assortment of goods and services. Market weights, in contrast, are based on the conversion of domestic currencies into the (U.S. dollar) exchange rate prevailing in the open market. Since purchasing power parity reflects the fact that goods and services that are not traded internationally tend to be cheaper in low-income countries than in high-income countries, the value of output in low-income countries tends to be higher using purchasing power parity than using market rates.[5]

TABLE 3.1
Annual Growth Rates of Output and Population *(in percent)*

	1960s	1970s	1980s	1990s	2000s	1960–2012
Market-weighted output						
World	4.92	4.16	3.18	2.59	2.73	3.44
Advanced economies	4.79	3.49	2.98	2.40	1.55	2.92
Emerging market economies	5.77	5.66	4.24	3.65	5.63	5.01
Other developing economies	5.52	5.17	1.81	1.71	4.90	3.85
Purchasing-power-parity-weighted output						
World	5.07	4.46	3.22	2.92	3.67	3.83
Advanced economies	5.02	3.61	2.90	2.54	1.58	3.00
Emerging market economies	5.15	5.88	4.24	3.80	6.11	5.10
Other developing economies	5.24	6.33	1.96	2.19	5.14	4.21
Population						
World	1.98	1.92	1.71	1.50	1.24	1.64
Advanced economies	1.06	0.82	0.58	0.68	0.62	0.74
Emerging market economies	2.24	2.10	1.79	1.44	1.04	1.67
Other developing economies	2.51	2.43	2.45	2.32	2.21	2.37
Market-weighted output *(per capita)*						
World	2.95	2.24	1.47	1.09	1.49	1.81
Advanced economies	3.73	2.67	2.39	1.72	0.93	2.18
Emerging market economies	3.53	3.56	2.45	2.21	4.59	3.34
Other developing economies	3.01	2.74	−0.64	−0.60	2.70	1.48
Purchasing-power-parity-weighted output *(per capita)*						
World	3.09	2.54	1.51	1.42	2.42	2.19
Advanced economies	3.96	2.79	2.31	1.85	0.96	2.26
Emerging market economies	2.91	3.78	2.45	2.36	5.07	3.42
Other developing economies	2.72	3.89	−0.49	−0.13	2.93	1.83

Note: Market-weighted (purchasing-power-parity [PPP]-weighted) output is the gross domestic product growth rate of the respective group using market (PPP) exchange rates. Per capita market-weighted (PPP-weighted) output growth rate is the difference between market-weighted (PPP-weighted) output growth and population growth. Each column corresponds to the country group average in the respective decade. The 2000s period includes 2000–12.

A quick glance at the data clearly shows the benefits of employing a per capita measure (Table 3.1). The average growth of world GDP (using purchasing-power-parity weights) is 3.8 percent during 1960–2012, but it fluctuates over time (from 5 percent in the 1960s to 2.9 percent in the 1990s). Output and population growth rates differ substantially across country groups. For example, output growth is on average 3 percent in advanced economies and 5 percent in emerging market economies. Average population growth is 0.7 percent in advanced economies but much larger in other groups: 1.7 percent in emerging market economies and 2.4 percent in other developing economies. Average population growth has declined both globally and in different groups of economies over time. Nonetheless, average global GDP growth picked up during the early 2000s because growth in emerging market and other developing economies accelerated markedly after registering consecutive declines during the previous four decades.

We use two methods to identify the turning points in global activity: a statistical method and a judgmental method. Both are widely used in the context of national business cycles. Although the two methods use different information sets, both rely on the "classical" definition of a business cycle: economic expansions, marked by increases in many measures of economic activity, followed by broad contractions in activity. These complementary methods help us arrive at our definitions of the global recession and recovery.

Statistical Method

In deciding when a particular country is in recession, economists often use statistical procedures to date the peaks and troughs of a key indicator of economic activity, such as the country's real GDP. The specific dating method we use provides a simple but effective procedure to identify turning points.[6] Moreover, it is convenient because the turning points identified are robust to the inclusion of newly available data.[7]

The algorithm requires a search for local maxima and minima over a given period. It then selects pairs of adjacent, locally absolute maxima and minima that meet certain censoring rules (Figure 3.1). Our methodology requires a minimum two-year duration of a cycle and a minimum one-year duration of each of the cyclical phases. A complete cycle goes from one peak to the next with its two phases: the recession phase (from peak to trough) and the expansion phase (from trough to the next peak).[8]

These censoring rules imply that a global recession takes place when the growth rate of our measure of global economic activity is negative. However, this is a purely mechanical rule for identifying a global recession. In reality, many other factors affect the evolution of global economic activity in real time. It is precisely because of this reason that institutions such as the National Bureau of Economic Research (NBER) in the United States and the Centre for Economic Policy Research (CEPR) in the United Kingdom use a comprehensive set of indicators of activity and employ a judgmental approach to identifying the turning points of national and regional cycles.[9]

Judgmental Method

An alternate method for identifying business cycles also has a long history and finds its roots in the pioneering work of Arthur Burns and Wesley Mitchell (1947), who laid the methodological foundations of the analysis of business cycles in the United States. They define a national business cycle to "consist[s] of expansions occurring at about the same time in many economic activities,

FIGURE 3.1
Evolution of a National Business Cycle

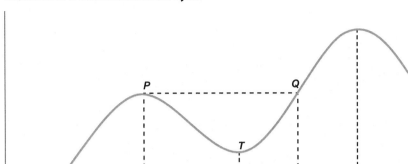

Note: This schematic represents a complete national business cycle comprising of two phases: an expansion and a recession. The expansion is the phase of the cycle between a trough and the following peak whereas the recession is between a peak and the following trough. P is the "peak" and T the "trough" of the cycle. Q is the point where the level of output reaches its previous peak and a recovery phase is completed (as implied by some definitions in the literature).

followed by similar general recessions, contractions, and revivals which merge into the expansion phase of the next cycle."

In 1978, the NBER established its Business Cycle Dating Committee to determine the dates of recessions in the United States. The CEPR has performed a similar task for the euro area since 2002. In contrast to a purely statistical approach, the NBER and CEPR date business cycle peaks and troughs by looking at a broad set of economic indicators and reaching a judgment on whether a preponderance of the evidence points to a recession.[10]

The NBER uses GDP, industrial production, retail sales, employment, disposable income, and initial claims for unemployment insurance. Because these indicators can present conflicting signals about the direction of an economy, the judgmental approach can sometimes be difficult to employ in real time. The CEPR's task is even more complex because, in addition to looking at multiple national indicators, it has to make a determination of whether the euro area as a whole is in recession.

We apply the judgmental method at the global level by looking at several indicators of global activity—real GDP per capita, industrial production, unemployment, trade and capital flows, and energy consumption. We focus on these indicators since the global analogs of some of the variables used by the NBER and CEPR are not available for a large number of countries over a long period. However, the measures we employ capture the essential information at the global level provided by the main variables used by these institutions. Moreover, our measures provide a broad perspective on the evolution of global business cycles. In addition to the standard activity measures, such as GDP, industrial production, and unemployment, the other variables we use capture changes in global trade and financial (capital) flows and global energy (oil) consumption.

DEFINING GLOBAL RECESSION AND GLOBAL RECOVERY

Armed with these two approaches, we can now define the concepts of global recession and global recovery. A global recession is a contraction in world real GDP per capita accompanied by a broad decline in various other measures of global economic activity. A global recession begins just after the world economy reaches a peak of activity and ends when it reaches its trough. Since we use annual data, a global recession lasts at least one year.[11]

The recovery phase from a recession has been widely studied for national business cycles.[12] Recovery is often defined as the early part of the expansion phase that follows a recession. In parallel, a global recovery is a broad rebound in worldwide activity during one to three years following a global recession. It simply refers to the period of increasing economic activity after a global recession. We consider the recovery phase to be associated with the first year following the trough of the global business cycle. We also examine the recovery in the first three years following a global recession, considering the possibility that a global recovery can take longer than a year.

A global recession is a contraction in world real GDP per capita accompanied by a broad decline in various other measures of global economic activity. A global recession begins just after the world economy reaches a peak of activity and ends when it reaches its trough.

BUILDING ON AN EARLIER CONTRIBUTION

We are not the first ones to define a global recession. Kenneth Rogoff, former IMF chief economist, and his coauthors defined the concept of global recession in a short piece they wrote for the IMF's *World Economic Outlook* in 2002. Their objective was to figure out whether the 2001 worldwide downturn was a global recession.[13]

As we do here, they also considered a measure of GDP per capita to identify episodes that could be labeled as global recessions. They also noted that the GDP per capita measure is an important metric, but it was at the same time a rather conservative one to pin down global recessions. They emphasized the relevance of the judgmental method and showed how it could be used in the context of the global economy. However, they focused on only two measures of global activity (output and industrial production), whereas we use a more comprehensive set of activity indicators. Moreover, their brief analysis did not cover global recoveries as we do here.

Our book on global recessions and recoveries was motivated by the events that have transformed the global economy since 2006. However, our approach to these concepts was certainly inspired by the work of Rogoff and his col-leagues.[14] As we explain in the next chapter, the dates of global recessions they identify correspond with ours. We also reach the same conclusion about the classification of the 2001 episode, as we discuss in Chapter 4.

TIME TO GET TO WORK

This chapter provides a disciplined framework for identifying global reces-sions and recoveries. It is time to put this framework into practice and get to the real work of determining the dates of global recessions and recoveries and documenting the events around these turning points.

PART II

Learning about
the Four Episodes

For a generation the world has enjoyed its greatest boom. It is now suffering its greatest inflation and could shortly be struggling with its greatest slump.

The Economist (1974a)

The world is in recession because its bankers overlent to inefficient borrowers, and its governments may be going to overprotect against efficient producers now.

The Economist (1982a)

[G]lobal activity is projected to contract by 1.3 percent in 2009. This represents the deepest post–World War II recession by far. Moreover, the downturn is truly global: output per capita is projected to decline in countries representing three-quarters of the global economy.

Olivier Blanchard and José Viñals (2009)

CHAPTER 4

Dates and Events: What Happened When?

Can one claim good knowledge of the U.S. economy without a serious understanding of the U.S. business cycle and its turning points? No! Similarly, a true understanding of the global economy requires a good grasp of the global business cycle and its turning points. In this chapter, we first determine the turning points of the global cycle. These ultimately correspond to the dates of global recessions, recoveries, and expansions. We then provide a brief narrative of the major events that coincided with the turning points of the global cycle. We conclude with a short analysis of the implications of global recessions for macroeconomics.

TURNING POINTS OF THE GLOBAL BUSINESS CYCLE

We first describe the turning points that we identify using each methodology.

Turning Points Using the Statistical Method

The statistical algorithm identifies four troughs in global economic activity since 1960, and these correspond to declines in world real gross domestic product (GDP) per capita and constitute global recessions: 1975, 1982, 1991, and 2009 (Figures 4.1 and 4.2). The use of market weights rather than purchasing-power-parity weights, which tilts the weighting toward advanced economies, does not affect the set of troughs, with one exception. Using market weights, the trough of the 1991 episode shifts to 1993 because of the recessions in many European countries during the European Exchange Rate Mechanism (ERM) crisis of 1992–93. With both weights, the dates of peaks in the global business cycle are 1974, 1981, 1990, and 2008.

The implication of these findings is that when measured by market weights, the duration of the 1991 global recession is two years but the duration of other episodes is just one year. With the purchasing-power-parity weights, the duration of all four global recessions is one year. This finding echoes the results from the literature on the features of national recessions. A recent study reports that the average duration of roughly 250 recessions in 44 advanced and emerging market economies since 1960 is also about one year.[1]

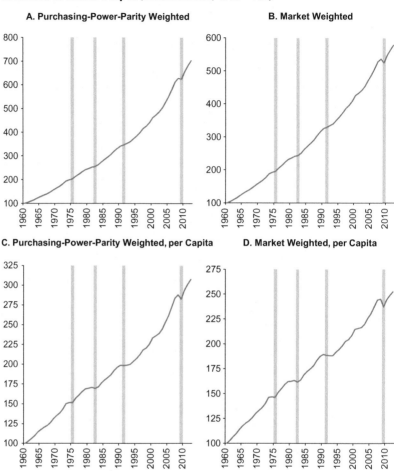

FIGURE 4.1
Evolution of World Output *(index numbers, 1960 = 100)*

Note: Shaded bars indicate global recessions.

Can we identify a global recession with a simple threshold associated with the growth of world GDP? The answer appears to be no, as Figure 4.2 shows the difficulty of using a growth threshold (such as 3 percent growth in world GDP) to identify a global recession.[2] If one assumes that a global recession takes place when world real GDP growth (with purchasing-power-parity weights) is less than 3 percent, the world economy was in recession for 14 years during 1960–2012, and 20 years using market weights over the same period.[3] If one uses growth rates per capita (with purchasing-power-parity weights) and assumes that the threshold is 1 percent, there were nine years of global recession since 1960.[4] With the use of market weights, there were 13 years of global recession. The growth of world GDP needs to fall below roughly 1.3 percent to register a contraction given the average rate of

FIGURE 4.2
Growth of World Output *(in percent)*

A. World Output Growth

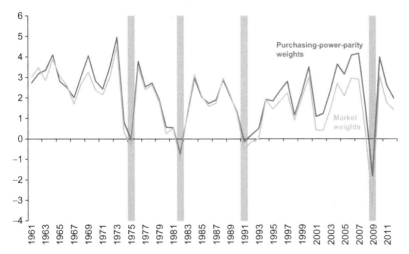

B. World Output Growth per Capita

Note: Each panel shows the percent change from a year earlier. World output growth is the weighted average of the growth rate of real gross domestic product of each country (using the purchasing-power-parity or market weights). World output growth per capita is the difference between world real output growth and world population growth. Shaded bars indicate global recessions.

population growth in the 2000s.[5] But it is important to recognize that this statistic is time variant, with substantial changes from one decade to another.[6]

Turning Points Using the Judgmental Method

The judgmental method is applied at the global level by looking at several indicators of global activity: real GDP per capita, industrial production, trade, capital flows, oil consumption, and unemployment. Figure 4.3 shows the

FIGURE 4.3
Evolution of Global Activity Variables *(in percent)*

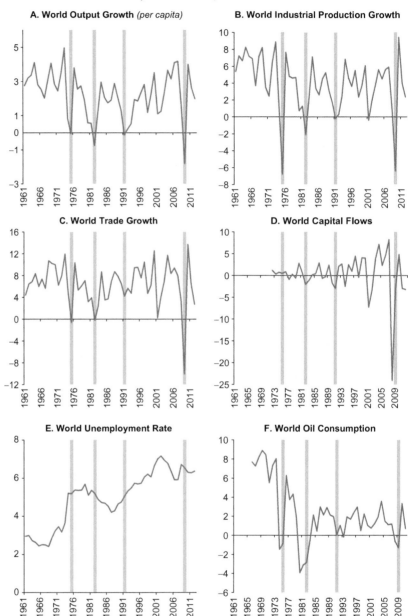

Note: World output growth is the difference between the purchasing-power-parity-weighted output growth rate and the population growth rate. World industrial production growth is the purchasing-power-parity-weighted industrial production growth of all countries. World trade growth is the growth rate of exports and imports of all countries. World capital flows correspond to the change in the ratio of total capital flows to gross domestic product, where total capital flows is the absolute sum of total inflows and total outflows. World unemployment rate is the labor-force-weighted unemployment rate of all countries. World oil consumption is the change in oil consumption. Shaded bars indicate global recessions.

FIGURE 4.4

Evolution of World Consumption and Investment *(in percent)*

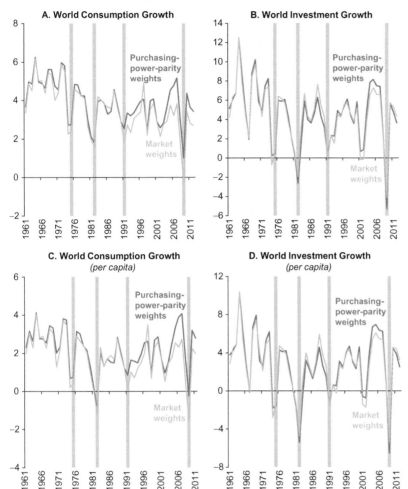

Note: Each panel shows the percent change from a year earlier. World consumption (investment) growth is the weighted average of the growth rate of consumption (investment) of each country (using the purchasing-power-parity or market weights for output). Per capita world consumption (investment) growth is the difference between world consumption (investment) growth and world population growth. Shaded bars indicate global recessions.

evolution of these indicators. The behavior of most indicators points to an obvious contraction in global economic activity after it peaked in the preceding year.[7] These periods also coincide with declining growth in global consumption and investment and sharp downturns in global credit and asset and commodity prices (Figures 4.4, 4.5, and 4.6). We discuss the behavior of these variables during the global recessions and recoveries in more detail in the next two chapters.

FIGURE 4.5

Evolution of World Credit, House Prices, and Equity Prices *(in percent)*

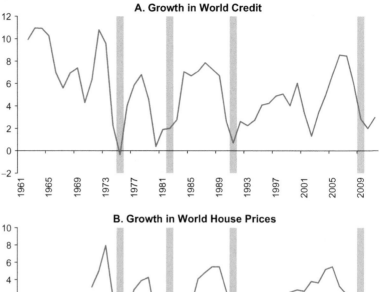

A. Growth in World Credit

B. Growth in World House Prices

C. Growth in World Equity Prices

Note: Each panel shows the four-quarter average of market-weighted growth rates of respective variables for advanced and emerging market economies. All variables are in real terms. House price data start in 1970. Growth in world credit and world equity prices start in 1962; the market weights are three-year rolling averages. Shaded bars indicate global recessions.

FIGURE 4.6
Evolution of World Commodity Prices *(in percent)*

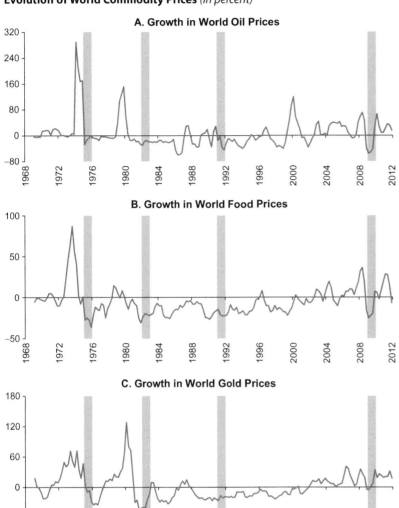

Note: Each panel presents the year-over-year growth rate of the respective real commodity price. The real growth rate of commodity price corresponds to the nominal growth rate deflated by world inflation, which is the year-over-year growth rate of the world consumer price index. Shaded bars indicate global recessions.

IS IT JUST A U.S. RECESSION? NO!

It is natural to ask whether the global recessions we identified were always accompanied by recessions in the United States. Although the four global recessions indeed coincided with recessions in the United States, not every U.S. recession was associated with a global recession. Specifically, the United

States experienced eight recessions during 1960–2014 whereas the global economy experienced only four.[8] In other words, a recession in the United States does not necessarily imply a global recession.

EVENTS SURROUNDING THE GLOBAL RECESSIONS

The four turning points we identify coincided with severe economic and financial disruptions in many countries around the world—these were periods of collapse for the world economy. Before we document the main properties of the global recessions and recoveries in the next two chapters, we briefly describe the major events that took place around these critical turning points.[9] Our objective is not to pinpoint the causes of the global recessions but simply to remind readers of the gravity and complexity of the events that coincided with these episodes.

The world economy faced unique challenges during each episode. The underlying shocks that led to the collapse of the world economy worked differently in each of the four episodes. A truly global shock—a sharp increase in oil prices—drove the 1975 recession. A series of global and national shocks, including the oil price shock in 1979, and subsequent policies and events—especially the Volcker disinflation and the Latin American debt crisis—played significant roles in the 1982 episode.

However, there were also multiple similarities in how the global economy descended into these full-blown recessions. A number of countries experienced financial crises during the global recessions.[10] While the 1991 event coincided with a wide range of global and national shocks, it became a worldwide event through transmission of various national shocks across borders: financial disruptions in the United States, Japan, and several Scandinavian countries; exchange rate crises in many advanced European economies; German unification; and the collapse of the Soviet Union in eastern Europe. The 2009 global recession started with problems in the U.S. financial sector in 2007, but it rapidly spread to other advanced economies and some emerging market economies through trade and financial linkages.

We now turn to a brief narrative of each global recession. In the notes at the end of the book, we provide a rich set of excerpts taken from media reports around the years of global recessions. These show that each global recession brought memories of the Great Depression of the 1930s and often led to pessimistic predictions about the future of the world economy. Appendix E also includes a detailed timeline of events around global recessions.

An interactive timeline of the 1975 global recession.

The global recession of 1975 followed the first major oil price shock the world economy had ever experienced.[11] Oil prices shot up fourfold following the Arab oil embargo that began in October 1973, when Egypt, Syria,

Tunisia, and Arab members of the Organization of the Petroleum Exporting Countries (OPEC) initiated the embargo to protest U.S. support to Israel in the Arab-Israeli conflict. Although the embargo ended in March 1974, the supply shock associated with the sharp rise in oil prices quickly translated into a substantial increase in inflation and a sharp decline in output in a number of countries. Specifically, the global recession of 1975 marked the beginning of a prolonged period of stagflation, with low output growth and high inflation in the United States. In addition, the Group of Seven countries except Germany—Canada, France, Italy, Japan, the United Kingdom, and the United States—experienced relatively high inflation.[12] As we describe later, sharp movements in oil prices also appear to have played important roles in the recessions of 1982 and 1991.[13]

The global recession of 1975 followed the first major oil price shock the world economy had ever experienced and ushered in a period of stagflation.

Oil-importing countries have since taken numerous steps to reduce their vulnerability to such shocks. They increased the number of sources from which they import oil, making them less vulnerable to disruptions from any one source, and substituted other sources such as natural gas and renewables, including solar and wind. In advanced and emerging market economies, there have also been increases in energy efficiency, with a steady decline in the amount of energy needed to generate a dollar of income.

Moreover, central banks have become much better at anchoring inflation expectations by communicating that oil price increases do not alter longer-run inflation prospects. The public in many countries is therefore much less fearful of the inflationary consequences of higher oil prices. Increases in oil prices are no longer expected to feed a wage-price spiral, as they did in the 1970s. Nevertheless, while countries have built up some ability to withstand oil shocks, they remain vulnerable to severe supply disruptions or to the uncertainty induced by extreme oil price volatility.

The global recession in 1982 was associated with a variety of events, including a rapid increase in oil prices, tight monetary policies in several advanced economies, and the Latin American debt crisis.[14] A second major oil price shock hit the global economy in 1979 during the Iranian revolution as prices jumped almost threefold. Inflation then reached new highs in several advanced economies (reaching 13.5 percent in the United States and 17 percent in the United Kingdom in 1980).

An interactive timeline of the 1982 global recession.

After the 1975 global recession, many advanced economies implemented accommodative policies for a prolonged period to revive economic growth. However, several started to pursue contractionary monetary policies to reduce inflation in the early 1980s.[15] These coincided with a sharp decline in activity along with a significant increase in the rate of unemployment in the United States and several other advanced economies during 1982–83.

The global recession in 1982 was associated with a variety of events, including a rapid increase in oil prices, tight monetary policies in several advanced economies, and the Latin American debt crisis.

A number of Latin American countries accumulated large debts during the 1970s (mainly funded by the petrodollar windfall of the oil-exporting countries). However, the sharp increase in global interest rates and the collapse of commodity prices in the early 1980s made servicing this debt very difficult.[16] Mexico's default in August 1982 marked the beginning of the Latin American debt crisis and the region's decade-long stagnation (known as the "lost decade"). Debt crises afflicted a number of countries in the region, including Argentina, Mexico, and Venezuela in 1982 and Brazil and Chile in 1983.[17]

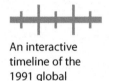

An interactive timeline of the 1991 global recession.

The 1991 global recession also reflected a host of problems in many corners of the world: difficulties in U.S. credit markets, banking and currency crises in Europe and the challenges of east Europe's economies transitioning away from communism, the bursting of Japan's asset price bubble, and uncertainty stemming from the first Gulf War and the subsequent increase in the price of oil.[18] The U.S. savings and loan crisis persisted from the mid-1980s to the mid-1990s, and close to 25 percent of financial institutions providing savings and loan services failed.[19] These developments coincided with a prolonged period of depressed activity in the U.S. housing market and a credit crunch that began in 1990. Unemployment started to increase in 1989, and the economy went into recession in July 1990.[20]

The early 1990s were an extremely challenging period for many countries in Europe. First, there were severe banking crises in several Scandinavian countries in early 1991. Finland, Norway, and Sweden had liberalized their financial sectors in the 1980s and enjoyed rapid growth accompanied by a significant expansion of credit before going through deep recessions largely because of these crises.

Second, the ERM among 11 European currencies disintegrated in 1992, and the ensuing crisis coincided with a sharp decline in activity in many of the member countries.[21] The ERM was simply a managed float in which currencies were allowed to fluctuate within predetermined bands. Although the system had worked well for a long time, several members of the ERM ran into competitiveness problems and their currencies faced speculative attacks after Germany increased interest rates in 1992 to control inflation (following unification in 1990). Ireland, Italy, Portugal, Spain, and the United Kingdom were all forced to devalue their currencies in 1992–93 and then experienced deep recessions.

The 1991 global recession reflected a host of problems, including difficulties in U.S. credit markets, banking and currency crises in Europe and the challenges of eastern Europe's transition, the bursting of Japan's asset price bubble, and the uncertainty stemming from the first Gulf War and the subsequent increase in the price of oil.

Third, the transition to market economies by the former communist bloc countries in eastern Europe also caused difficulties in the early 1990s. In particular, output in these economies fell significantly at the start of the transition, by 40 percent on average before it bottomed out.[22]

Finally, after enjoying robust growth and soaring asset prices during the 1980s, Japan experienced a recession in the early 1990s that was accompanied by a collapse in equity and house prices. The recession began a prolonged period of stagnation—Japan's own lost decade. In addition, the first Gulf War (August 2, 1990–February 28, 1991) pitted a U.S.-led international coalition against Iraq following Iraq's invasion of Kuwait, and the associated increase in oil prices hurt global activity.[23]

The 2009 global recession followed the worst financial crisis since the stock market crash of October 1929 and the subsequent Great Depression of the 1930s. Although financial crises have always been a recurrent feature of global recessions, the latest episode included an unusually large number of severe crises in advanced economies. The crisis started in mid-2007 in the major advanced economies after an extended period of macroeconomic stability accompanied by financial exuberance. The buildup to the crisis featured asset price and credit booms in a number of countries; a dramatic expansion in the volume and variety of marginal loans, particularly in mortgage markets; and a period of relatively lax regulation and supervision of financial markets and institutions.[24]

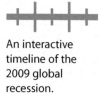

An interactive timeline of the 2009 global recession.

Although the U.S. mortgage markets were at the epicenter, the financial crisis quickly spread to other financial market segments in many other countries and turned into a global crisis after the collapse in September 2008 of the investment bank Lehman Brothers, which had a very large international exposure.[25] A number of financial institutions failed in the United States and Europe (we list some of them in Appendix E). The pervasive interconnectedness of national and international financial markets, with the United States at the core, helped transmit the crisis to other advanced, emerging market, and developing economies.[26]

The 2009 global recession followed the worst financial crisis since the stock market crash of October 1929 and the subsequent Great Depression of the 1930s. This latest episode included an unusually large number of severe crises in advanced economies.

The crisis led to prolonged asset price busts and credit crunches, a collapse in global trade, and highly synchronized recessions in many countries around the world in 2009. Banking crises erupted in many European countries in 2008 and turned into a regionwide sovereign debt crisis in 2011–12. A FOCUS box at the end of the chapter provides additional information on the similarities and differences between the 2007–09 global financial crisis and earlier ones.[27] While they were somewhat peripheral to the bigger story of the financial crisis, oil prices also increased sharply (spiking to $133 a barrel in July 2008 from $53 in January 2007) in the run-up to the global recession.

TRUE TURNING POINTS FOR MACROECONOMICS

Global recessions have not been turning points only for the world economy, but by sparking a rethinking of macroeconomic theories and policies, they have also been transformative events for the economics profession. For example, prior to the 1975 recession, the dominant macroeconomic framework was the Keynesian approach to policymaking, which emphasized the importance of movements in aggregate demand as the main source of economic fluctuations. This view naturally lent support to the use of macroeconomic policies to stimulate aggregate demand to fine-tune business cycle fluctuations. Under the standard Keynesian framework, the coexistence of inflation and stagnation in activity was considered impossible.

Global recessions have not been turning points only for the world economy, but by sparking a rethinking of macroeconomic theories and policies, they have also been transformative events for the economics profession.

During the 1975 global recession and the ensuing recovery, many advanced economies did in fact experience both high inflation and stagnation, a phenomenon known as stagflation. As a consequence, macroeconomics went through a period of soul-searching, and new theories were developed that gave more prominence to the shocks originating on the supply (production) side of the economy.[28] Other theories showed how policies that affect nominal variables (and target aggregate demand) can have only temporary effects on macroeconomic outcomes in environments with rational agents and flexible prices.[29]

The 1982 and 1991 episodes were also important turning points for macroeconomics. The global recession of 1982, for example, led to a serious assessment of monetary policy, especially in advanced economies.[30] There was substantial progress in the design and objectives of monetary policies as inflation increasingly became the key concern of central bankers. The global economy enjoyed a period of "Great Moderation" from the mid-1980s until the global financial crisis. Some argued that improvements in monetary policy played an important role in delivering stable output and inflation outcomes during this period.[31]

As discussed, the 1991 episode was an amalgam of adverse events, including problems in credit and housing markets in the United States, banking crises in several Scandinavian countries, currency crises in many European countries, the bursting of the Japanese asset price bubble, and the structural and cyclical problems of eastern European transition economies. These events intensified research on the linkages between credit markets and the real economy, determinants of exchange rate movements, and the sustainability of currency unions. New research led to revolutionary changes in the institutional structures of central banks and the design of monetary policies. During the 1990s, a number of countries undertook reforms to increase the independence of their central banks. Many central banks adopted inflation targeting as the foundation of their monetary policies. A new line of research focused

07:07

Former IMF historian James Boughton puts the 2009 global financial crisis in a historical context.

on a wide range of problems associated with the transition of eastern European countries to market economies.

The latest recession was a truly dramatic turning point because it showed the limitations of macroeconomic models to analyze the implications of financial intermediaries and instruments for activity. Moreover, debates on economic policies in the wake of the crisis have clearly illustrated the constraints of available policy measures to cope with the devastating effects of the global recession.[32] In subsequent chapters, we provide a detailed discussion of these policy issues.

FOCUSING NEXT ON THE EFFECTS

This chapter describes the main events that took place around global recessions and shows the complex circumstances that led to the collapses of the world economy. We now turn to the sad stories of these collapses by presenting an empirical analysis of their main features in the next chapter.

FOCUS

THE GLOBAL FINANCIAL CRISIS

The proximate cause of the 2009 global recession was the financial crisis that started in the United States in 2007 and quickly spread around the world through financial and trade linkages. The crisis had multiple and interlinked causes, some common to past crises and others more unique.[33]

How Similar?

There are at least four elements common to financial crises. The first is rapid appreciation of asset prices. The pattern of "exuberant" asset prices in the United States and other advanced economies prior to the 2007–09 crisis is reminiscent of other crises, including the so-called Big Five banking crises (Finland, 1991; Japan, 1992; Norway, 1987; Sweden, 1991; and Spain, 1977).

The second common element is credit booms or, more generally, rapid financial expansion. Much research has documented how episodes of unusually sharp credit expansions end in crisis (Mendoza and Terrones 2012). As in past episodes, international financial integration helped facilitate credit expansion in various corners of the world in the run-up to the Great Recession.

The third is the emergence of systemic risks. In the United States and other advanced economies, systemic risk arose from the housing sectors. In other countries, particularly in emerging Europe, it arose from the large amounts of credit extended in foreign currency.

The final common element is a failure of regulation and supervision to restrict excessive market behavior. As in many previous episodes, the large credit expansions before 2007 were associated with poorly supervised and unregulated financial innovation, and as in many previous episodes, the result was a crisis.

How Different?

The latest episode is unique in many respects. First, problems in the household sector played a more prominent role than in previous financial crises. Most previous episodes stemmed from problems in the public sector (such as the Latin American debt crisis of the 1980s) or the corporate sector (such as the Asian financial crisis of the late 1990s). In many countries, however, the latest crisis largely originated from "overextended" households. This had major implications for how the crisis was transmitted from the financial to the real sector and complicated the design of resolution mechanisms and policy responses.

Second, leverage increased sharply in the financial sector, directly so among commercial banks in Europe and through the shadow banking system (investment banks and non-deposit-taking institutions) in the United States. High leverage limited the ability of financial systems to absorb even small losses and contributed to the rapid decline in confidence and increase in counterparty risk early in the crisis.

Third, there has been a dramatic increase in the extent of international financial integration over the past three decades, and global finance now involves many players from various markets and different countries. Many financial instruments that originate in the United States are held in other advanced economies and by the official sector in several emerging market economies. While increased financial integration has conferred many benefits, these extensive links meant the crisis in U.S. financial markets quickly turned into a full-fledged global crisis and made a coordinated solution much more difficult.

Finally, financial instruments have become more complex and opaque over time. Securitization, spurred by the use of innovative (and highly complex) financial instruments, has been critical in the rapid expansion of credit, particularly mortgage credit, in the United States. However, the increased recourse to securitization and the expansion of the originate-and-distribute model has exacerbated agency problems—that is, the problems with motivating one party (the agent, in this case the financial institution) to act in the interests of another (the principal, in this case the investor). The distribution model led to widespread reliance on ratings for the pricing of credit risk. Moreover, investors were often unable or unwilling to fully assess underlying values and risks. This lack of understanding quickly led to a confidence crisis during 2007–09.

The Organization for Economic Cooperation and Development . . . sharply cut its forecast for the world economy, warning that failure to end the euro crisis and avert a fiscal impasse in the United States could cause a global recession.

Stephen Castle (2012)

The global economy experiences a recession every six years or so, and the frequency of global recessions tends to increase when global indebtedness is high. Given that the last global recession was four years ago, and also given that the global economy is significantly more indebted today than it was four years ago, we believe there is now a greater than 60 percent probability that we will experience another global recession in the next three to five years.

Saumil H. Parikh (2013)

CHAPTER 5

Global Recessions:
Sad Stories of Collapse

The 2009 global recession clearly showed that our knowledge of the main features of such episodes is quite limited. How do activity variables behave during a global recession? What happens to credit and asset prices? What are the main differences and similarities among the four global recessions? This chapter answers these questions. We document the main regularities of global recessions and then outline the specific features of the 2009 global recession. In addition to the four global recessions, we analyze the two global downturns during which the world economy slowed significantly but was able to escape falling into an outright recession.

GLOBAL RECESSIONS: MAIN SIMILARITIES

There are surprising similarities in how the world economy experienced a period of collapse during each of the four global recessions. The evolution of the main indicators of world activity point to these similarities (Figure 5.1 and Table 5.1A). For example, world output, industrial production, trade, capital flows, and oil consumption often started to slow a year before the peak of each global cycle.

Output, industrial production, trade, capital flows, asset prices, and oil consumption slow two years before a global recession. Employment, inflation, and interest rates fall during the recession's first year.

The unemployment rate increased most sharply in the year of recession as growth collapsed. Asset prices and credit typically began decelerating about two years ahead of the global recessions. Inflation and nominal interest rates fell during the year of the global recession (Figure 5.2 and Table 5.1B). The latest global recession followed a similar pattern, although most indicators contracted much more sharply.

Real Economy

The four global recessions display noticeable quantitative regularities in the behavior of the real economy (Tables 5.1A and 5.1B).

- *Contraction in gross domestic product (GDP) per capita.* The decline in GDP per capita (purchasing-power-parity weighted) in a typical global recession is about 0.7 percent, which is 3 percentage points lower than average annual growth of the world economy (2.4 percent) during the years of expansion over 1960–2012.

FIGURE 5.1
Global Recessions: Activity Variables

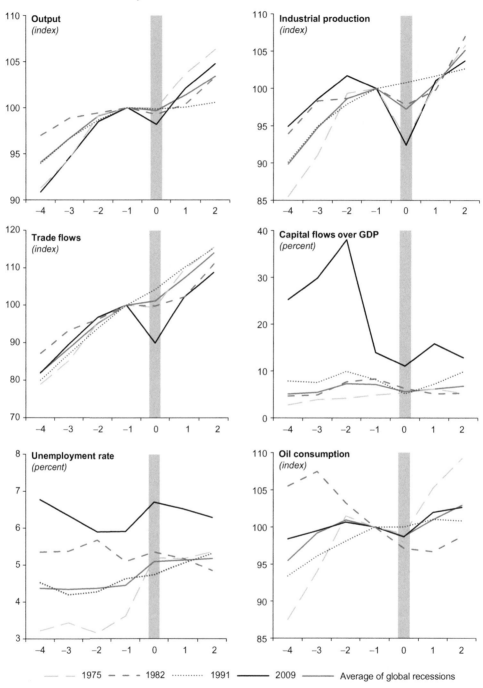

Note: Time 0 denotes the year of the respective global recession (shaded with gray). All variables are in annual frequency. Aggregates for output are purchasing-power-parity-weighted per capita real output indices. Aggregates for industrial production are purchasing-power-parity-weighted industrial production of advanced and emerging market economies. Aggregates for trade are trade-weighted total trade flow indices. Aggregates for unemployment rate are labor-force-weighted unemployment rates in percent. Output, industrial production, trade, and oil consumption are index numbers equal to 100 one period before the global recession year.

TABLE 5.1A

Global Recessions: Activity Variables (percent change unless otherwise noted)

Variable	Average 1972–74	1975	Average 1979–81	1982	Average 1988–90	1991	Average 2006–08	2009	Average All Global Recessions	Average Non-Recession Years 1960–2012	Average Three Years Before Recession	Average 1960–2012
Total output (PW)	5.08	1.82	2.74	1.01	3.79	1.50	4.44	-0.57	0.94	4.07	4.01	3.83
Total output (MW)	4.62	1.54	2.59	0.74	3.81	1.13	3.27	-1.97	0.36	3.70	3.57	3.44
Output per capita (PW)	3.09	-0.07	1.01	-0.74	2.09	-0.14	3.26	-1.81	-0.69	2.43	2.36	2.19
Output per capita (MW)	2.62	-0.35	0.86	-1.02	2.11	-0.50	2.09	-3.22	-1.27	2.06	1.92	1.81
Trade flows	8.22	-0.59	4.71	-0.23	7.72	4.19	6.91	-10.08	-1.68	7.01	6.89	6.34
Capital flows over GDP	0.71	0.44	0.93	-2.06	0.10	-3.00	-3.77	-2.91	-1.88	0.29	-0.51	0.17
Oil consumption	4.61	-0.90	-1.74	-2.87	2.31	0.01	0.54	-1.32	-1.27	2.31	1.43	2.25
Unemployment (labor weighted)	0.13	1.58	-0.08	0.26	0.04	0.11	-0.28	0.79	0.68	-0.02	-0.05	0.08
Industrial production (PW)	5.41	-6.85	2.12	-2.21	3.54	0.81	1.78	-7.58	-3.96	3.99	3.21	3.36
Consumption (PW)	4.83	2.73	3.09	1.79	3.72	2.53	4.28	1.00	2.01	4.05	3.98	3.90
Investment (PW)	5.30	0.42	2.24	-2.63	4.60	0.25	5.63	-5.30	-1.81	5.04	4.44	4.51
Consumption per capita (PW)	2.74	0.74	1.23	-0.99	2.02	0.85	3.23	-0.24	0.09	2.33	2.30	2.16
Investment per capita (PW)	3.21	-1.57	0.34	-5.42	2.88	-1.41	4.46	-6.54	-3.74	3.30	2.72	2.76

Note: All variables except industrial production are in annual frequency; industrial production is in quarterly frequency, and year-over-year growth rates are annualized as the average of four quarters. For unemployment, labor-weighted changes in levels are reported. The "Average Three Years Before Recession" column reflects the average of the three years before global recessions. PW is the purchasing-power-parity-weighted average of the same variable of each country, and MW is the market-weighted average of the same variable of each country. The 1991 recession lasted until 1993 with market weights; all other recessions lasted one year.

TABLE 5.1B
Global Recessions: Financial Variables and Commodity Prices *(percent change unless otherwise noted)*

	Average 1972–74	1975	Average 1979–81	1982	Average 1988–90	1991	Average 2006–08	2009	Average All Global Recessions	Average Non-Recession Years 1960–2012	Average Three Years Before Recession	Average 1960–2012
Financial Variables												
Credit	7.54	−0.34	2.29	2.00	5.53	0.68	7.73	3.10	1.36	5.58	5.77	5.25
House prices	5.04	−3.90	1.37	−3.23	4.59	−0.06	1.53	−2.38	−2.39	1.55	3.13	1.24
Equity prices	−5.32	−4.69	−0.64	−9.44	5.55	−1.41	6.97	−14.52	−7.52	4.76	1.64	3.79
Inflation rate	3.21	0.76	0.61	−1.02	0.24	−0.38	0.46	−3.33	−0.99	−1.21	1.13	−1.17
Nominal short-term interest rates	1.25	−2.33	1.99	−1.36	0.64	−1.83	0.04	−2.14	−1.91	0.07	0.98	−0.08
Real short-term interest rates	−1.17	−0.41	0.88	0.61	0.37	−0.56	−0.38	1.19	0.21	−0.02	−0.07	0.00
LIBOR overnight	2.05	−4.28	3.15	−7.10	0.50	−2.35	−0.31	−2.08	−3.95	0.30	1.35	−0.04
Commodity Prices												
Oil prices	71.76	−12.06	32.13	−20.06	−8.00	−24.69	20.91	−29.40	−21.55	7.59	29.20	6.15
Food prices	24.97	−29.03	−7.33	−21.37	−15.63	−20.06	12.76	−14.99	−21.36	−3.13	3.69	−5.29
Gold prices	43.38	−10.15	26.83	−28.85	−20.37	−20.32	20.55	10.01	−12.33	2.53	17.59	1.58

Note: All variables are in quarterly frequency and year-over-year growth rates are annualized as the average of four quarters. For inflation, nominal and real short-term interest rates, and London interbank offered rate (LIBOR) overnight rate, the year-over-year changes in levels are reported. "Average Three Years Before Recession" column reflects the average of the three years before global recessions. MW is the market-weighted average of the same variable for each country. The 1991 recession lasted until 1993 with market weights; all other recessions lasted one year.

FIGURE 5.2

Global Recessions: Financial Variables, Interest Rates, and Inflation

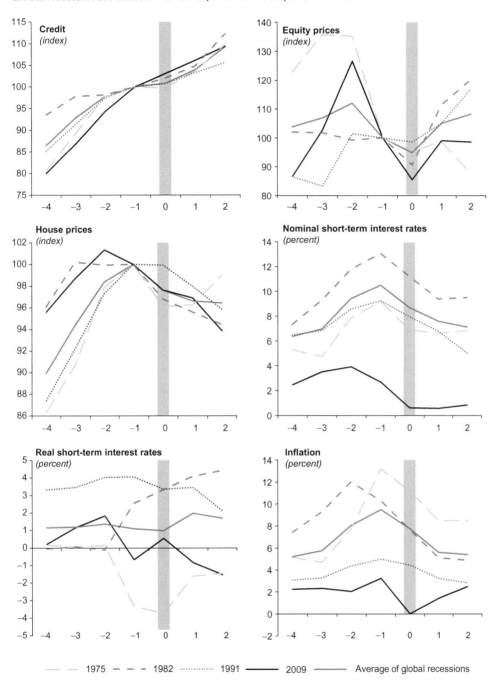

Note: Time 0 denotes the year of the respective global recession (shaded with gray). All variables are in annual frequency. All variables are market weighted by gross domestic product in U.S. dollars. Credit, equity, and house price figures are for advanced and emerging market economies and are index numbers equal to 100 one period before the global recession year. Nominal and real short-term interest rates and inflation are only for advanced economies. Inflation is the change in the consumer price index.

- *The deepest episode is 2009.* The 2009 global recession was by far the deepest in five decades, and as such called the "Great Recession."[1] If total real GDP (rather than per capita) is used as the main metric of economic activity, 2009 was the global economy's only contraction since 1960. There were sharper declines in almost all indicators in 1975 and 1982 than in 1991; in 1991, in fact, world trade grew strongly despite the recession. During the 1991 global recession, only one-third of the advanced economies in our sample experienced national recessions, whereas growth contracted in almost all advanced economies during the 2009 global recession. Chapter 6 analyzes the extent of synchronization of national recessions in more detail.

- *Not much higher growth three years prior to global recessions.* Growth does not appear to be higher before global recessions, with average growth over the three years prior to these episodes comparable with growth in other years. However, when one focuses on a five-year rolling-window average of world growth, it is possible to conclude that the global economy went through relatively more vibrant periods two to three years prior to the 1991 and 2009 episodes. In particular, growth in world output per capita picked up noticeably prior to those two global recessions (Figure 5.3).

FIGURE 5.3

Growth of World Output: Rolling Average *(in percent, per capita, five-year rolling window)*

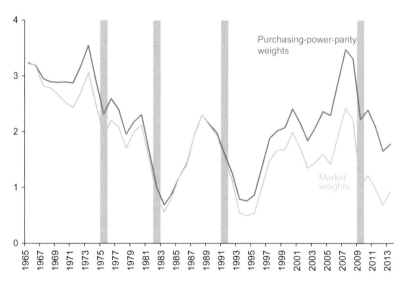

Note: Each line shows the five-year rolling-window average of the percent change from a year earlier. World output growth per capita is the difference between world real output growth and world population growth. World output growth is the weighted average of the growth rate of real output of each country (using the purchasing-power-parity or market weights). Shaded bars indicate global recessions.

- *Broad decline in activity.* Investment, industrial production, and trade often decline much more than output during global recessions. Although consumption on average holds up well (consumption per capita declined in 1982 and 2009, but continued to grow in the two other episodes), the growth of consumption is much smaller than during other years. Given that consumption is the most relevant variable for welfare, much lower consumption growth during global recessions is another indication of the substantial welfare losses associated with these episodes. There are significant declines in both oil consumption and prices during global recessions after noticeable increases in both before these episodes (except the 1991 episode, during which global oil consumption did not change much).

- *Sharp rise in unemployment.* Global unemployment picks up significantly during global recessions. The surge in unemployment was particularly severe during the 1975 and 2009 episodes.[2]

What can explain the much larger contraction in activity during the 2009 global recession compared with previous recessions? In Chapters 6 and 7, we focus on the following factors: the highly synchronized nature of the 2009 global recession and national recessions and the fact that these occurred alongside a severe global financial crisis.

01:17
The unprecedented reach of the 2009 global recession

Financial Markets

Financial markets tend to be depressed during global recessions (Figure 5.2). Although credit continues to expand, the average growth rate of credit is about one-fourth the annual average observed in nonrecession years (Table 5.1B). Both house and equity prices fall during a global recession. The average decline in equity prices is three times larger than the decline in house prices. When there is rapid credit growth prior to global recessions, house prices also tend to increase sharply.

Inflation and Interest Rates

Inflation falls as demand contracts rapidly (Figure 5.2). Nominal short-term rates also drop during global recessions as monetary policies become more accommodative. The behavior of short-term nominal rates during the 2009 global recession clearly shows its unique nature (as some countries quickly hit the zero lower bound). Although real short-term rates also tend to decline during the global recessions, there appears to be wide variation among the four episodes depending on the behavior of inflation and nominal interest rates. For example, real rates collapsed during the 1975 episode but went up during the 1982 recession. Policy rates (nominal short-term rates) increased in many advanced economies prior to the 1982 episode because of the reasons discussed in Chapter 3.

These results collectively indicate that the behavior of the main macroeconomic and financial variables during global recessions are comparable with those observed during national recessions. For example, much larger changes in investment, industrial production, and international trade relative to changes in output and relatively smooth patterns of consumption during global recessions are also observed during national recessions. The similarities across the four global recessions clearly show the value of studying these episodes.

THE 2009 GLOBAL RECESSION: COLLAPSE ALL OVER

The sharp declines in a wide range of economic indicators point to the severity of the 2009 global recession. Investment per capita declined in all the global recessions, along with the massive fall in output, but the decline in the last recession easily exceeded that during previous episodes.

The collapse of global trade and capital flows during the 2009 global recession is particularly striking. Although the globalization of national manufacturing chains has been a major force driving the growth of world trade during the past two decades, the same process appeared to be instrumental in the sharp contraction of cross-border trade flows. The decline in global trade during this episode dwarfs the decline during previous episodes. Indeed, the collapse of global trade was one reason the recession evoked fears of another Great Depression and provoked protectionist measures by some governments seeking to shield domestic industries from foreign competition.[3]

A number of recent studies examine the sharp decline of trade relative to output during the 2009 global recession. In addition to the importance of the rise of global manufacturing chains, these studies advance other potential explanations, including the sharp fall in trade credit, the dramatic decline in durable goods trade, significant movements in inventories, and the large magnitude of cross-border spillovers associated with demand shocks.[4]

Global capital flows also fell more sharply during the 2009 global recession. After overshadowing the growth of global trade flows over the past two decades, global capital flows reached unprecedented levels in 2007. However, these flows dried up rapidly in the last quarter of 2008 as the global financial crisis spread from advanced economies to emerging market and developing economies. Global capital flows also declined substantially in 1982 and 1991, but much less so than during the 2009 global recession. Recent research shows that these declines are also associated with country-specific features, including openness to financial and trade flows, the nature of financial linkages with the rest of the world (for example, bank flows were associated with much larger declines), and domestic macroeconomic conditions.[5]

01:35

The human costs of the 2009 global recession

The rate of global unemployment was higher during the 2009 global recession than during other episodes. Specifically, the unemployment rate increased about 2.5 percentage points in advanced economies (Figure 5.4).

FIGURE 5.4

Global Recessions: Selected Activity Variables by Country Group

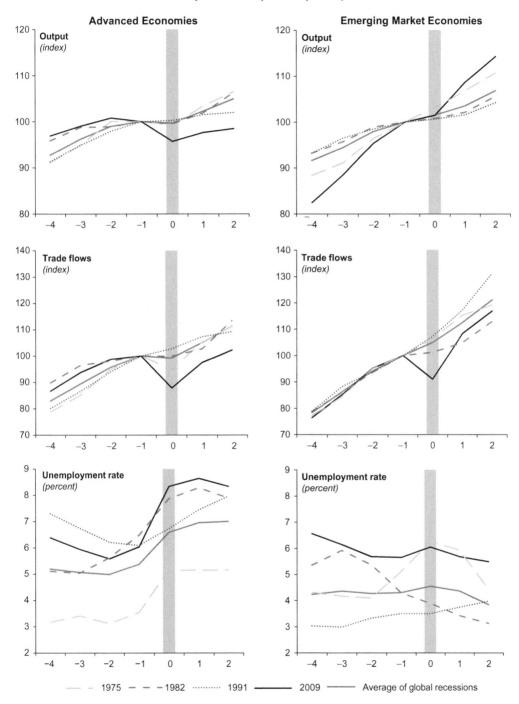

Note: Time 0 denotes the year of the respective global recession (shaded with gray). All variables are in annual frequency. Aggregates for output are purchasing-power-parity-weighted per capita real output indices. Aggregates for trade are trade-weighted total trade flow indices. Aggregates for unemployment rate are labor-force-weighted unemployment rates in percent. Output and trade are index numbers equal to 100 one period before the global recession year.

02:18

The U.S. housing crisis and its effects on American households

The 2009 global recession led to a worldwide increase of 23 million in the number of people unemployed.[6] We discuss this issue in detail in Chapter 5.

All the financial variables we focus on declined during 2009, although these declines were not necessarily larger than during previous episodes (Table 5.1B). When we analyze the behavior of these variables in the context of the decline prior to the global recession, however, the recent episode definitely stands out (Figure 5.2). Many countries experienced housing bubbles before the 2009 global recession and ended up with significant declines in house prices during the global recession.

DIFFERENT EFFECTS BY COUNTRY

Although aggregate data about the dynamics of global recessions provide a wealth of information, they also mask substantial variation in growth among different groups of countries. In advanced economies, GDP per capita contracted in three of the four global recessions, with 1991 the exception (Figure 5.4 and Table 5.2). Advanced economies were the main locus of the collapse in world GDP in 2009 (Figure 5.5). They went through deep recessions and experienced much larger declines in their GDP compared with previous episodes. In particular, real output per capita fell 4.3 percent, that is, roughly 7 percentage points lower than their average growth during the non-recession years.

The 2009 global recession was different for emerging market and developing economies than the previous three global recessions: output per capita actually grew. But while emerging market economies as a group performed relatively well during the latest global recession, there were sharp differences among the economies in different regions (detailed tables document the performance of different regions in Appendix F). Emerging Asia, for example, had the most favorable outcomes, with growth rates declining only modestly. China and India, the two largest economies in emerging Asia, maintained strong growth during the crisis. Output fell most sharply in emerging Europe due to the collapse of capital inflows, international trade, and domestic demand as many of these economies experienced financial crises. Somewhat surprisingly, economies in the Middle East and North Africa and in sub-Saharan Africa weathered the crisis relatively well. Their modest exposures to trade and financial flows from advanced economies may have limited the extent of spillovers from the global shocks. Economies in these regions had also improved their macroeconomic policies prior to the global recession, which gave them more space to respond to the global shock with countercyclical policy measures.

The brunt of the 2009 global recession fell on advanced economies.

What best explains the resilience of emerging market economies as a group during the 2009 global financial crisis? The literature emphasizes seven factors.[7] These factors are also useful in understanding differences in resilience across various groups of emerging market economies. First, emerging market

TABLE 5.2

Global Recessions: Activity Variables by Country Group *(percent change)*

Variable	Average 1972–74	1975	Average 1979–81	1982	Average 1988–90	1991	Average 2006–2008	2009	Average All Global Recessions	Average Non-Recession Years 1960–2012	Average Three Years Before Recession	Average 1960–2012
Advanced Economies												
Total output (PW)	4.10	0.05	2.13	0.06	3.78	1.12	1.72	−3.70	−0.62	3.30	2.93	3.00
Total output (MW)	3.99	0.05	2.16	0.01	3.86	1.15	1.73	−3.73	−0.63	3.22	2.94	2.92
Output per capita (PW)	3.22	−0.73	1.43	−0.52	3.08	0.28	1.05	−4.27	−1.31	2.56	2.20	2.26
Output per capita (MW)	3.11	−0.73	1.47	−0.56	3.17	0.31	1.07	−4.31	−1.32	2.47	2.20	2.18
Emerging Market Economies												
Total output (PW)	6.46	5.19	4.12	2.66	4.06	2.24	7.66	2.60	3.17	5.26	5.58	5.10
Total output (MW)	6.11	4.87	3.90	2.72	4.01	1.42	7.12	1.63	2.66	5.21	5.28	5.01
Output per capita (PW)	4.22	3.06	2.38	0.76	2.37	0.64	6.65	1.49	1.48	3.59	3.90	3.42
Output per capita (MW)	3.87	2.74	2.16	0.81	2.32	−0.19	6.10	0.53	0.97	3.54	3.61	3.34
Other Developing Economies												
Total output (PW)	8.11	3.97	2.54	1.96	2.88	1.40	6.09	1.79	2.28	4.37	4.91	4.21
Total output (MW)	5.55	4.13	2.62	1.21	2.43	−0.42	5.95	1.02	1.48	4.05	4.14	3.85
Output per capita (PW)	5.78	1.76	−0.17	−0.41	0.32	−0.96	4.13	−0.24	0.04	1.98	2.51	1.83
Output per capita (MW)	3.22	1.92	−0.09	−1.17	−0.13	−2.78	3.99	−1.01	−0.76	1.67	1.75	1.48

Note: All variables are in annual frequency. "Average Three Years Before Recession" column reflects the average of the three years before global recessions. PW is the purchasing-power-parity-weighted average of the same variable of each country, and MW is the market-weighted average of the same variable for each country. The 1991 recession lasted until 1993 with market weights; all other recessions lasted one year.

FIGURE 5.5

Contributions to Global Growth during Global Recessions

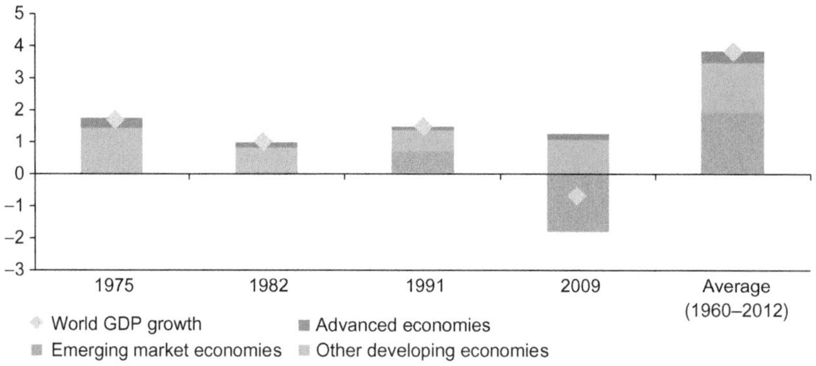

Note: Each bar presents the contributions of three country groups to world GDP growth (purchasing-power-parity weighted) in the respective time period. World GDP growth is purchasing-power-parity weighted.

economies have become less dependent on foreign finance and have shifted away from foreign-currency-denominated external debt. Second, they came into the crisis with much larger buffers of foreign exchange reserves.[8] Third, greater trade linkages among emerging market economies themselves increased their resilience by shielding them to some extent from slower growth in the advanced economies.

Fourth, emerging market economies also have more diversified production and export patterns. Fifth, their business cycles show signs of having diverged from those in the advanced economies as they increased their intragroup trade and financial linkages. Sixth, many emerging market economies have instituted more stable macroeconomic policies, including flexible exchange rate regimes.

Finally, in a number of emerging market economies, rising income levels per capita and a burgeoning middle class have increased the size and absorptive capacity of domestic markets, making them potentially less reliant on foreign trade to benefit from economies of scale in their production structures and also less susceptible to a collapse of exports.

Although emerging market economies as a group displayed resilience during the 2009 global crisis, many subsequently experienced what appears to be a synchronized slowdown. During 2010–14, growth rates in many emerging market economies were markedly lower than prior to the 2009 global financial crisis and are expected to decline in the medium term. This is a result of both external factors, including likely tightening of global financial conditions and weak global trade, and internal factors, including political uncertainty and challenges associated with macroeconomic and structural policies.

GLOBAL DOWNTURNS: CLOSE CALLS!

In addition to the four global recessions discussed here, the global economy experienced relatively low growth in 1998 and 2001. World output per capita (in purchasing-power-parity terms) grew slightly more than 1 percent in these two years (Figure 5.6 and Table 5.3A), the lowest growth rates the global economy registered during 1960–2012, except in the years of global recessions and the years before and after these episodes.

These downturns fall short of qualifying as a global recession, however. The statistical approach we use does not identify these episodes as troughs because world real GDP per capita did not contract in these years. In 1997–98, economic activity in many emerging market economies, particularly in Asia, declined sharply, but growth in advanced economies held up. In 2001, conversely, many advanced economies had mild slowdowns or recessions, but growth in major emerging market economies, such as China and India, remained robust.[9]

Moreover, during 1998 and 2001, the behavior of the other global indicators was rather mixed, supporting the inference from the statistical method that these episodes did not display the features of a global recession. For example, the main activity indicators we focus on did not suggest a broad-based weakness in the global economy in 1998.[10] In 2001, although industrial production did fall and the rate of global unemployment picked up slightly, both global trade flows and oil consumption increased.[11] Equity prices declined substantially in 2001, and prices of commodities declined significantly in both episodes (Table 5.3B).

FIGURE 5.6
Growth of World Output during Global Downturns *(in percent, per capita)*

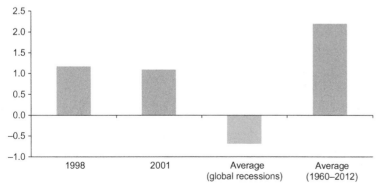

Note: Each bar shows world output growth per capita (purchasing-power-parity weighted) for the relevant period. Global downturn years are 1998 and 2001. Global recession years are 1975, 1982, 1991, and 2009.

TABLE 5.3A
Global Downturns: Activity Variables (percent change unless otherwise noted)

Variable	1998	2001	Average (global recessions)	Average (1960–2012)
Total output (PW)	2.55	2.31	0.94	3.83
Total output (MW)	2.31	1.65	0.36	3.44
Output per capita (PW)	1.17	1.09	−0.69	2.19
Output per capita (MW)	0.93	0.43	−1.27	1.81
Trade flows	4.70	0.25	−1.68	6.34
Capital flows over GDP	−0.44	−7.31	−1.88	0.12
Oil consumption	0.46	0.74	−1.27	2.03
Unemployment (labor weighted)	0.33	0.56	0.68	0.06
Industrial production (PW)	1.83	−1.85	−3.87	3.78
Consumption (PW)	2.42	2.89	2.01	3.90
Investment (PW)	4.41	0.63	−1.81	4.51
Consumption per capita (PW)	0.91	1.67	0.09	2.16
Investment per capita (PW)	3.02	−0.58	−3.74	2.76

Note: All variables except industrial production are in annual frequency. Industrial production is in quarterly frequency, and year-over-year growth rates are annualized as the average of four quarters. For unemployment, labor-weighted changes in levels are reported. Global downturn years are 1998 and 2001. PW is the purchasing-power-parity-weighted average of the same variable for each country, and MW is the market-weighted average of the same variable for each country.

TABLE 5.3B
Global Downturns: Financial Variables and Commodity Prices (percent change unless otherwise noted)

Variable	1998	2001	Average (global recessions)	Average (1960–2012)
Financial Variables				
Credit (MW)	5.06	3.34	1.29	5.25
House prices (MW)	1.06	2.67	−2.44	1.24
Equity prices (MW)	9.07	−15.06	−7.63	3.79
Inflation rate (MW)	−0.52	−0.21	−1.04	−1.17
Nominal short-term interest rates (MW)	0.24	−0.89	−1.94	−0.08
Real short-term interest rates (MW)	1.08	−0.75	0.22	0.00
LIBOR overnight	0.06	0.00	−3.95	−0.04
Commodity Prices				
Oil prices	−35.63	−16.92	−21.55	6.15
Food prices	−15.04	−5.90	−21.34	−5.29
Gold prices	−15.66	−6.75	−12.33	1.58

Note: All variables are in quarterly frequency, and year-over-year growth rates are annualized as the average of four quarters. For inflation, nominal and real short-term interest rates, and London interbank offered rate (LIBOR) overnight rate, the year-over-year changes in levels are reported. All variables except nominal short-term interest rates, LIBOR overnight, and inflation rate are in real terms. MW is the market-weighted average of the same variable for each country.

These results confirm the earlier finding by Kenneth Rogoff and his coauthors about the 2001 episode. Specifically, they also concluded that the 2001 episode "falls somewhere short of a global recession, certainly in comparison with earlier episodes . . . That said, it was a close call."[12]

HOW OFTEN? HOW LIKELY?

The quotes at the beginning of this chapter show that it is easy to make casual statements about the frequency and likelihood of global recessions.[13] Using the disciplined analysis of these episodes we present here, we are able to reach some better informed conclusions about the frequency and likelihood of global recessions. Considering the four global recessions and two global slowdowns we identify since 1960, one can observe that the global economy comes to the verge of a recession or a slowdown over a cycle lasting nine years. This implies that during 1960–2014 the likelihood of a global recession in any given year was about 7 percent (4/55) and the likelihood of a global recession or a downturn was slightly higher than 11 percent (6/55).

WHAT HAPPENS AFTER GLOBAL RECESSIONS?

The world economy experiences periods of collapse during global recessions but eventually finds its footing and rebounds. We became acquainted with the main features of global recessions in this chapter; it is time to delve into the characteristics of global recoveries, which are periods of revival for the world economy.

The recovery on which the fate of so many businesses depends has faltered in most major economies. Bankruptcies break new records. The revival in demand in the industrial world this year may soon putter out.

The Economist (1982b)

Many commentators are suggesting that the recent data . . . indicate that the "green shoots" of an economic recovery are clearly visible. While there do seem to be some signs of improvement . . . the most recent data may still suggest that the global economic contraction is still in full swing with a very severe, deep and protracted U-shaped recession.

Nouriel Roubini (2009)

CHAPTER 6

Global Recoveries: Tales of Revival

Strong recoveries are all alike; every weak recovery has its own story. However, our knowledge about the evolution of global recoveries is limited. How does the world economy recover after a global recession? Has the ongoing recovery after the 2009 global recession been different? This chapter documents the main similarities of global recoveries and presents the specific features of the recovery following the Great Recession.

GLOBAL RECOVERIES: MAIN SIMILARITIES

A recovery at the national level is often defined as the early part of an expansion phase in the business cycle. We define a global recovery as the period—usually the first year—of increasing economic activity following a global recession. In addition, we study the first three years following a global recession, given the possibility that a global recovery can take longer than one year. We focus on the recoveries that followed the global recessions of 1975, 1982, 1991, and 2009.

A global recovery is the period—usually the first year—of increasing economic activity following a global recession.

Real Economy

The periods of revivals after global recessions display many similarities (Figure 6.1 and Tables 6.1A and 6.1B).[1]

- *A broad rebound in activity.* A typical global recovery is accompanied by a broad rebound in economic activity, generally driven by a pickup in consumption, investment, industrial production, and international trade. How do these variables respond to changes in world output? To answer this, we calculate the changes in these variables in response to a 1 percentage point change in the growth rate of global output per capita. The results indicate that in response to such an increase in world gross domestic product (GDP) growth per capita, growth in world consumption per capita increases by 0.8 percentage point, investment by

FIGURE 6.1

Global Recoveries: Activity Variables

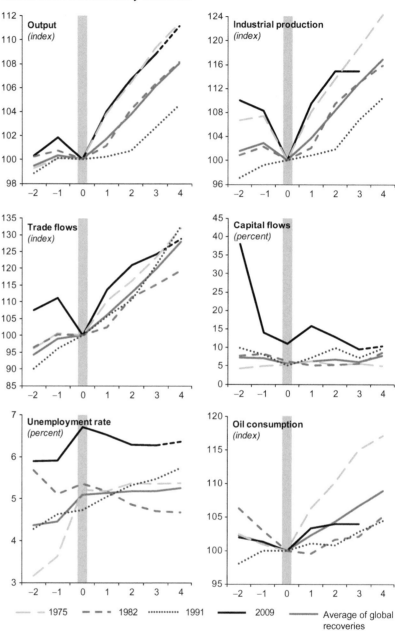

Note: Time 0 denotes the year of the respective global recession (shaded with gray). All variables are in annual frequency. Aggregates for output are purchasing-power-parity-weighted per capita real output indices. Aggregates for industrial production are purchasing-power-parity-weighted industrial production of advanced and emerging market economies. Aggregates for trade are trade-weighted total trade flow indices. Aggregates for unemployment rate are labor-force-weighted unemployment rates in percent. Output, industrial production, trade, and oil consumption are index numbers equal to 100 in the global recession year. For the latest recovery, data for 2013 (year 4) are based on the IMF's *World Economic Outlook* forecasts.

TABLE 6.1A

Global Recoveries: Activity Variables *(percent change unless otherwise noted)*

Variable	1976	Average 1976–78	1983	Average 1983–85	1992	Average 1992–94	2010	Average 2010–12	Average of First Years	Average of First Three Years	Average 1960–2012
Total output (PW)	5.43	4.74	2.91	3.78	1.97	2.44	5.17	4.02	3.87	3.74	3.83
Total output (MW)	5.15	4.57	3.00	3.88	1.61	2.15	4.25	3.25	3.50	3.46	3.44
Output per capita (PW)	3.79	3.02	1.16	2.05	0.21	0.88	3.99	2.86	2.29	2.20	2.19
Output per capita (MW)	3.52	2.85	1.25	2.16	−0.15	0.59	3.07	2.09	1.92	1.92	1.81
Trade flows	10.33	7.25	2.41	4.86	5.68	6.61	13.67	7.59	8.02	6.58	6.34
Capital flows	0.85	0.07	−1.12	−0.19	2.09	0.72	4.79	−0.47	1.65	0.03	0.17
Oil consumption	6.25	4.76	−0.47	0.69	1.02	0.91	3.32	1.33	2.53	1.92	2.25
Unemployment (labor weighted)	−0.03	0.05	−0.17	−0.22	0.32	0.25	−0.18	−0.15	−0.01	−0.02	0.08
Industrial production (PW)	8.08	5.93	2.10	4.17	0.89	2.23	9.36	5.98	5.11	4.36	3.36
Consumption (PW)	4.82	4.62	3.92	3.92	3.34	3.30	4.36	3.80	4.11	3.91	3.90
Investment (PW)	5.94	5.96	1.57	3.82	2.33	3.17	5.64	4.67	3.87	4.40	4.51
Consumption per capita (PW)	3.14	2.84	2.04	1.68	1.63	1.56	3.18	2.75	2.50	2.21	2.16
Investment per capita (PW)	4.26	4.19	−0.55	1.62	0.62	1.41	4.47	3.62	2.20	2.71	2.76

Note: All variables except industrial production are in annual frequency. Industrial production is in quarterly frequency, and year-over-year growth rates are annualized as the average of four quarters. For unemployment, labor-weighted changes in levels are reported. "Average of First Three Years" column reflects the average of the three years following the global recessions. PW is the purchasing-power-parity-weighted average of the same variable for each country, and MW is the market-weighted average of the same variable for each country.

TABLE 6.1B

Global Recoveries: Financial Variables and Commodity Prices *(percent change unless otherwise noted)*

Variable	1976	Average 1976–78	1983	Average 1983–85	1992	Average 1992–94	2010	Average 2010–12	Average of First Years	Average of First Three Years	Average 1960–2012
Financial Variables											
Credit (MW)	4.04	5.57	2.76	5.50	2.61	2.53	2.97	3.18	3.10	4.17	5.25
House prices (MW)	0.16	2.30	-1.23	-0.49	-1.96	-1.53	-0.74	-1.29	-0.94	-0.17	1.24
Equity prices (MW)	3.45	-3.52	22.93	15.94	6.47	9.56	15.90	4.28	12.18	8.54	3.79
Inflation rate (MW)	2.37	-0.72	1.65	2.44	-1.19	-0.55	1.55	0.55	1.10	0.57	-1.17
Nominal short-term interest rates (MW)	-0.29	0.15	-1.43	-0.71	-1.47	-1.05	0.04	0.09	-0.79	-0.60	-0.08
Real short-term interest rates (MW)	2.13	1.20	0.17	0.18	0.48	-0.15	-1.51	-0.47	0.32	0.39	0.00
LIBOR overnight	-1.91	0.70	-3.29	-1.52	-2.19	-0.51	0.00	-0.03	-1.84	-0.80	-0.04
Commodity Prices											
Oil prices	-9.63	-6.71	-19.86	-18.17	-16.02	-21.98	28.19	16.37	-4.33	-12.80	6.15
Food prices	-15.97	-8.53	-14.45	-17.55	-15.66	-17.09	7.82	5.14	-9.56	-13.18	-5.29
Gold prices	-30.23	-1.80	-2.48	-17.85	-19.13	-15.69	21.79	16.97	-7.51	-10.71	1.58

Note: All variables are in quarterly frequency, and year-over-year growth rates are annualized as the average of four quarters. For inflation, nominal and real short-term interest rates, and London interbank offered rate (LIBOR) overnight rate, the year-over-year changes in levels are reported. "Average of First Three Years" column reflects the average of the three years following the global recessions. MW is the market-weighted average of the same variable for each country.

FIGURE 6.2
Sensitivity of Global Activity Variables

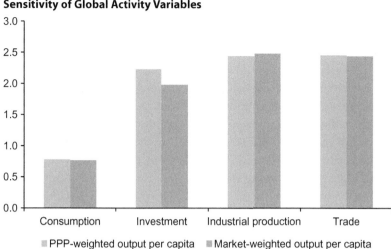

Note: Each bar represents the sensitivity of the respective variable to a 1 percentage point change in world GDP per capita. For example, the growth rate of global consumption per capita increases about 0.8 percentage points when the growth rate of global output per capita increases 1 percentage point. Details of these calculations are presented in Appendix G. PPP = purchasing power parity.

2.2 percentage points, industrial production by 2.4 percentage points, and trade by 2.5 percentage points (Figure 6.2).[2] Most indicators of global activity also start growing in the first year of a recovery. In particular, industrial production, trade, and capital flows quickly rebound during the first year.

- *Some recoveries are stronger than others.* The global recovery from the 1975 recession was the strongest in terms of average output growth in the first three years of the recovery. As we discuss in detail below, the latest episode featured an even stronger rebound in global industrial production and trade during the first three years. The global recovery following the 1991 recession was the weakest, partly reflecting sluggish growth in consumption, investment, industrial production, and trade flows.

- *Similar growth performance.* The average growth over the three years following a global recession is close to the average growth of the global economy in a typical year.

- *Weak labor markets.* Notwithstanding the pickup in activity, the rate of global unemployment often remains high in the year after a trough and tends to be more persistent than most other indicators. For example, during the weak recovery following the 1991 recession the global unemployment rate grew four years in a row.

Financial Markets

Global financial markets become healthier as recoveries strengthen over time (Figure 6.3). Although global equity prices on average pick up quickly in the first year of a recovery, house prices tend to stay depressed for two to three years. Credit also takes longer to attain the types of growth rates observed during nonrecession periods. Although creditless recoveries observed in national economies do not take place at the global level, the growth of credit tends to be much weaker during global recoveries than the annual average during the nonrecession years (Table 6.1B).

There appear to be differences in the behavior of financial markets during the four global recoveries. Housing markets were mostly depressed during recoveries following the last three global recessions. In contrast, average growth in equity markets was much larger during the first year of the global recoveries than in other years. Equity markets stayed weak during the recovery after the 1975 recession, reflecting a long period of stagflation in several major advanced economies.

Inflation and Interest Rates

Inflation tends to decline during global recoveries (Figure 6.3). Nominal short-term rates stay low because monetary policies often remain accommodative. In fact, nominal short-term rates have declined in the first year of every global recovery. Real short-term rates tend to pick up, but patterns appear to vary widely across episodes depending on the behavior of inflation and nominal interest rates.

THE LATEST RECOVERY: WEAKER OR STRONGER?

Although the ongoing trajectory of global GDP growth since 2009 was quite similar to the period following the 1975 global recession, there was an even stronger rebound in industrial production and trade in the first three years. The first year of the latest recovery was the strongest among the four episodes (measured in GDP per capita in purchasing-power-parity terms).[3] The robustness of the global recovery surprised many observers who expected a much weaker outcome, as the major advanced economies continued to experience the adverse effects of the financial crisis. The qualitative behavior of unemployment during the latest global recovery follows that during the previous episodes. The behavior of credit and equity markets has also been similar to that of the previous episodes.

The current global recovery is significantly different from the previous three episodes in at least five major dimensions. First, one of its most distinguishing features has been its uneven nature, with major differences in the performance of advanced economies and emerging market economies (Figure 6.4 and Table 6.2). Advanced economies were the engines of previous global recoveries, but the emerging market economies have accounted for the lion's share of global growth since the 2009 global recession (Figure 6.5).

FIGURE 6.3

Global Recoveries: Financial Variables, Interest Rates, and Inflation

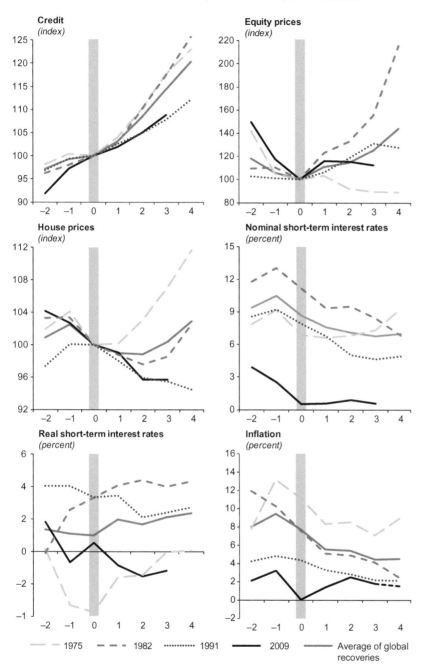

Note: Time 0 denotes the year of the respective global recession (shaded with gray). All variables are in annual frequency. All variables are market weighted by output in U.S. dollars. Credit, equity, and house prices are for advanced and emerging market economies and are index numbers equal to 100 in the global recession year. Nominal and real short-term interest rates and inflation are only for advanced economies. Inflation is the change in the consumer price index.

FIGURE 6.4

Global Recoveries: Selected Activity Variables by Country Group

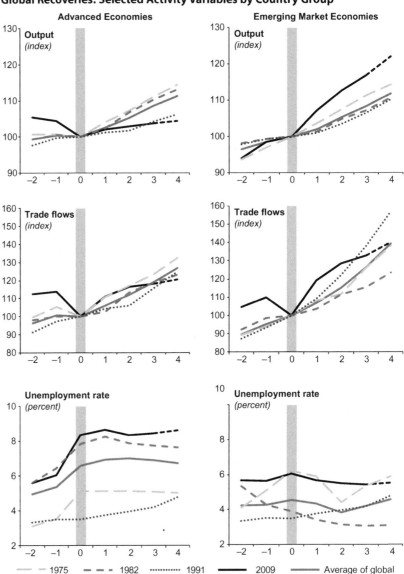

Note: Time 0 denotes the year of the respective global recession (shaded with gray). All variables are in annual frequency. Aggregates for output are purchasing-power-parity-weighted per capita real output indices. Aggregates for trade are trade-weighted total trade flow indices. Aggregates for unemployment rate are labor-force-weighted unemployment rates in percent. Output and trade are index numbers equal to 100 in the global recession year. For the latest recovery, data for 2013 (year 4) are based on the IMF's *World Economic Outlook* forecasts.

TABLE 6.2
Global Recoveries: Activity Variables by Country Group *(percent change)*

Variable	1976	Average 1976–78	1983	Average 1983–85	1992	Average 1992–94	2010	Average 2010–12	Average of First Years	Average of First Three Years	Average 1960–2012
Advanced Economies											
Total output (PW)	4.80	4.23	2.92	3.85	1.98	2.10	2.54	1.71	3.06	2.97	3.00
Total output (MW)	4.80	4.23	3.04	4.03	1.84	1.92	2.57	1.71	3.06	2.97	2.92
Output per capita (PW)	4.13	3.58	2.40	3.34	1.23	1.38	2.02	1.21	2.45	2.38	2.26
Output per capita (MW)	4.13	3.58	2.53	3.52	1.10	1.21	2.05	1.21	2.45	2.38	2.18
Emerging Market Economies											
Total output (PW)	5.37	5.50	3.20	4.15	2.49	3.64	8.11	6.35	4.79	4.91	5.10
Total output (MW)	4.95	5.29	3.53	4.24	1.88	3.90	7.81	6.12	4.55	4.89	5.01
Output per capita (PW)	3.60	3.65	1.34	2.34	0.94	2.13	7.06	5.34	3.23	3.36	3.42
Output per capita (MW)	3.19	3.44	1.67	2.43	0.33	2.39	6.77	5.10	2.99	3.34	3.34
Other Developing Economies											
Total output (PW)	9.64	5.79	1.89	2.08	−0.15	0.20	5.15	4.73	4.13	3.20	4.21
Total output (MW)	8.72	5.49	1.26	1.72	−2.29	−0.33	4.89	4.64	3.15	2.88	3.85
Output per capita (PW)	7.45	3.42	−0.61	−0.45	−3.42	−2.19	3.20	2.79	1.65	0.89	1.83
Output per capita (MW)	6.53	3.12	−1.25	−0.81	−5.55	−2.72	2.94	2.69	0.67	0.57	1.48

Note: PW is the purchasing-power-parity-weighted average of the same variable for each country, and MW is the market-weighted average of the same variable for each country.

FIGURE 6.5

Contributions to Global Growth during Global Recoveries *(in percent)*

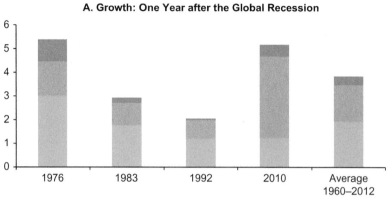

A. Growth: One Year after the Global Recession

■ Advanced economies   ■ Emerging market economies   ■ Other developing economies

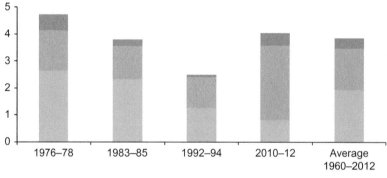

B. Growth: Average of Three Years after the Global Recession

■ Advanced economies   ■ Emerging market economies   ■ Other developing economies

Note: Each bar represents the contribution of each country group to world GDP growth (purchasing-power-parity weighted) in the respective time periods.

01:55

The role of emerging market economies in the 2009 global recession

Moreover, emerging market economies, as a group, have enjoyed their strongest recovery to date. Although they were also severely affected by the collapse of global trade in 2009, they delivered strong growth in 2010, largely driven by buoyant domestic demand, vibrant financial markets, and expansionary policies. However, as discussed in Chapter 5, average growth in emerging market economies during 2010–14 was quite high but was significantly lower than during 2003–08.

The strong performance of emerging market economies during the early years of the recovery also reflects structural improvements such as better-regulated financial systems and stronger macroeconomic frameworks, which allowed them to pursue more credible and effective countercyclical policies. However, there were differences in the strength of recovery across regions as well (see detailed tables in Appendix H).[4]

Second, for advanced economies, the latest recovery appears to be the weakest during the postwar era (Figure 6.6).[5] This partly reflects the legacy of

FIGURE 6.6

Global Recoveries: World and Advanced Economies

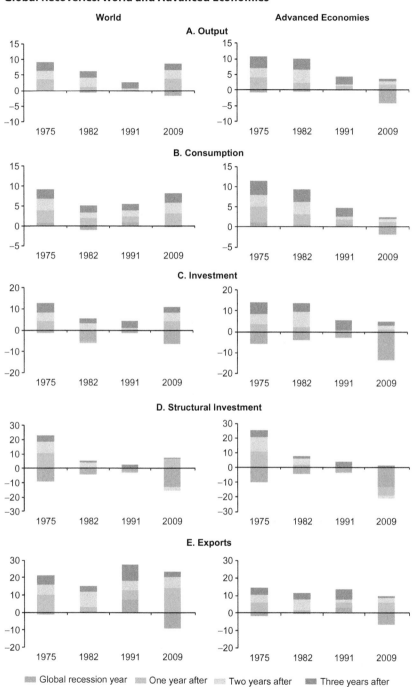

Note: Each bar represents the percent change in the respective variable during the years of the global recessions and the global recoveries. The variables for output, consumption, investment, and structural investment are the purchasing-power-parity-weighted averages and are in per capita terms. Output, consumption, and investment are in real terms. Structural investment and exports are in current U.S. dollars.

the global financial crisis, particularly the need for balance sheet repair in both the household and the financial sectors. Some advanced economies in the euro area also struggled to finance their public debt and experienced severe sovereign debt crises. Compared with previous episodes, the growth rates of consumption and investment have also been much smaller. We discuss the role played by financial disruptions in explaining the sluggish nature of the ongoing recovery in advanced economies in Chapter 7.

Third, the deterioration in labor markets was worse during the latest global recovery than during previous episodes, and it was much more pronounced in advanced economies. Consistent with weak income growth in these economies, unemployment fell only very slowly during the recovery, suggesting that the jobless nature of the two previous recoveries also characterizes the latest episode. In emerging market economies, in contrast, unemployment rates slightly declined on average in the first three years of recovery.

Among the advanced economies, increases in the unemployment rate varied considerably across countries during the recession. Three factors account for this: the extent of growth (or lack thereof) in incomes, structural bottlenecks, and the impact of macroeconomic and labor market policies. Structural factors may have played a supporting role in some countries, particularly where the collapse of the housing sector was a major reason for the drop in output. The role of policies, especially labor market policies such as work sharing, has been important in some specific cases (for example, in Germany, where unemployment declined). However, the growth factor was by far most important in explaining the differential performance of labor markets across countries.[6]

Fourth, cumulative growth in investment was quite small during 2010–12. Contrary to previous global recoveries, there was a contraction in investment in structures in the first three years of the latest recovery. The decline in the growth rate of investment in structures in advanced economies was especially severe because of the deterioration in credit and housing markets. Indeed, this has been the first time that house prices in the United States collapsed nationally. Housing markets in many advanced economies remained weak during 2009–14, and residential investment stayed depressed as households struggled to improve their balance sheets.

Fifth, this recovery has been different because uncertainty in the advanced economies has been unusually high and volatile whereas the previous episodes coincided with steady declines in uncertainty. We analyze the role of uncertainty in explaining macroeconomic outcomes in Chapter 8.

Finally, the latest recovery differs from the earlier episodes in the evolution of fiscal and monetary policies: these policies were aligned in previous recoveries, but they diverged in the latest episode. We present a detailed analysis of this divergence and its implications in Chapter 9.

IS IT 1992 ALL OVER AGAIN?

Despite the marked difference in the severity of the 1991 and 2009 global recessions, their underlying causes and the evolution of activity during the following recoveries share remarkable similarities for the group of advanced economies.

Both recoveries were preceded by recessions associated with severe disruptions in credit and housing markets in the major advanced economies. In particular, the global recovery following the 1991 recession was adversely affected by the ripple effects of a collapse in credit and asset markets in the United States and Japan.[7] Similarly, the deep 2009 global recession was associated with substantial problems in credit and housing markets in the United States and a number of other advanced economies, including Ireland, Spain, and the United Kingdom.

Both the 1991 and 2009 global recessions were attended by financial crises, and the ensuing recoveries were weak and protracted.

Both recoveries were also slowed by challenges in Europe (Figure 6.7). Specifically, the latest recovery and the one in the early 1990s were hampered by financial market problems in the advanced European economies, driven by their desire to protect the exchange rate mechanisms that they designed—the managed float regime of the European Exchange Rate Mechanism (ERM) in the earlier episode and the euro more recently. As Chapter 3 documents, the earlier recovery was shaped by downturns in many European countries during the ERM crisis of 1992–93, when interest rates were raised to defend the exchange rate arrangement after the 1991 global recession. This further depressed economic activity and credit and housing markets.[8]

The recent recovery lost its momentum in late 2011 as the financial crises in some euro area countries intensified and threatened growth in other parts of the world. Challenges associated with sovereign debt markets in some countries in the euro area exposed the flaws in the design of monetary union and led many member countries to resort to the use of contractionary fiscal policies amid a protracted period of balance sheet repair.[9] The euro area suffered a double-dip recession that started in the third quarter of 2011. After experiencing its longest recession ever, the euro area began growing again, albeit at a very low rate, in the second quarter of 2013. Several countries again fell into recession or experienced weak growth during 2014.

A speech in July 2012 by European Central Bank (ECB) President Mario Draghi marked a critical turning point in the euro area crisis as he sent a strong signal about the ECB's policy line when he said that "the ECB is ready to do whatever it takes to preserve the euro. And believe me, it will be enough."[10] Financial markets in Europe stayed relatively calm since the ECB employed its Outright Monetary Transactions program in September 2012 to lower the borrowing costs of EU periphery countries. However, corporate and household debt both remained high, which dampened growth during 2014.

02:45

The devastating effects of the crisis have lingered, particularly in Europe.

FIGURE 6.7
Global Recoveries: Euro Area

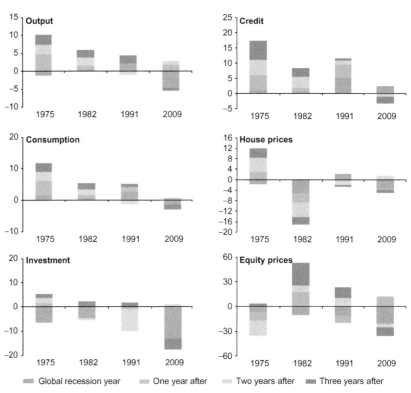

Note: Each bar represents the percent change in the respective variable in the years of the global recessions and recoveries. Growth rates of output, consumption, and investment are the purchasing-power-parity-weighted averages and are in per capita terms. Growth rates of real credit, real house prices, and real equity prices are market weighted by output in U.S. dollars.

There was substantial volatility in world oil markets during the global recessions of both 1991 and 2009. Oil prices increased rapidly in the 1991 episode, mainly because of the Gulf War. Likewise, oil prices escalated during the 2009 global recession to unprecedented levels in a short time. Although prices declined during the recovery following the 1991 recession (and other episodes), oil prices remained elevated through mid-2014, which was a drag on the recovery process. However, oil prices rapidly declined in the second half of 2014.

The recoveries following the 1991 and 2009 global recessions were both characterized by meager growth in advanced economies. In part, this was the result of disappointing growth in domestic consumption and investment, which in turn was driven by the legacies of the financial crisis in advanced economies—namely, the need to mend household balance sheets, weak credit expansion, and lingering problems in housing markets. Persistently high unemployment also marked both of these recoveries.

LARGE AND PERSISTENT HUMAN AND SOCIAL COSTS

Adverse macroeconomic events, such as national recessions and crises, often carry significant human and societal costs. These have far-reaching implications, including the loss of jobs and lifetime incomes, increased poverty and inequality, loss of human capital, discouraged workers and lower labor force participation, weaker health outcomes, lower fertility rates, and a loss of social cohesion.[11]

Global recessions are periods of collapse for the world economy. This is not simply because of the decline in income per capita but also because of the enormous social and human toll they inflict. The world economy has been able to deliver growth in income per capita in the year following each global recession since 1960. However, the large social and human costs of these episodes have always left scars extending well beyond the period of recession and recovery.

In the 2009 global recession, for example, the adverse effects on labor markets were particularly pronounced, and it turned into a "jobs crisis" in many parts of the world.[12] The number of people unemployed globally rose from 178 million in 2007 to 212 million in 2009. In 2014, seven years after the beginning of the global financial crisis, the global jobless totaled a staggering 201 million. The large and persistent social and human costs make all the more important a rigorous understanding of the sources of global recessions and policy responses to cope with them.

05:32
The large social and human costs of global recessions have always left scars extending well beyond the period of recession and recovery.

GLOBAL EXPANSIONS: WHAT HAPPENS BETWEEN GLOBAL RECESSIONS?

A global recovery is the early stage of the expansion phase in the global business cycle, and between two global recessions there is an expansion phase.[13] We now briefly discuss the key features of global expansions.

The world economy experienced four expansions since the 1974 recession: 1975–81, 1983–90, 1992–2008, and one that started in 2010. The duration of the first three global expansions varied, with a minimum of 7 and a maximum of 17 years. The longest global expansion, 1992–2008, accompanied the information technology revolution and the economic transformation of China and many other emerging market economies.[14] Although the longest expansion featured the "Great Moderation" in macroeconomic volatility, the period also included the 1998 and 2001 global downturns during which the world economy came close to experiencing a recession. The latest global expansion turned six years old in 2015.

The world economy registered 2 percent per capita GDP growth on average during the first three expansions (Figures 6.8 and 6.9). The latest expansion has seen relatively higher average growth so far primarily because of the vibrancy of emerging market economies. However, the average rate of global unemployment has been higher than during previous expansions, and

03:20
The global expansion from 1992 to 2008 featured the economic rise of Asia.

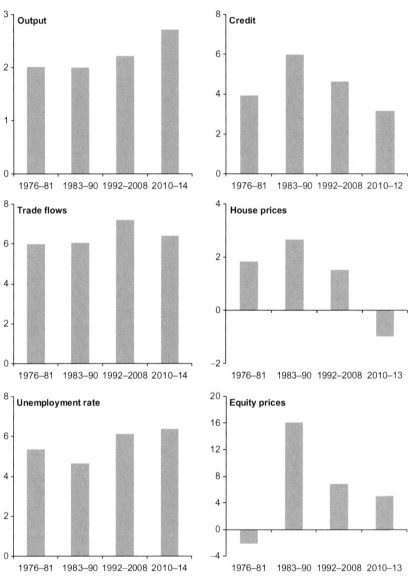

FIGURE 6.8

Global Expansions: Activity and Financial Variables

Note: Each bar represents the average growth of the respective variable during the years of the global expansions. Growth rate of output is the purchasing-power-parity-weighted averages and is in per capita terms. Aggregates for trade are trade-weighted total trade flow indices. Aggregates for unemployment rate are labor-force-weighted unemployment rates in percent. Growth rates of real credit, real house prices, and real equity prices are market weighted by output in U.S. dollars.

credit and housing markets have performed worse in the aftermath of the 2009 global recession.

THE COLLAPSE OF 2009 UNDER A MICROSCOPE

There has been much discussion about what made the 2009 global recession so severe and the recovery so weak in advanced economies. In Part III

FIGURE 6.9

Global Expansions: Activity Variables by Country Group

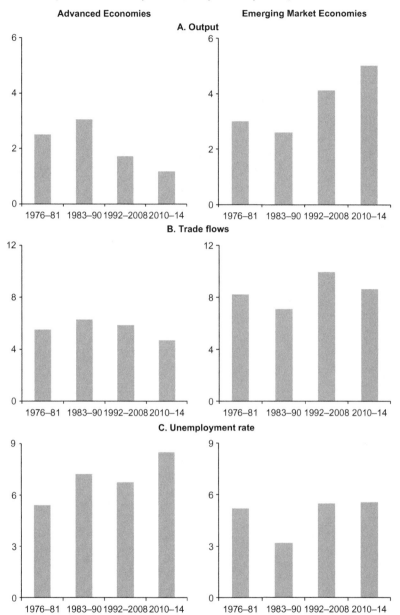

Note: Each bar represents the average growth of the respective variable during the years of the global expansions. Growth rate of output is the purchasing-power-parity-weighted averages and is in per capita terms. Aggregates for trade are trade-weighted total trade flow indices. Aggregates for unemployment rate are labor-force-weighted unemployment rates in percent.

we closely examine the main factors that explain the depth of the recession and the sluggish nature of the recovery. We start with an examination of the implications of the highly synchronized nature of the 2009 global recession.

PART III

The Great Recession under a Microscope

The probability is growing that the global economy . . . will experience a serious recession. Recent developments suggest that all G7 economies are already in recession or close to tipping into one. Other advanced economies or emerging markets . . . are also nearing a recessionary hard landing. When they reach it, there will be a sharp slowdown in the BRICs [Brazil, Russia, India, China] and other emerging markets.

Nouriel Roubini (2008)

As the United States and many other large economies slip in unison, the reality of integrated markets is being underscored: just as globaliza-tion spreads prosperity—linking cotton farmers in Texas to textile mills in China—the same forces spread hurt when times go bad.

Peter S. Goodman (2008)

The truth is that the synchronization of the world business cycle is something of a mystery.

Paul Krugman (2008b)

CHAPTER 7

Synchronization of Recessions

One of the most distinguishing features of the 2009 global recession was its unprecedented reach, with almost all advanced economies and a significant number of emerging market and developing economies experiencing synchronized contractions in activity. How synchronized are national recessions around global recessions? Are highly synchronized recessions associated with deeper downturns and weaker recoveries? And what happens to financial markets during highly synchronized recessions?

GLOBALIZATION AND SYNCHRONIZATION

Globalization, which is often associated with rising trade and financial linkages, has gathered momentum over the past three decades. These linkages have become increasingly more forceful in transmitting economic shocks across borders. Indeed, an often repeated view in the media in recent years is that globalization has changed the nature of global business cycles. However, the economic literature is inconclusive about the role globalization plays in the synchronization of national business cycles, as we discuss in a FOCUS box at the end of this chapter. Against this backdrop, the latest global recession has led to intensive discussions about the severity and duration of synchronized recessions.

The proportion of countries in recession rose sharply during the four global recessions.

SYNCHRONIZATION DURING GLOBAL RECESSIONS

Not surprisingly, the proportion of countries in recession rose sharply during the four global recessions. We measure the extent of synchronization by the proportion of countries in recession in each year (Figure 7.1, panel A). This metric suggests that the proportion of countries in recession reached a local peak during each global recession. Interestingly, this proportion has increased over time: it was close to 40 percent in the 1975 episode and about 65 percent in the 2009 global recession. The proportion of countries in recession started picking up ahead of the recession year. During the 1998 and 2001 global downturns, that proportion was relatively low at about 20–25 percent.

01:55

Global recessions have become increasingly synchronized.

We also consider a measure that tracks yearly fluctuations in the GDP-weighted fraction of countries that experienced a decline in real GDP. Since countries are weighted by their purchasing power parity, those that are larger

FIGURE 7.1
Synchronization of Recessions

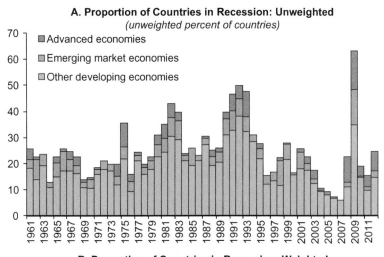

A. Proportion of Countries in Recession: Unweighted
(unweighted percent of countries)

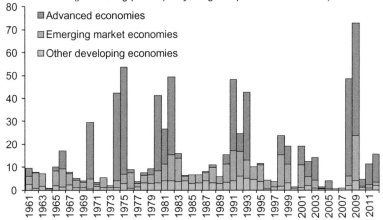

B. Proportion of Countries in Recession: Weighted
(purchasing-power-parity-weighted percent of countries)

Note: Panel A shows the proportion of countries in recession, defined as a contraction in GDP (unweighted). Panel B shows the purchasing-power-parity-weighted proportion of countries in recession, defined as a contraction in GDP. Data are in annual frequency and include 163 countries. Global recession years are 1975, 1982, 1991, and 2009.

in economic size receive a greater weight with this measure (Figure 7.1, panel B). The weighted fraction of countries in recession was about 50 percent in the first three global recessions, but rose to more than 75 percent in the latest episode.

In addition, we study the growth distribution of economies during global recessions and recoveries (Figures 7.2 and 7.3). The 2009 global recession stands out as the most painful; more than 60 percent of countries grew by less than 2 percent a year.[1] The distributions of average growth during the recoveries (the first three years after a recession) suggest that the recoveries after the

FIGURE 7.2
Global Recessions: Distribution of Output Growth *(percent of countries)*

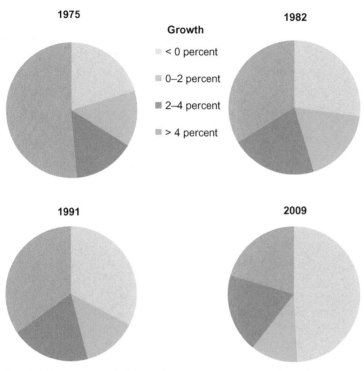

Note: Each chart represents the fraction of countries with various annual growth rates during the respective global recession years. The sample includes 163 countries.

1975 and 2009 episodes were associated with better cross-sectional growth outcomes.

Declines in output in advanced economies largely drove the 1975 recession, but emerging market and developing economies played a role in the other episodes. In 1982, recessions in many Latin American countries contributed to the decline in global activity, whereas in 1991 declines in the eastern European transition economies worsened the performance of the world economy. The 1991 recession was a multiyear episode in which the 1990–91 U.S. recession was followed by recessions among European countries during the European Exchange Rate Mechanism crisis. In both the 1982 and 1991 episodes, the number of countries in recession remained high in the aftermath of the global recession.

The 2006–07 period stands out for the historically low number of countries in recession. However, this was followed by a sharp reversal of fortune. In 2009, almost all advanced economies and roughly half the emerging market and developing economies were in recession. The degree of

In 2009, almost all advanced economies and roughly half the emerging market and developing economies were in recession, reflecting the depth of the global financial crisis and much stronger international trade and financial linkages.

FIGURE 7.3

Global Recoveries: Distribution of Output Growth *(percent of countries)*

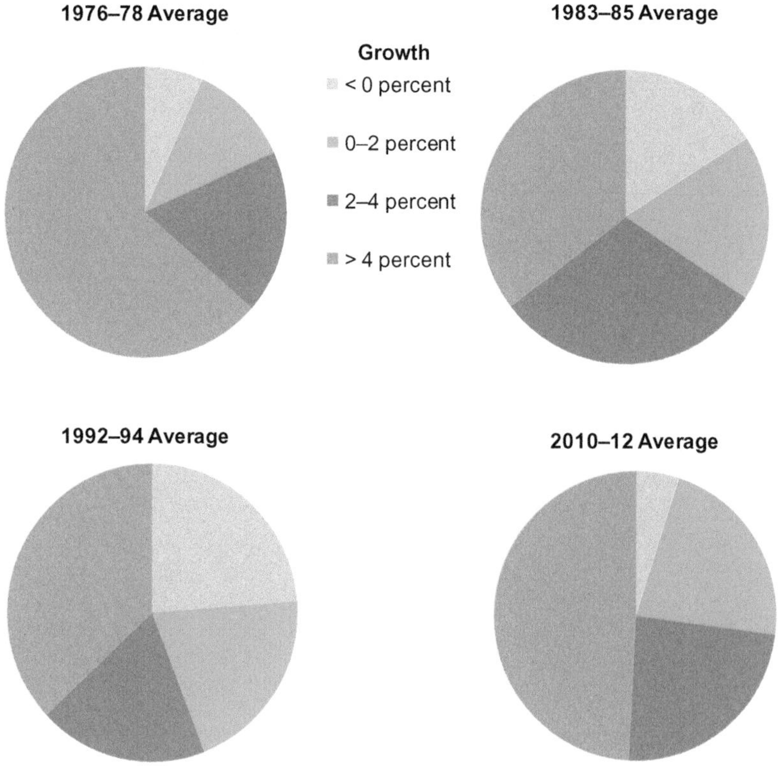

Note: Each chart represents the fraction of countries with various annual growth rates during the respective global recovery years. The sample includes 163 countries.

synchronicity of this recession was the highest during the past 50 years, possibly reflecting the depth of the global financial crisis and much stronger international trade and financial linkages.[2] Even though the 2009 global recession was clearly driven by sharp declines in activity in advanced economies as a result of the global financial crisis, recessions in a number of emerging market and developing economies also contributed to its depth and synchronicity.

WHEN SYNCHRONIZED, RECESSIONS ARE DEEPER AND RECOVERIES ARE WEAKER

Are highly synchronized recessions different from others? Yes, for at least three reasons. First, it is not possible to rely on external demand for growth during synchronized recessions with a number of countries simultaneously suffering from weak demand. Second, the major advanced economies typically contract during synchronized global recessions, which can affect expectations about future global growth and further depress consumption and investment.

FIGURE 7.4
Synchronization of Recessions and Financial Downturns *(in percent)*

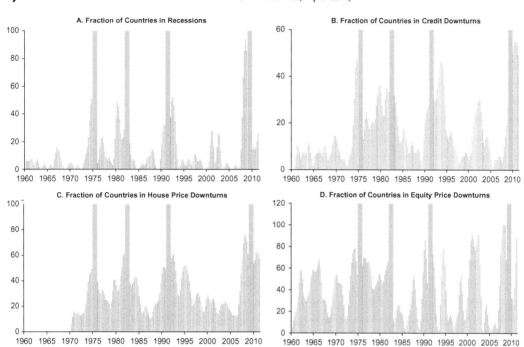

Note: Each bar represents the share of countries experiencing recessions or financial downturns. The figures include complete as well as ongoing episodes. The sample contains the quarterly data for advanced economies. Global recession years (1975, 1982, 1991, and 2009) are shaded in gray.

Third, synchronized recessions often coincide with severe disruptions in financial markets. Credit conditions tighten and asset prices drop, weakening the balance sheets of households, corporations, financial institutions, and sovereigns. This, in turn, hurts consumption and investment and causes output to decline sharply.

To analyze whether synchronized recessions are different, we use quarterly data for a core set of advanced economies. This data set provides a sharper picture of the duration and amplitude of recessions. Highly synchronized recessions are defined as those in which 10 or more of the 21 advanced economies in our sample are simultaneously in recession.[3] As expected, highly synchronized recessions in advanced economies are also closely aligned with the global recessions (Figure 7.4). Highly synchronized recessions are longer and deeper than others: the average duration of a highly synchronized recession is 40 percent and its amplitude is 45 percent greater than those of other recessions (Figure 7.5).

Recoveries from synchronous recessions are very slow on average, with output taking 50 percent longer to attain its previous peak than recoveries after other recessions (Figure 7.6). In highly synchronized recessions, it is

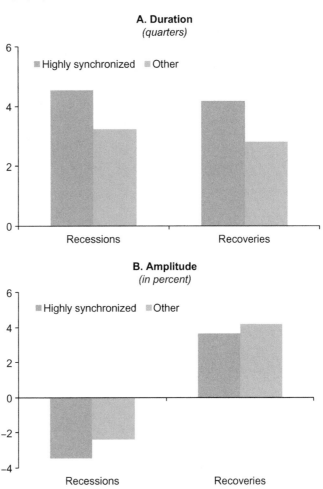

FIGURE 7.5

Highly Synchronized Recessions: Duration and Amplitude

A. Duration
(quarters)

B. Amplitude
(in percent)

Note: The duration of a recession is the number of quarters from peak to trough. The duration of a recovery is the number of quarters it takes output to reach the level of the previous peak starting from the trough. The amplitude of a recession is the change in output from peak to trough, whereas the amplitude of a recovery is the change in output in four quarters following the trough. Duration refers to the average of all episodes, and amplitude is the median of all episodes. Highly synchronized recessions are defined as those during which 10 or more of the 21 advanced economies in the sample are in recession at the same time.

difficult for an aggregate recovery to be driven by a turnaround in net exports. Private consumption stagnates, investment growth declines, and the rate of unemployment remains high for an extended period. Exports are typically more sluggish, and financial markets struggle after highly synchronized recessions (Figure 7.7). Credit growth also stays weak, unlike during other recoveries when credit and investment growth often recovers rapidly.[4]

FIGURE 7.6

Highly Synchronized Recessions: Activity Variables *(in percent)*

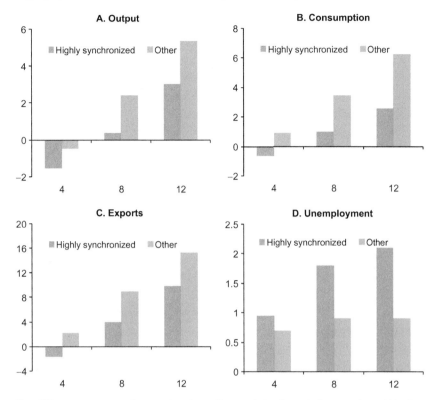

Note: All figures except unemployment show the median cumulative change in the respective variable after the indicated number of quarters from the time of the peak of output. The unemployment figure shows the median difference in the unemployment rate from the level of the unemployment rate at the peak of output. Highly synchronized recessions are defined as those during which 10 or more of the 21 advanced economies in the sample are in recession at the same time.

FIGURE 7.7

Highly Synchronized Recessions: Financial Variables *(in percent)*

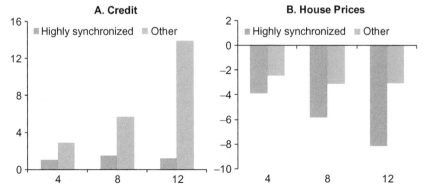

Note: These figures show the median total change of the respective variable after the indicated number of quarters (horizontal axis) from the time of the peak of output. Highly synchronized recessions are defined as those during which 10 or more of the 21 advanced economies in the sample are in recession at the same time.

SYNCHRONIZATION OF FINANCIAL DOWNTURNS

Economists have long studied the interactions between different types of cycles and that research has had important policy implications. For example, extensive study of the linkages between business cycles and inflation cycles has led economists to warn of the risks of higher inflation if monetary policy is lax and an economy is producing more goods and services than its potential. Conversely, economists warn of deflation if monetary policy is tight and the level of economic activity is less than its potential.

The recent global financial crisis has shifted attention away from the previous focus on the linkages between business cycles and inflation cycles and toward the effects and policy implications of cycles in financial markets. A number of advanced economies experienced booms in credit availability, housing, and equity prices during the upturn in the financial cycle prior to the crisis, with the global economy putting in its best performance of the past four decades. At the same time, however, risks were building, and the subsequent downturn of the cycle was dramatic, with severe credit crunches and asset price busts leading to the deepest global recession since the Great Depression of the 1930s.

Indeed, global recessions, especially the last three episodes, coincided with financial disruptions and crises in a number of countries (Figure 7.4, Appendix D).[5] This is also evident in the fact that the proportion of countries experiencing recessions around the world is highly correlated with the fraction of those going through credit contractions or downturns in housing markets (Figure 7.4).[6]

In particular, synchronized credit contractions are closely associated with global recessions. House price declines are also highly synchronized across countries, especially during periods of global recessions. Equity prices exhibit the highest degree of synchronization, reflecting the extensive integration of financial markets. However, the popular saying that "Wall Street has predicted nine of the last five recessions" resonates here, as the proportion of countries experiencing bear equity markets frequently exceeds the proportion of countries in a recession.[7]

What are the implications of this coincidence of financial cycles across countries? Synchronized downturns have more adverse implications than other downturns. For example, in highly synchronized downturns, equity prices drop by about 40 percent, compared with 18 percent for other downturns.

When one financial variable experiences a synchronized downturn, other financial aggregates also perform worse. House prices drop much more during synchronized credit downturns, while credit grows less during synchronized housing downturns. It is well known that globally synchronized downturns tend to result in much larger declines in equity prices, and our findings extend this observation to other financial market segments.[8]

FROM SYNCHRONIZATION TO CRISES

Given the highly synchronized nature of the four global recessions, it is no surprise that these were periods of collapse for the world economy. The 2009 global recession was a true collapse with an unprecedented degree of synchronization. This was one of the main explanations for its depth and the weakness of the ensuing recovery. A number of studies also argue that the 2007–08 global financial crisis played a major role in shaping the recession and recovery. We study this issue next.

FOCUS

LINKAGES BETWEEN GLOBALIZATION AND SYNCHRONIZATION

There is no consistent theoretical prediction across different models about how globalization affects the degree to which business cycles are synchronized.[9] The effects of trade and financial integration depend, in different models, on the level of development, the nature of shocks, and the pattern of specialization.

Trade Linkages

International trade linkages generate both demand- and supply-side spillovers across countries, which can increase the degree of business cycle synchronization. For example, on the demand side, an investment or consumption boom in one country can increase demand for imports, boosting economies abroad. On the supply side, a positive shock to output in tradable goods leads to lower prices; hence, imported inputs for other countries become cheaper.

However, both classical and "new" trade theories imply that increased trade linkages lead to increased specialization. How does this affect the degree of synchronization? The answer depends on the nature of specialization (intra- versus interindustry) and the types of shocks (common versus country specific). If stronger trade linkages are associated with increased interindustry specialization across countries, then the impact of increased trade depends on the nature of shocks. If industry-specific shocks are more important in driving business cycles, then the degree of international business cycle synchronization should decrease (Krugman 1993). If common shocks, which might be associated with changes in demand and/or supply conditions, are more dominant than industry-specific shocks, then this would lead to a higher degree of business cycle synchronization (Frankel and Rose 1998).

Financial Linkages

The effects of financial integration on cross-country correlations of output growth are also ambiguous in theory. Financial integration could reduce cross-country output correlations by stimulating the specialization of production through the reallocation of capital in a manner consistent with the comparative advantage of countries. However, financial linkages could result in a higher degree of business cycle synchronization by generating large demand-side effects as the changes in equity prices affect the dynamics of wealth. Furthermore, contagion effects transmitted through financial linkages could also increase cross-country spillovers of macroeconomic fluctuations (Claessens and Forbes 2001; Forbes 2013).

Recent empirical studies are unable to provide a concrete explanation for the impact of stronger global linkages on the synchronization of business cycles. Some employ cross-country or cross-region panel regressions to assess the role of global linkages in explaining the degree of the synchronization of business cycles in advanced economies (Kose and Yi 2006). While Imbs (2004) finds that the extent of financial linkages, sectoral similarity, and the volume of intra-industry trade all have a positive impact on business cycle correlations, Baxter and Kouparitsas (2005) and Otto, Voss, and Willard (2001) document that international trade is the most important transmission channel for business cycle fluctuations.

Kose, Prasad, and Terrones (2003a) find that both trade and financial linkages have a positive impact on cross-country output and consumption correlations. Imbs (2006) reports that financial linkages lead to higher output and consumption correlations in advanced economies. This effect appears to be much smaller for developing economies (Kose, Prasad, and Terrones 2003a). Jansen and Stokman (2004) find that countries with stronger foreign direct investment linkages had more correlated business cycles in the second half of the 1990s. Kalemli-Ozcan, Papaioannou, and Peydró (2013) report a strong negative effect of banking integration on the degree of output synchronization during tranquil times.

In sum, there is empirical evidence suggesting that both trade and financial linkages tend to increase the degree of business cycle synchronization. However, the impact of such linkages on synchronization is also influenced by the composition of trade and financial flows, the nature of shocks, and country-specific features.

There is a belief among policy makers that serious recessions associated with financial crises are necessarily followed by slow recoveries—like the one we've experienced since mid-2009. But this widespread belief is mistaken.

Michael Bordo (2012)

The current weak recovery is unusual because it followed a deep recession. And the fact that the recession was associated with a financial crisis does not invalidate the historical regularity that deep recessions are usually followed by V-shaped recoveries.

John B. Taylor (2013b)

[R]ecessions associated with systemic banking crises tend to be deep and protracted and . . . this pattern is evident across both history and countries.

Carmen M. Reinhart and Kenneth S. Rogoff (2012c)

CHAPTER 8

Double Whammy: Crisis and Recession

The 2009 global recession was a true collapse. It coincided with a global financial crisis and took a heavy toll on the world economy. Are recessions associated with financial crises deeper and longer? And are recoveries that follow such recessions weaker and more protracted?

DIFFERENT? OR NOT?

Many countries experienced financial crises during the global recessions and downturns (Figure 8.1). The latest episode was no exception, but it differed in that there were financial crises in a large number of major advanced economies. The financial crisis was followed by the deepest global recession and the weakest recovery in many of these economies since the Great Depression.

01:36
President Obama describes the effects of the 2009 financial crisis on the real economy.

Researchers have vigorously debated whether these unpleasant characteristics are related to the severe financial crises in several advanced economies during 2007–09.[1] On one side, a number of researchers show that recessions with severe financial market problems often lead to larger contractions in output and last longer. Moreover, they claim that recoveries following such recessions tend to be weaker and slower.[2] On the other side, some argue that there is no difference between recoveries following recessions accompanied by financial crises and recoveries following other recessions.[3]

RECESSIONS, RECOVERIES, AND FINANCIAL CRISES

To assess whether recessions and recoveries are different when they are associated with financial crises, we employ quarterly data for a core group of advanced economies as in the previous chapter. We use a simple "dating" rule to determine whether a specific recession is associated with a financial crisis. In particular, if a recession started at the same time as or after the beginning of a financial crisis, we consider that recession to be associated with the respective financial crisis. This rule describes a timing association between the two events, but does not imply a causal link. Of the 122 recessions in our sample, 15 are associated with financial crises.[4]

Recessions associated with financial crises are longer and generally more costly than others. Those associated with the "Big Five" financial crises were

FIGURE 8.1
Financial Crises around Global Recessions and Downturns
(number of crises)

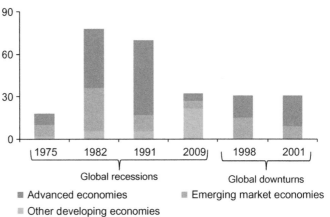

Note: Each bar represents the total number of financial crises that started in the year of the respective global recession or downturn or within two years before or after these events. Financial crises include currency, debt, and banking crises.

01:25

Recessions associated with financial crises are often longer and generally more costly than others.

particularly costly (Figure 8.2).[5] Financial crises are also followed by weak recoveries: it takes as much time to recover to the level of activity reached in the previous peak as the recession itself lasted, whereas cumulative GDP growth in the four quarters after the trough is typically lower than following other types of recessions. For example, cumulative growth one year after the trough for a recession with a financial crisis is 2.5 percentage points lower than in other cases, after controlling for the severity and duration of the previous recession.

WHY DO CRISES PRODUCE DIFFERENT CYCLICAL OUTCOMES?

What mechanisms differentiate recessions and recoveries associated with financial crises from those without? A FOCUS box at the end of this chapter summarizes the rich literature that documents that financial crises can prolong and deepen recessions through a variety of channels. To illustrate, sharp declines in asset prices can reduce the net worth of firms and households, limiting their capacity to borrow, invest, and spend. This leads to further drops in asset prices. Banks and other financial institutions might restrict lending when their capital bases diminish during crises, resulting in protracted and deeper recessions.

The substantial changes in the main components of output during recessions reinforce this conclusion. Consumption and investment usually decline much more sharply, leading to more pronounced drops in overall output and employment during recessions coinciding with financial market problems. Moreover, the rate of unemployment typically registers a larger increase during recessions accompanied by financial crises.

FIGURE 8.2

Recessions and Recoveries with Financial Crises: Output

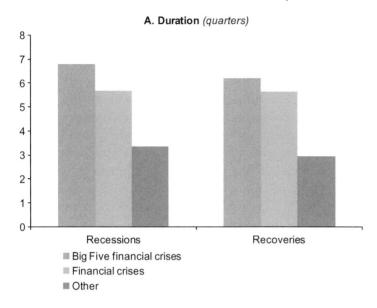

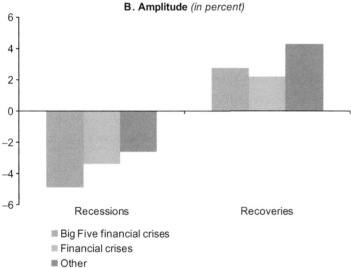

Note: The duration of a recession is the number of quarters from peak to trough. The duration of a recovery is the number of quarters it takes for output to get to the level of the previous peak from the trough. The amplitude of a recession is the change in output from peak to trough, whereas the amplitude of a recovery is the change in output in four quarters following the trough. Duration refers to the average of all episodes, and amplitude is the median of all episodes. Recessions refer to recessions associated with financial crises. Recoveries refer to recoveries that follow recessions associated with financial crises. "Big Five financial crises" refers to the average of recessions associated with the Big Five financial crises: Finland (1990–93), Japan (1993), Norway (1988), Spain (1978–79), and Sweden (1990–93). "Financial crises" refers to the average of recessions associated with financial crises. "Other" refers to the average of other recessions.

EBULLIENT EXPANSIONS PRIOR TO FINANCIAL CRISES

The nature of expansions that precede financial crises is also an important factor in determining the implications of the associated recessions. These episodes have often been associated with overheated goods and labor markets (Figure 8.3). Relative to other expansions, labor market participation is elevated, nominal wage growth is high, and unemployment is low.

In addition, financial markets have often been exuberant, with credit and asset price booms during expansions prior to financial crises (Figure 8.4). The growth rates of credit and asset prices during expansions preceding financial crises are higher than during other expansions.[6] Rapid credit growth has typically been associated with shifts in household saving rates and a deterioration in the quality of balance sheets. For example, household saving rates out of disposable income have been noticeably lower in expansions before financial crises. However, after a financial crisis strikes, saving rates increase substantially, especially during recessions.

Taken together, the behavior of these variables suggests that expansions prior to financial crises may be driven by overly optimistic expectations for growth in income and wealth. The result is often overvalued goods, services, and, in particular, asset prices. For a period, this buoyancy appears to confirm optimistic expectations. But when expectations are eventually disappointed, restoring household balance sheets and downward price movements requires sharp adjustments in private behavior. Not surprisingly, a key reason recessions associated with financial crises are so much worse is the resultant decline in private consumption.

RECOVERIES AFTER CRISES LOOK DIFFERENT TOO

Recoveries following financial crises appear to be weaker in many dimensions. The weakness in private demand tends to persist during expansions that follow recessions associated with financial crises (Figure 8.5). Private consumption typically grows more slowly than during other recoveries, and private investment continues to decline after the end of the recession trough. Thus, output growth is sluggish and the unemployment rate continues to rise by more than usual. Although the recovery of domestic private demand from financial crises is weaker than usual, economies hit by financial crises have typically benefited from relatively strong demand in the rest of the world, which has historically helped them export their way out of recession.

Financial markets often experience prolonged busts during recoveries following recessions associated with financial crises (Figure 8.6). Credit growth falters, whereas in other recoveries it is steady and strong. Asset prices are generally weaker; in particular, house prices experience a prolonged decline.

What are the implications of these trends for the dynamics of recoveries after financial crises? First, households and firms either perceive a stronger

FIGURE 8.3

Expansions prior to Financial Crises: Activity Variables *(in percent)*

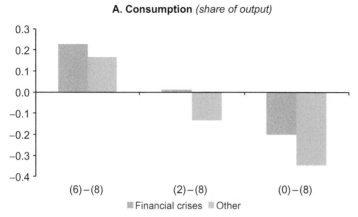

A. Consumption *(share of output)*

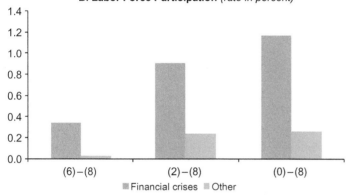

B. Labor Force Participation *(rate in percent)*

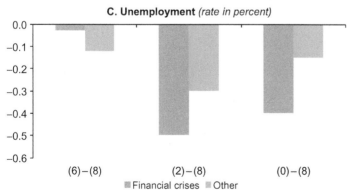

C. Unemployment *(rate in percent)*

Note: Each panel shows the median change in the level of the respective variable in the period denoted relative to eight periods before the peak in output. (6)–(8) indicates the change in the respective variable between six periods before and eight periods before the peak in output. (2)–(8) indicates the change in the respective variable between two periods before and eight periods before the peak in output. (0)–(8) indicates the change in the respective variable between the time at the peak in output and eight periods before the peak in output. "Financial crises" refers to the recessions with financial crises. "Other" refers to all other recessions.

FIGURE 8.4

Expansions prior to Financial Crises: Financial Variables *(in percent)*

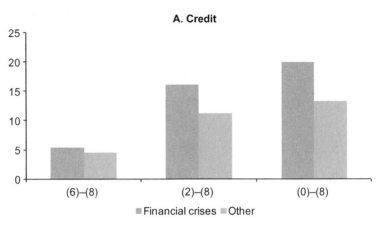

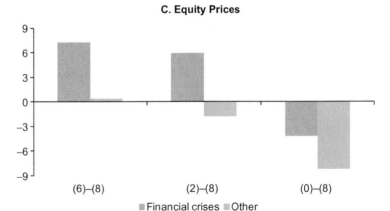

Note: Panels show the median change in the level of the respective variable in the period denoted relative to eight periods before the peak in output. (6)–(8) indicates the change in the respective variable between six periods before and eight periods before the peak in output. (2)–(8) indicates the change in the respective variable between two periods before and eight periods before the peak in output. (0)–(8) indicates the change in the respective variable between the time at the peak in output and eight periods before the peak in output. "Financial crises" refers to the recessions with financial crises. "Other" refers to all other recessions.

FIGURE 8.5

Recoveries following Financial Crises: Activity Variables *(in percent)*

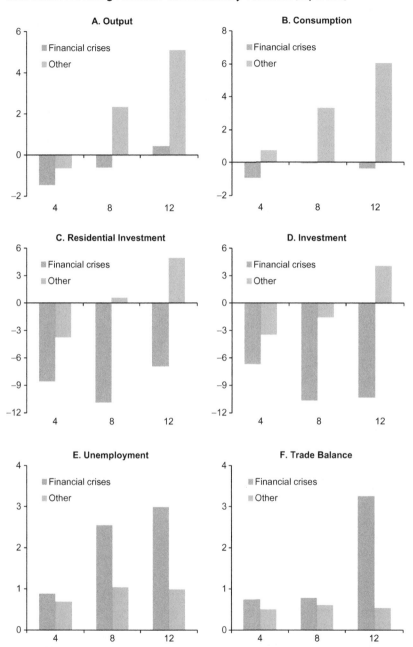

Note: Panels show the median change of the respective variable 4, 8, and 12 quarters after the start of the recession. "Financial crises" refers to the recoveries following recessions associated with financial crises. "Other" refers to all other recoveries.

FIGURE 8.6

Recoveries following Financial Crises: Financial Variables *(in percent)*

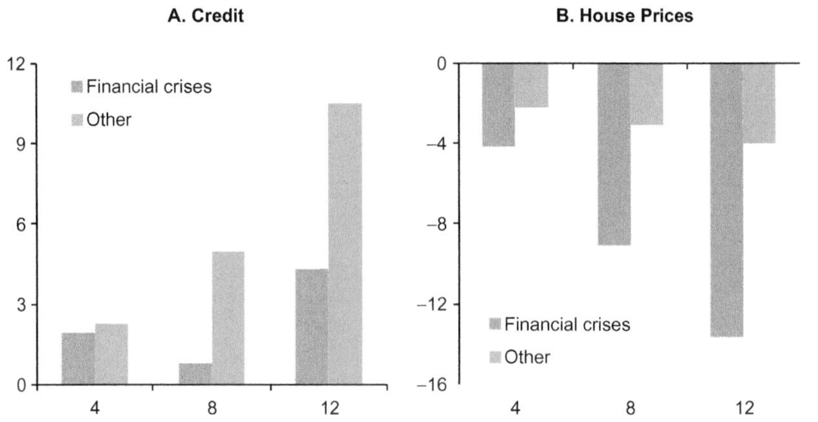

A. Credit   B. House Prices

Note: Panels show the median change of the respective variable 4, 8, and 12 quarters after the start of the recession. "Financial crises" refers to the recoveries following recessions associated with financial crises. "Other" refers to all other recoveries.

need to restore their balance sheets after a period of overleveraging or are forced to do so by sharp reductions in credit supply. Private consumption growth is likely to be weak until households perceive that they are more financially secure.

Second, expenditures with long planning horizons—notably real estate and capital investment—suffer more markedly from the aftereffects of financial crises. This appears to be strongly associated with weak credit growth. Further, industries that depend heavily on external credit recover much more slowly after these types of recessions.

MEDIUM-TERM IMPLICATIONS: IT GETS UGLY

Financial crises tend to have a long-lasting impact on the level of output. Recent research documents that although the growth of output eventually returns to its precrisis rate, the level of output stays below the precrisis trend over the medium term.[7] Specifically, the level of output on average stays about 10 percent below its precrisis trend seven years after a systemic financial crisis in a large number of advanced and emerging market economies.

Declines in the employment rate, the capital-to-labor ratio, and productivity all contribute to the low level of output following financial crises. In the short term, the output loss stems from the decline in total factor productivity.[8] In the medium term, losses associated with capital and employment are the major factors keeping the level of output below the precrisis trend.

The long-lasting impact of the 2009 global recession has been particularly visible (Figure 8.7). In addition to the United States and the United Kingdom,

02:33
Turmoil on Wall Street hits Main Street

FIGURE 8.7

Global Recoveries: Evolution of Output in Major Advanced Economies

(rate per capita in percent)

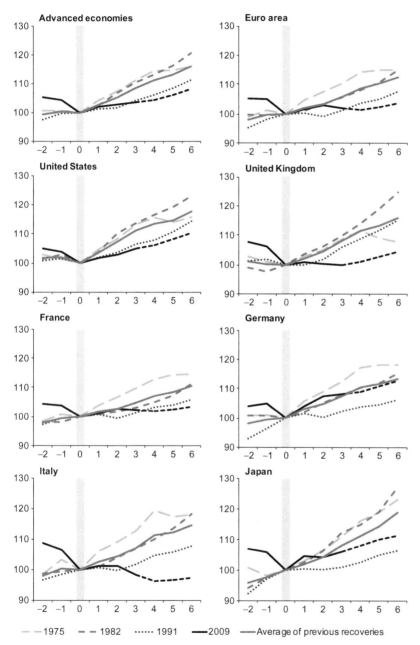

Note: Time 0 denotes the year of the respective global recession (shaded with gray). Aggregates for euro area and advanced economies are purchasing-power-parity-weighted per capita real output indices. Output index numbers are equal to 100 in the global recession year. For the 2009 episode, data for the 2013–15 period are based on the IMF's *World Economic Outlook* forecasts.

many euro area economies struggled to deliver growth that can lead to sizable improvements in income per capita and in labor markets.

Many commentators recognized early the likely adverse implications of the latest global financial crisis over the medium term. For example, in 2009, Carmen Reinhart and Kenneth Rogoff, in an influential book and a series of papers, claimed that the recovery following the 2009 episode would be very weak.[9] In 2009, Mohammed El-Erian and Bill Gross (both then with the Pacific Investment Management Company) argued that the global economy had entered into a "new normal" phase.[10] They claimed that, in this new phase and for the foreseeable future, the world would experience very slow growth, and the engine of growth would be the systemically important emerging market economies instead of the major advanced ones.[11]

AND THE LONG-TERM IMPLICATIONS: PESSIMISTS GALORE

Six years after the global financial crisis, some observers claimed that advanced economies faced what appeared to be a period of "secular stagnation." The implication is that, following severe financial crises, countries can experience an extended period of sluggish growth and low levels of output and employment in an environment with low real interest rates. Moreover, adverse feedback loops between price and wage deflation can further worsen economic conditions.

The growth forecasts for the advanced economies in September 2008, just before the collapse of Lehman Brothers, have indeed proved quite optimistic (Figure 8.8). In 2015, forecasts from both the IMF and World Bank still suggested that most of these economies were likely to experience much lower growth in the foreseeable future relative to their precrisis trends. Moreover, global real interest rates, which had been declining since 1980, were still expected to remain low.[12]

Lawrence Summers, the former U.S. Treasury secretary, was first to raise the notion that the United States and other advanced economies have been suffering from secular stagnation, setting off a vigorous debate among economists.[13] Summers cited many factors that could lead to secular stagnation after a financial crisis: depressed investment and consumption demand, higher risk aversion, increased costs of financial intermediation, debt overhang, and declining costs of durable goods. In a series of articles, Summers made a case for a large fiscal stimulus program to avert stagnation by building up infrastructure and promoting investment in the energy sector in the United States to increase demand.

Recent research also concludes that, in light of the Japanese experience after its banking crisis in the 1990s, some major euro area economies are likely to suffer long stagnation because of delays in the implementation of necessary bank recapitalization and structural reforms.[14]

FIGURE 8.8
Output Projections

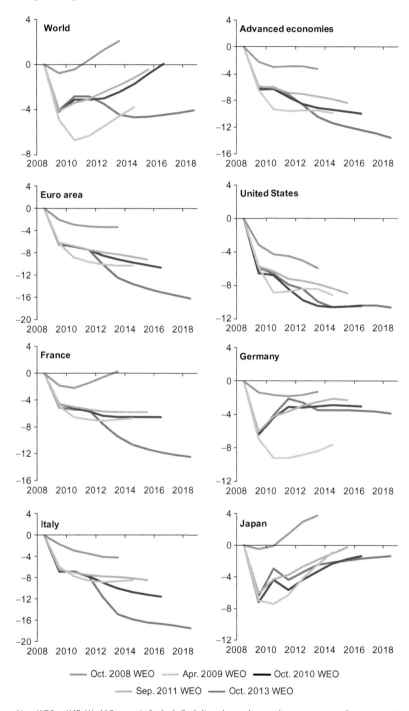

        ⸻ Oct. 2008 WEO   ⸻ Apr. 2009 WEO   ⸻ Oct. 2010 WEO
              ⸻ Sep. 2011 WEO   ⸻ Oct. 2013 WEO

Note: WEO = IMF, *World Economic Outlook*. Each line shows the gap between output from respective
    projections and output generated using precrisis average growth between 1996 and 2006. Output
    level in 2008 is equal to 100.

Others consider the case for secular stagnation to be weak.[15] Kenneth Rogoff claims that weak growth performance since the Great Recession has been similar to the typical dynamics observed following a systemic financial crisis. He emphasizes a different reason for the slow growth after the crisis: the failure of governments to eliminate unsustainable debt levels in the U.S. mortgage markets and in European periphery economies. John Taylor, a Treasury undersecretary for international affairs in the Bush administration, finds a culprit in policy uncertainty, which he says made firms reluctant to invest. Taylor considers policy uncertainty to be a major reason for the slow growth during the latest recovery in the United States. There are also broader discussions about how emerging market and developing economies can face various growth challenges in the future.[16]

HAVE WE BEEN HERE BEFORE? YOU BET!

There were many predictions of an extended period of low growth following earlier global recessions.[17]

And, as discussed, the recovery after the 1991 global recession—also associated with financial crises—was long and weak. Since 2010, global activity has gradually strengthened and is expected to improve further in the medium term, according to the forecasts at the time of the writing of this book.

However, the global economy faces multiple downside risks, including challenges associated with the transition from unconventional monetary policies, deflationary pressures, fragile growth prospects in the euro area, and a synchronized slowdown in emerging market economies. And there are still concerns about the durability of global financial stability. The bottom line is that it remains to be seen whether advanced economies will continue their expansion or experience a longer period of stagnation in the coming years.

It remains to be seen whether advanced economies will continue their expansion or experience a longer period of stagnation.

LOOMING UNCERTAINTY: NOT GOOD EITHER

This chapter explains how recessions accompanied by financial crises differ from those that are not and how the recoveries that follow such episodes are longer and weaker. High levels of uncertainty are another factor prominently cited to explain the sluggish nature of the ongoing recovery; we turn now to the role of uncertainty.

FOCUS

FINANCIAL DISRUPTIONS AND ACTIVITY

Economic developments over the past two decades show vividly that gyrations in financial markets greatly influence real activity around the world. Following the largest housing bubble in its modern history, Japan experienced a massive asset market crash in the early 1990s, which marked the start of its "lost decade." After prolonged credit booms, many emerging market economies in Asia faced deep financial crises in the second half of the 1990s. The equity market booms of the late 1990s in a number of advanced economies ended with simultaneous busts and recessions. The recent global financial crisis was similar to the earlier episodes. However, the Great Recession was truly seismic, with severe credit crunches and asset price busts leading to the deepest global recession since the Great Depression of the 1930s.

Financial Frictions and Output

A rich research program has explored the interactions between the financial sector and the real economy. For example, Fisher (1933) and Keynes (1936) were among the first to emphasize these interactions during the Great Depression.[18] Basic economic theory suggests that, in a world without financial frictions, macroeconomic developments and financial conditions interact closely through wealth and substitution effects (Cochrane 2006).[19]

However, in the presence of financial frictions, these linkages can be amplified through various channels, including the "financial accelerator" and related mechanisms. According to these mechanisms, decreases (or increases) in asset prices worsen a household's or a business's net worth, reducing (or increasing) its capacity to borrow, invest, and consume. This process, in turn, can be amplified and propagated across corporations and households, leading to further decreases (increases) in asset prices over time, thereby creating general equilibrium effects (Bernanke and Gertler 1989; Bernanke, Gertler, and Gilchrist 1999; Kiyotaki and Moore 1997). Many theoretical models emphasize the roles played by movements in credit and asset prices (house and equity) in shaping the evolution of macroeconomic aggregates over the business cycle.

A number of studies examine the roles of asset prices and credit in transmitting and amplifying shocks. For example, some recent studies analyze specifically how endogenous developments in housing markets can magnify and transmit various types of shocks to the real economy in dynamic stochastic general equilibrium models.[20] Other studies consider how movements in equity prices can be associated with leverage cycles that are in turn closely related to movements in the real economy (Adrian and Shin 2008; Mendoza 2010). More recently, the emphasis has been on how shocks to the supply of financing can lead to real effects, including recessions and recoveries (Gertler and Kiyotaki 2010; Brunnermeier and Sannikov 2012). In addition to these theoretical studies, empirical work emphasizes the importance of house prices and credit dynamics in shaping business cycles (Leamer 2007; Mendoza and Terrones 2008).

Implications of Asset Price Busts

Claessens, Kose, and Terrones (2012) document the significant role played by asset price busts and the growth of house prices prior to recessions in determining the duration and depth of recessions. The growth of equity prices prior to recessions does not appear to be significantly related to the depth of recessions, and recoveries accompanied by equity booms are not necessarily stronger than those without such booms.

What explains the relatively more important role of housing markets in shaping the length and magnitude of cyclical outcomes? First, housing represents a large share of wealth for most households. Houses are also an important form of collateral against which households can borrow and adjust their consumption patterns (as house prices vary). In contrast, equity ownership is a smaller share of wealth for many households and is typically more concentrated among wealthy households who likely make much smaller adjustments in their consumption over the business cycle. Moreover, equity wealth cannot be used as collateral as easily as housing wealth.

Second, equity prices are more volatile than house prices, implying that changes in house prices are more likely to be permanent than those in equity prices (Cecchetti 2006; Kishor 2007). With changes in wealth seeming more permanent, households tend to adjust their consumption more when house prices increase (decline), leading to larger increases (declines) in output during recoveries (recessions) associated with house price booms (busts) (Helbling and Terrones 2004). In studies using micro data, housing wealth has indeed been found to have a larger effect on consumption than equity wealth.[21]

Consequently, house price adjustments often have a greater effect on aggregate consumption and output than equity prices do. Empirical studies also indicate that the importance of housing extends also to changes in the main components of output. Consumption and investment usually decline sharply during recessions coinciding with house price busts, which are in turn accompanied by more pronounced drops in employment. Recessions with house price busts tend to be significantly longer and deeper.

Uncertainty is largely behind the dramatic collapse in demand. Given the uncertainty, why build a new plant, or introduce a new product now? Better to pause until the smoke clears.

Olivier Blanchard (2009c)

Participants noted that elevated uncertainty about employment prospects continued to weigh on consumption spending. A number of business contacts indicated that they were holding back on hiring and spending plans because of uncertainty about future fiscal and regulatory policies.

Federal Open Market Committee (2010)

CHAPTER 9

Uncertainty: How Bad Is It?

This chapter explores the role of uncertainty in driving macroeconomic outcomes. It addresses three questions: How is uncertainty measured? How does it evolve over the business cycle? And what is the impact of uncertainty on growth and business cycles? We analyze the main features of various measures of uncertainty, examine the links between uncertainty and growth and business cycles in advanced economies, and interpret the evidence in light of findings from recent research.

SOMETHING OF A MYSTERY

Some economists and politicians argue that the two years of harsh times visited on the United States and euro area during the Great Recession should have been followed by rapid recoveries. Milton Friedman, the late Nobel Prize–winning economist, called this the "guitar-string" theory of recessions. When a guitar string is pulled down and released, it bounces back—and the harder the string is pulled down, the faster it returns.[1]

The recent recovery in advanced economies has been accompanied by bouts of elevated uncertainty.

However, the economic performance in many advanced countries since the Great Recession has not followed that theory. Instead, the deep recessions were followed by recoveries that have been disappointingly weak and slow. To push Friedman's metaphor further, the guitar string seems to have been pulled down so hard that it snapped.

These developments are something of a mystery. Why has the latest recovery been so slow? As we documented in the previous chapter, some argue that recoveries following financial crises tend to be slow because the legacy of the crisis—balance sheet repair, weak credit expansion, and lingering problems in housing markets—weighs on activity. Considering the evidence, this argument certainly has its merits.

However, the latest recovery in advanced economies has been different from the earlier ones in at least one important dimension—it has been accompanied by bouts of elevated uncertainty, whether associated with financial crises or not. This suggests a complementary explanation for the anemic recovery, one that emphasizes the roles played by macroeconomic and policy uncertainty in curtailing economic activity and is unrelated to the fact that the 2009 global recession was associated with a financial crisis.

Economic uncertainty refers to an environment in which little or nothing is known about the future state of the economy. There are many sources of economic uncertainty, including changes in economic and financial policies and regulations, differing views on growth prospects, and productivity movements, as well as potential wars, acts of terrorism, and natural disasters.

How important is uncertainty in slowing the latest recovery? This question has led to intense debates. On one side, recent research shows that uncertainty has indeed risen in the United States and the euro area since 2007, and the increase in uncertainty appears to have negative effects on activity at both macro and micro levels.[2] Businesses have been uncertain about the fiscal and regulatory environment in the United States and Europe, and this has probably been one factor causing them to postpone investment and hiring. For example, a 2014 survey by the National Association for Business Economics reported that the "vast majority" of a large panel of business economists "feels that uncertainty about fiscal policy is holding back the pace of economic recovery."[3] On the other side, some argue that the standard measures of macroeconomic and policy uncertainty suffer from various problems and that it is unclear whether uncertainty has a causal effect on activity.

02:27

Lawrence Summers on "hysteresis" and why the long-term economic costs of the Great Recession will be so high.

MEASURING UNCERTAINTY

Quantifying uncertainty is a challenge because it is not an observable variable but is one that is deduced from other variables. In the language of statistics, uncertainty is a latent variable. However, it is possible to gauge uncertainty indirectly using a number of measures that emphasize distinct aspects of uncertainty that an economy faces over time.

Some of these measures focus on macroeconomic uncertainty, including the volatility of stock returns, dispersion in unemployment forecasts, and the prevalence of terms such as "economic uncertainty" in the media. Others consider uncertainty at the microeconomic level, using indicators that capture variation across sectoral output, firm sales, stock returns, and dispersion among forecasts by managers in manufacturing firms.

Because we are concerned primarily with macroeconomic uncertainty, we concentrate on four measures based on the volatility of stock returns and economic policy. The first is the monthly standard deviation of daily stock returns in each advanced economy in our sample of 21 countries. This measure captures uncertainty associated with firm profits and has also been shown to be a good proxy for aggregate uncertainty.

The second is the Chicago Board Options Exchange S&P 100 Volatility Index, which is an indicator of the implied volatility of equity prices calculated from prices of Standard & Poor's (S&P) 100 options. The third gauges uncertainty over economic policies in the United States and the euro area and is a weighted average of the following indicators: the frequency with which terms like "economic policy" and "uncertainty" appear together in the media, the number of tax provisions that will expire in coming years, and the dispersion of forecasts of future government outlays and inflation. The fourth, which represents uncertainty at the global level, captures common movements in the first measure using data for some major advanced economies with the longest available series.

UNCERTAINTY: HERE, THERE, AND EVERYWHERE

Regardless of which measures are used, both macroeconomic and policy uncertainty tend to rise during global recessions (Figure 9.1). Policy uncertainty in the United States and the euro area has remained relatively high since the 2007–09 global financial crisis. The euro area experienced significantly higher uncertainty because of severe sovereign debt problems in some member states. In the United States, uncertainty was driven primarily by wrangling over fiscal policy (including taxes and government spending), long-term structural issues (such as health care and regulatory policies), and entitlement programs (such as the government-sponsored retirement plan Social Security and the old-age health plan Medicare) during 2010–12 (Figure 9.2).[4]

Interestingly, monetary policy uncertainty does not appear to be a major factor behind the rise in policy uncertainty, possibly because of low and stable inflation and interest rates. Moreover, uncertainty has been unusually high and volatile throughout the lethargic global recovery, which contrasts with the recoveries following the other three global recessions (Figure 9.3), which were all accompanied by steady declines in uncertainty.

At the national level, uncertainty about the economy runs contrary to the business cycle. During expansions, macroeconomic uncertainty is generally much lower than during recessions, regardless of the measure used (Figure 9.4). Likewise, microeconomic uncertainty about specific industries or companies, measured by the volatility of movements in plant-level productivity in the United States, also behaves countercyclically and reached a post-1970 high during the Great Recession.[5]

UNCERTAINTY AND ACTIVITY: UNDERSTANDING THE LINKAGES

It is difficult to establish a causal link between uncertainty and the business cycle. Does uncertainty drive recessions, or do recessions lead to uncertainty? Empirical findings on this question have been mixed.[6] However, economic theory points to clear channels through which uncertainty can negatively affect growth. Some uncertainty is intrinsic to the business cycle: firms and households will learn only over time which sectors fare better or worse—and for how long—in response to the shocks that cause recessions. On the demand side, for example, when faced with high uncertainty, firms reduce investment and delay projects as they gather new information, because investment is often

FIGURE 9.1
Evolution of Uncertainty

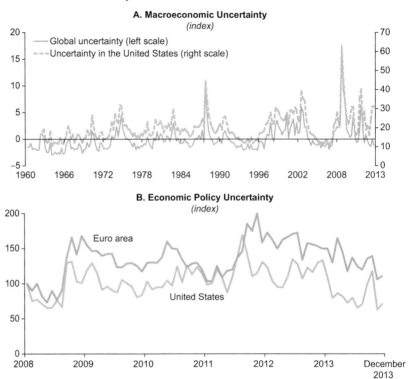

A. Macroeconomic Uncertainty
(index)

B. Economic Policy Uncertainty
(index)

Note: Uncertainty in the United States refers to the Chicago Board Options Exchange S&P 100 Volatility Index (VXO), which is calculated from S&P 100 calls and puts. Global uncertainty is the estimated dynamic common factor of the country-specific uncertainty measure using the series for Italy, Japan, and the United States (these countries have had series of stock market indices since 1960), and country-specific uncertainty refers to the monthly standard deviation of daily stock returns in each country. Daily returns are calculated using each country's stock price index; time coverage varies across economies. Economic policy uncertainty is an index of policy uncertainty for the United States and the euro area.

FIGURE 9.2
Sources of Policy Uncertainty *(in percent of total, January 2010–October 2012)*

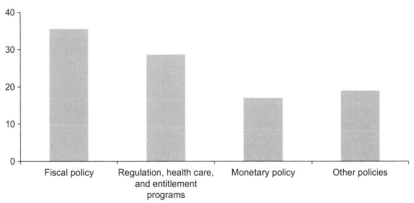

Note: Each bar shows the proportion of policy uncertainty accounted for by the respective policy variable. Fiscal policy refers to uncertainty associated with taxes and government expenditures, whereas "Other policies" refers to uncertainty associated with national security, trade, sovereign debt, and currency.

FIGURE 9.3

Uncertainty during Global Recoveries *(index)*

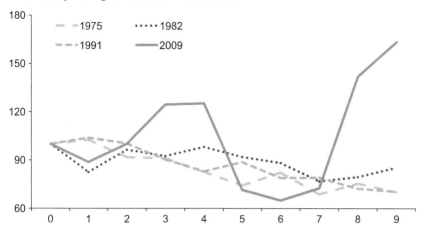

Note: Uncertainty refers to the monthly standard deviation of daily stock returns in the United States. Each line represents the evolution of uncertainty starting three quarters after uncertainty reached its peak during the respective global recession. The uncertainty measure is equal to 100 three quarters after uncertainty reached its peak during the respective global recession. Time 0 refers to February 1975, March 1983, March 1991, and March 2009.

FIGURE 9.4

Uncertainty over the Business Cycle *(in percent)*

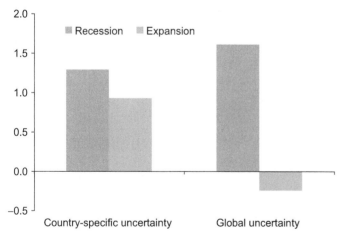

Note: This figure shows the average country-specific and global uncertainty levels during expansions and recessions. Country-specific uncertainty refers to the monthly standard deviation of daily stock returns in each advanced economy. Global uncertainty is the common factor of the country-specific uncertainty for three advanced economies (Italy, Japan, United States) for which data are available for 1960–2012.

When faced with high uncertainty, firms reduce investment and delay projects as they gather new information.

costly to reverse.[7] The response of households to high uncertainty is similar: they reduce their consumption of durable goods as they wait for less uncertain times. On the supply side, firms' hiring plans are also hurt by higher uncertainty, reflecting the high costs of adjusting personnel.

Financial market problems, such as those since 2007, can amplify the negative impact of uncertainty on growth. For example, uncertainty leads to a decline in expected returns on projects financed with debt and makes it harder to assess the value of collateral. As a result, creditors charge higher interest rates and limit lending during uncertain times, which reduces firms' ability to borrow. The decline in borrowing causes investment to contract, especially for credit-constrained firms, and slows productivity growth because of reduced spending on research and development. These factors together can translate into a significant reduction in output growth.[8]

The impact of uncertainty differs across sectors and countries. Sectors producing durable goods, including machinery and equipment, automobiles, houses, and furniture, are often most affected by increased uncertainty. The impact of uncertainty on consumption and investment is larger in emerging market economies than in advanced economies, possibly because financial markets and institutions are less developed.[9]

WHAT IS THE IMPACT OF UNCERTAINTY ON GROWTH?

Empirical evidence suggests that uncertainty tends to be detrimental to economic growth.[10] For example, a 1 standard deviation increase in uncertainty is associated with a decline in output growth of between 0.4 and 1.25 percentage points depending on the measure used for macroeconomic uncertainty. There have indeed been multiple episodes during which uncertainty rose by 1 standard deviation or more, including at the onset of the 2009 global recession and during the recent debt crisis in the euro area. High uncertainty tends to be associated with a larger drop in investment than in output and consumption growth. These findings lend support to the validity of different channels through which uncertainty hurts economic activity. They are also consistent with recent studies that document a negative relationship between growth and uncertainty.[11]

Uncertainty tends to be detrimental to economic growth.

Policy-induced uncertainty, which is also negatively associated with growth, has increased to record levels since the 2009 global recession. Specifically, the sharp increase in policy uncertainty between 2006 and 2011 may have stymied growth in advanced economies. Empirical evidence indicates that such a large increase in policy uncertainty is associated with a highly persistent and significant decline in output (Figure 9.5).[12] The adverse impact of uncertainty on economic growth works mainly through two channels.

FIGURE 9.5
Impact of Policy Uncertainty on Growth *(in percent)*

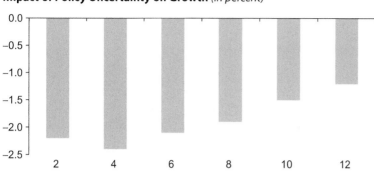

Note: This figure shows that gross domestic product (GDP) declines 2.2 percent in the second quarter in response to an increase in policy uncertainty in the first quarter, 2.4 percent in the fourth quarter, and so on. The increase in uncertainty is assumed to be equal to the change from 2006 until 2011. These results are based on a vector autoregression model, which is estimated using quarterly data from 1985 to 2011, including policy uncertainty, GDP, the S&P 500 Index, the federal funds rate, employment, investment, and consumption.

First, it directly affects the behavior of households and firms, which postpone investment and consumption decisions when uncertainty about future policies is elevated. Second, it breeds macroeconomic uncertainty, which in turn tends to reduce growth.

UNCERTAINTY, RECESSIONS, AND RECOVERIES

The degree of economic uncertainty also appears to be related to the depth of recessions and the strength of recoveries. Recessions accompanied by high uncertainty are often deeper than other recessions (Figure 9.6). Similarly, recoveries that coincide with periods of elevated uncertainty are weaker than other recoveries. The unusually high levels of uncertainty since the latest financial crisis and the associated episodes of deep recessions and weak recoveries play an important role in explaining these findings. Moreover, the latest recovery in advanced economies has coincided with lower cumulative growth in consumption and investment, along with a sharp and sustained contraction in investment in structures, as uncertainty has remained high.

Recessions accompanied by high uncertainty are often deeper than other recessions.

Uncertainty shocks account for about one-third of business cycle variation in advanced economies and up to half of cyclical volatility in emerging market and other developing economies, implying that these shocks play a sizable role in driving the dynamics of recessions and expansions. Other relevant research concludes that shocks associated with uncertainty and financial disruptions were the primary factors that led to the 2009 global recession.[13]

This chapter documents that high uncertainty historically coincides with periods of lower growth and that a pickup in uncertainty appears to increase

FIGURE 9.6

Role of Uncertainty: Recessions and Recoveries *(in percent)*

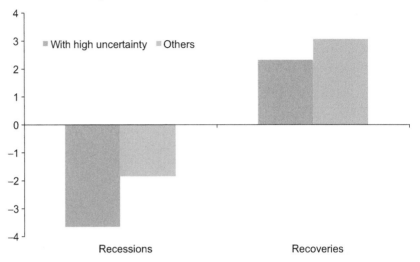

Note: This figure shows the amplitude of recessions and recoveries associated with and not associated with high uncertainty. A recession is associated with high uncertainty if the level of uncertainty falls in the top quartile of uncertainty measured at the trough of all recessions. A recovery is associated with high uncertainty if the level of uncertainty during the recovery is in the top quartile of the average uncertainty of all recovery episodes. The amplitude of a recession is the percent decline in output from peak to trough. The amplitude of a recovery is the one-year change in output from the trough of the recession. The statistics refer to the median of all episodes. Uncertainty refers to country-specific uncertainty, which is the monthly standard deviation of daily stock returns in each country. Daily returns are calculated using each country's stock price index; time coverage varies across economies.

the likelihood of a global recession. It is difficult for policymakers to overcome the intrinsic uncertainty economies typically face over the business cycle. However, uncertainty about economic policy was unusually high during the latest recovery, and it appears to have contributed significantly to macroeconomic uncertainty.

ON THE HORIZON: POLICIES

00:19

Mario Draghi, president of the European Central Bank, pledges to preserve the euro.

Policymakers can reduce policy-induced uncertainty by implementing bold and timely measures. Have the policy measures been sufficient to mitigate the severe impact of the 2009 global recession? In the next chapter, we trace the evolution of policies during global recessions and recoveries and document another unusual feature of the latest global recovery: the great divergence between fiscal and monetary policies in advanced economies.

[F]ollowing fiscal rules blindly . . . is a recipe for disappointment and political conflict. Fiscal stabilization that supports growth is welcome. Premature fiscal stabilization that undermines it is yet another folly.

Martin Wolf (2010c)

The (Great) Depression teaches us that tax cuts and increases in government spending can help heal a depressed economy, but only if they are used on a sufficiently large scale. It shows that when interest rates are at zero, monetary policy can still be effective, but it will likely take a regime shift. Policy needs to be dramatic enough that it changes people's expectations about future prices and output growth.

Christina Romer (2013)

The basic notion that what we need is more stimulus (uncertainty-creating activism) is badly misplaced. We are displacing a very large amount of private investment with the aggregate stimulus.

Alan Greenspan (2013)

We should be looking for a better balance between monetary and other growth-promoting policies, including fiscal policy.

Ben S. Bernanke (2015e)

CHAPTER 10

The Great Divergence of Policies

The 2009 global recession and the ensuing recovery have opened a new chapter in the long debate on the role of economic policies in stabilizing macroeconomic fluctuations and promoting growth. This debate became more passionate after some advanced economies withdrew large fiscal stimulus programs they implemented early in the crisis. How have fiscal and monetary policies evolved during global recessions and recoveries? Is the latest episode different from the previous ones?

THE DEBATE ON POLICIES AND CYCLES

Do expansionary fiscal and monetary policies help a country recover from a recession? Or do these policies hamper growth while sowing the seeds of the next crisis? There has been a robust debate on these questions since the 2007–09 global financial crisis, especially in advanced economies.

The latest global recovery has followed an unusual path compared with the three previous global recoveries.

Some economists argue that macroeconomic policies implemented during 2008–09 were instrumental in preventing another Great Depression and that the recovery would have been even weaker if the large monetary and fiscal stimulus had not been in place. If anything, they claim that the fiscal stimulus in the United States during 2008–09 was insufficient given the depth of the recession, and that it was a major mistake to withdraw the stimulus before a durable pickup in the real economy. Some commentators also suggest that the Federal Reserve should have been much more aggressive. Specifically, they argue that the Federal Reserve should have attempted to create moderate inflation for a short period to help accelerate both the private sector deleveraging process and the healing of housing market problems.[1]

Others bring a totally different perspective: they claim that the weak recovery in advanced economies is a reflection of poorly designed macroeconomic policies. These policies led to rising public debt and increased uncertainty and expanded the boundaries of regulatory measures that weigh on growth.[2] As a result, the investment climate has deteriorated, undercutting new projects and hampering employment growth. Some have also been very critical of expansionary monetary policies implemented by the Federal Reserve.[3]

UNDERSTANDING THE GREAT DIVERGENCE

The latest global recovery has followed an unusual path compared with the three previous global recoveries. Specifically, the recovery following the Great Recession exhibited two types of divergence. The first is the sharp divergence of activity between advanced and emerging market economies, as documented in Chapter 6. In emerging market economies, this recovery has been the strongest. However, there is no question that the Great Recession has been followed by a "Not So Great Recovery" in advanced economies. In fact, the latest recovery has been the weakest so far for them, as discussed in earlier chapters.

There has been a divergence of activity between advanced and emerging market economies and a divergence of policies among advanced economies.

The second specific feature is the great divergence of monetary and fiscal policies, which became increasingly more pronounced during 2011–13. In particular, while the directions of fiscal and monetary policies were aligned in previous episodes, during the current recovery, these policies have marched in opposite directions, mainly in advanced economies.[4]

05:22

Sub-Saharan Africa survived the Great Recession reasonably well.

We now trace the evolution of fiscal and monetary policies during global recessions and recoveries. Since we focus on the cyclical properties of these policies, we use measures that provide a good reading of the cyclical policy stance. For fiscal policy, we consider the evolution of real primary government expenditures. For monetary policy, we examine the evolution of nominal short-term interest rates and the size of central bank assets.[5]

FISCAL POLICY: STIMULUS FIRST, BUT THEN AUSTERITY

In response to the large output and employment losses associated with the Great Recession, a number of advanced and emerging market economies employed wide-ranging expansionary fiscal policy measures during 2008–09.[6] These coordinated measures were instrumental in supporting aggregate global demand during the height of the global financial crisis. In some advanced economies, especially the United States, the fiscal stimulus that was introduced at the outset of the financial crisis was far larger than in previous recessions, reflecting the severity of the episode (Figure 10.1). In 2009, fiscal deficits went up to 9 percent of GDP in the advanced economies and to 4.5 percent of GDP in the emerging market economies.

However, as public debt and financing requirements in some advanced economies rose significantly, market pressures and political constraints forced some of these economies to withdraw fiscal support in 2010.[7] The change in policies led to an unprecedented outcome and set quite different paths for government expenditures in advanced economies than during past recoveries, when policy was decisively expansionary with increases in real primary

FIGURE 10.1

Government Expenditures: Country Groups *(index)*

Note: Indexed to 100 in the year before global recession. Zero is the time of the global recession year. Each line shows the purchasing-power-parity-weighted average of the countries in the respective group. Previous episodes refer to those prior to 2009. Line breaks for 2009 denote the IMF's *World Economic Outlook* forecasts.

government expenditures. Specifically, expenditures fell during the first two years of the latest global recovery and are projected to continue to decline modestly or to stabilize gradually. The pattern of contractionary fiscal policy also holds across the major advanced economies, with the euro area—particularly, the periphery economies that have experienced severe sovereign debt problems—and the United Kingdom showing sharp departures from the typical paths of government expenditures observed in the past episodes (Figure 10.2).[8]

In contrast, in emerging market economies, the ongoing recovery has been accompanied by a more expansionary fiscal policy stance than during past episodes (Figure 10.1). This was possible because these economies had stronger fiscal positions this time around than in the past.

MONETARY POLICY: ON STEROIDS

Monetary policy has played a key role in restoring financial sector health and mitigating the adverse effects of the Great Recession on the real economy. During the early stages of the global financial crisis, central banks in the major advanced economies sharply reduced interest rates, expanded their liquidity facilities, and started purchasing longer-term assets. To the extent that these measures were effective in improving the health of the financial sector, central bank actions also supported economic activity. Policy rates were brought virtually to zero, and a variety of unconventional monetary policy measures were introduced, including quantitative easing and "twisting" operations. These policies increased the size and altered the composition of central bank balance sheets. The combination of zero interest rates and the record expansion of central bank balance sheets is unprecedented.

02:02
U.K. Prime Minister Gordon Brown outlines the coordinated global response to the crisis undertaken by the Group of 20.

FIGURE 10.2

Government Expenditures: Countries and Regions *(index)*

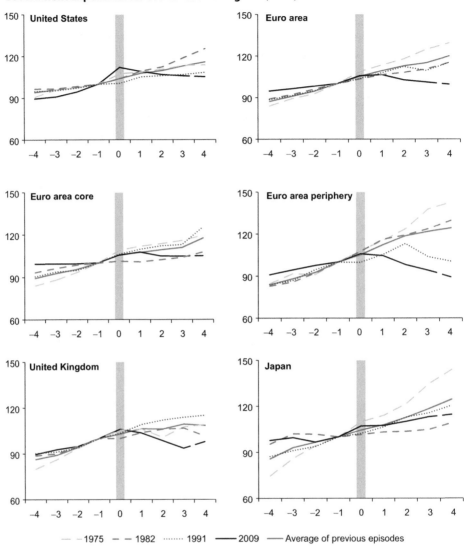

Note: Lines for the aggregates show the purchasing-power-parity-weighted average of the countries in the respective group. Euro area core includes France and Germany. Euro area periphery includes Greece, Ireland, Italy, Portugal, and Spain. Line breaks for 2009 denote the IMF's *World Economic Outlook* forecasts. Indexed to 100 in the year before global recession. Zero is the time of the global recession year. Previous episodes refer to those prior to 2009.

Monetary policies in advanced economies were exceptionally accommodative during the latest recovery compared with earlier episodes (Figure 10.3). In particular, policy rates remained at the zero lower bound, and central bank balance sheets in the major advanced economies continued to expand compared with earlier episodes (Figure 10.4). In addition, central banks began or intensified the use of forward guidance to provide information about the future direction of monetary policy to have a larger impact on expectations.

FIGURE 10.3
Interest Rates *(percent)*

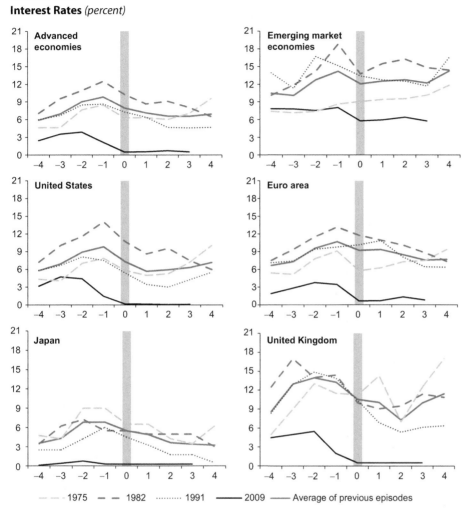

--- 1975   — — 1982   1991   —— 2009   —— Average of previous episodes

Note: Aggregates are market weighted by GDP in U.S. dollars; observations are excluded for countries experiencing inflation 50 percent greater than in the previous year. Interest rates refer to policy rates or three- or four-month Treasury
bill rates. Zero is the time of the global recession year. Previous episodes refer to those prior to 2009.

Monetary policy in emerging market economies was also more supportive of
economic activity than in the past, including through the non- or partially
sterilized purchases of international reserves.

THE GREAT DIVERGENCE IN POLICY EFFECTIVENESS

Interestingly, the great divergence of fiscal and monetary policies appears to
have coincided with a great divergence in policy effectiveness as well. The
zero lower bound on interest rates and the extent of financial disruption during the crisis limited the impact of expansionary monetary policies in
advanced economies. At the same time, the same zero lower bound and the

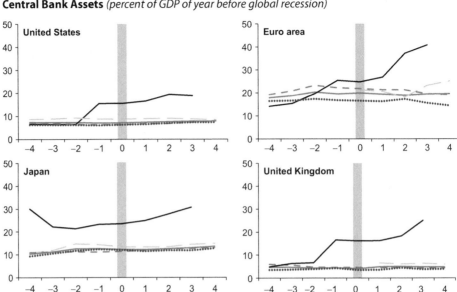

FIGURE 10.4
Central Bank Assets *(percent of GDP of year before global recession)*

Note: Euro area aggregate is market weighted by GDP in U.S. dollars. Zero denotes the year of the global recession. Previous episodes refer to those prior to 2009.

extent of slack in these economies tended to amplify the impact of contractionary fiscal policies. The divergence of policies and their effectiveness is thus one likely factor contributing to the sluggish nature of the recovery in advanced economies. We briefly summarize the sizable literature analyzing the roles of fiscal and monetary policies in a FOCUS box at the end of this chapter.

WHY DID POLICIES DIVERGE?

The stance of fiscal policy in the advanced economies during the latest global recession remains controversial. One view is that the fiscal stimulus at the onset of the recession was too small to engineer a robust recovery and that its subsequent withdrawal only made matters worse. Another view is that there are good reasons to employ contractionary fiscal policies. Specifically, caution about fiscal stimulus and the pace of consolidation in the latest recession and recovery are likely explained by high ratios of public debt to GDP and large deficits.

Advanced economies entered the Great Recession with much higher levels of debt than in the past (Figure 10.5). In fact, public debt in these economies reached record-high levels (Figure 10.6), with debt-to-GDP ratios larger than 100 percent in Japan, the United States, and many countries in Europe. The high debt levels reflect a combination of factors, including expansionary fiscal

FIGURE 10.5

Public Debt: Country Groups *(percent of GDP of year before global recession)*

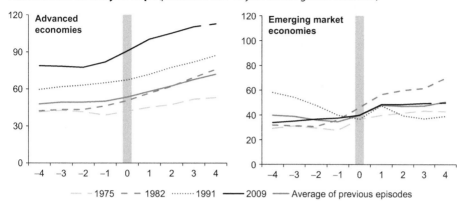

Note: Aggregates are market weighted by GDP in U.S. dollars and refer to public-debt-to-GDP ratios. Line breaks for the 2009 episode denote the IMF's *World Economic Outlook* forecasts. Zero is the time of the global recession year. Previous episodes refer to those prior to 2009.

policies in the run-up to the recession, financial sector support measures, and substantial revenue losses resulting from the severity of the Great Recession. In a number of countries, large debt levels also coincided with significant deficits. The deficit levels in some advanced economies have been large in part because of the collapse in revenues. Moreover, sovereign debt crises in some euro area periphery economies and challenges associated with market access put pressure on these economies to accelerate their fiscal consolidation plans.

At the same time, the aggressive stance of monetary policy was relatively easy to defend given historically low levels of inflation in advanced economies (Figure 10.6). There was indeed more room for monetary policy maneuvering because inflation rates were much lower in both advanced and emerging market economies at the beginning of the recession than in the past, and a number of central banks had undertaken a wide range of measures to avoid deflation (Figure 10.7).

WHAT IS THE RIGHT MIX OF POLICIES?

The evidence presented in this chapter does not in itself permit an assessment of whether the different policy mix pursued in the wake of the 2009 global recession was appropriate. The response may have been reasonable given the respective room available for fiscal and monetary policies in advanced economies. In particular, some advanced economies needed to improve their fiscal balances to reduce high levels of public debt to help reduce market pressures and mitigate the potential negative effects that high public debt can have on growth.[9]

FIGURE 10.6
Debt, Deficit, and Inflation: The Big Picture

A. Overall Deficit versus Net Debt
(percent of GDP)

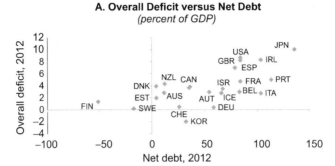

B. Gross Domestic Debt
(2012 U.S. dollar GDP-weighted average, percent of GDP)

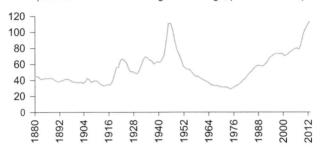

C. Debt-to-GDP Ratios in 2012
(percent of GDP)

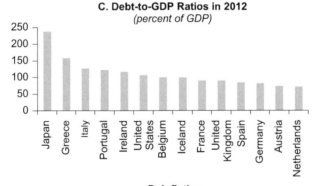

D. Inflation
(market weighted, in percent)

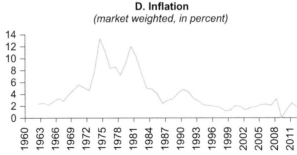

Note: Panel A plots the overall deficit and net debt of advanced economies in 2012. Panel B plots the gross domestic debt as a percentage of GDP in advanced economies. Panel C shows the debt-to-GDP ratios of selected advanced economies in 2012. Panel D shows the market-weighted inflation for advanced and emerging market economies (observations are excluded for countries experiencing inflation greater than 50 percent). AUS: Australia, AUT: Austria, BEL: Belgium, CAN: Canada, CHE: Switzerland, DEU: Germany, DNK: Denmark, EST: Estonia, ESP: Spain, FIN: Finland, FRA: France, GBR: Great Britain, ICE: Iceland, IRL: Ireland, ISR: Israel, ITA: Italy, JPN: Japan, KOR: Korea, NZL: New Zealand, PRT: Portugal, SWE: Sweden, USA: United States of America.

FIGURE 10.7
Inflation: Country Groups *(percent)*

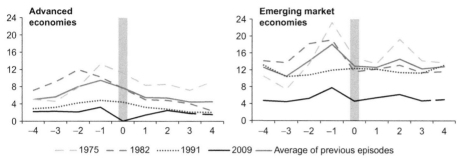

Note: Aggregates are market weighted by GDP in U.S. dollars. Observations are excluded for countries experiencing inflation 50 percent greater than in the previous year. Line breaks for the 2009 recession denote the IMF's *World Economic Outlook* forecasts (2013). Zero is the time of the global recession year. Previous episodes refer to those prior to 2009.

However, there are also obvious concerns. Even though monetary policy has been effective, policymakers had to resort to unconventional measures. Even with these measures, the zero bound on interest rates and the extent of financial disruption during the crisis have reduced the traction of monetary policy. Together with the extent of slack in these economies, this may have amplified the impact of contractionary fiscal policies. Policymakers therefore may run the risk of overburdening monetary policy.

WINDS OF CHANGE

Both monetary and fiscal policies underwent a transition in major advanced economies starting in late 2013. For example, the Federal Reserve took its first steps to normalize its monetary policy by gradually reducing its bond purchases as activity picked up and labor markets started to improve in the United States.[10] Although the Federal Reserve stopped its quantitative easing policy in 2014, both the European Central Bank and the Bank of Japan continued their expansionary policies at the time of writing this book. In addition, there were also some slight changes on the fiscal policy front in many advanced economies.[11] In late 2013, policymakers in the United States reached a two-year budget deal that reduced automatic spending cuts. Some advanced economies have recently slowed down fiscal consolidation plans.

SUPPORT FROM GLOBAL GROWTH: NEXT IN LINE

Each factor we studied in Part III played a unique role in shaping the dynamics of the 2009 global recession and subsequent recovery. We return to this issue in the last chapter to provide a synthesis of their roles. Before that, however, we turn in the next chapter to a brief analysis of the relationship between global and national cycles.

FOCUS

IMPACT OF POLICIES ON ACTIVITY

Economists have vigorously debated the effectiveness of fiscal and monetary policies in mitigating macroeconomic fluctuations. Much of this debate centers on the impact of active, or discretionary, policies rather than policies that automatically respond to the business cycle.[12] This section briefly surveys the literature analyzing various aspects of these policies in the context of the 2009 global recession.

Fiscal Policy

The debate over the role of fiscal policy has been particularly intense, and estimates of how output responds to discretionary changes in policy vary substantially depending on the methodology employed, the sample of countries, and the period under investigation. The growing consensus, however, is that discretionary fiscal policy does have a positive impact on economic activity, although the magnitude varies over the phases of the business cycle.[13] The debt crisis in some advanced economies, especially in the euro area, brought to the fore questions about the optimal composition and speed of fiscal consolidation in a context of depressed economic activity (Blanchard and Leigh 2013a). Recent evidence suggests that public investment can have an important effect on output when the economy is operating below full employment and monetary policy is accommodative (Abiad, Furceri, and Topalova 2015).

Monetary Policy

There has also been a debate about the effectiveness of discretionary monetary policy in influencing economic activity. Some argue that, in a world with flexible prices and rational agents, monetary policy cannot systematically affect economic activity.[14]

Others, however, claim that in a world with sticky prices, monetary policy can have a short-term impact on economic activity. This view has been very influential and led to the design of monetary policy rules, such as the Taylor rule, aimed at stabilizing activity and inflation. One problem with the empirical literature examining the effectiveness of monetary policy has been the lack of good proxies for discretionary monetary policies. This issue was partly addressed recently, and there is evidence that contractionary monetary policy shocks have a negative impact on output and inflation (Romer and Romer 2004).

The effectiveness of monetary and fiscal policies has also been debated in the context of a zero lower bound in interest rates. The standard Keynesian models imply that monetary policy becomes ineffective if the economy is in a liquidity trap—a situation in which the monetary authority is unable to further reduce already low interest rates because agents hoard all available cash as they expect deflation. Some studies suggest, however, that monetary policy could be effective even when the economy hits the zero lower bound if the policy measures can influence the expected path of monetary policy (Eggertsson and Woodford 2003). Werning (2012) argues that in such a circumstance the optimal nominal interest rate should be kept at zero longer than warranted by the current inflation rate. This would promote inflation and stimulate future output after the economy recovers from the trap. And this, in turn, could lead to an increase in consumption, ameliorating the negative output gap.[15]

Effectiveness of Unconventional Policies

Central banks facing the zero lower bound have expanded and changed the composition of their balance sheets in recent years. In some cases, central banks, through their lending operations, became active financial intermediaries.[16]

How effective have unconventional monetary policies been in the advanced economies? There is evidence that these measures have helped reduce long-term interest rates.[17] For example, D'Amico and others (2012) report that the large-scale asset purchases conducted in the United States were instrumental in reducing long-term rates.[18] The reduction in long-term rates helped boost equity prices, shoring up the process of economic recovery (Kiley 2013). However, these findings should be interpreted with caution given the uncertainty associated with the effects and the fact that it is still too soon to reach definitive conclusions (IMF 2013c).

Some argue that there are major risks associated with the unprecedented policy measures adopted by the central banks. In particular, there are questions about the impact of forward guidance, the implications of a prolonged period of low interest rates, financial stability risks stemming from unconventional policies, the credibility of central banks, and the best strategies to exit from these policies.[19]

PART **IV**

Living with the
Global Cycle

[T]here is a danger that recession will feed on itself and that confidence in the future will be progressively sapped throughout the world as caution follows disappointment.

Max Wilkinson (1982)

Last summer economists in America and Britain agonized about the risk of recession. Now that it has happened they have turned their attention to another "R-word": recovery. To most people a recession sounds bad, a recovery good. But in some ways a recession can, like a strict diet, be good for an economy's health. Recession can cleanse the economy of imbalances and clear the system for a strong recovery.

The Economist (1991)

CHAPTER 11

A Complex Affair: Global and National Cycles

The 2009 global recession forced a reconsideration of the linkages between the global business cycle and national cycles. Some countries were able to weather the global storm rather effectively, but others went through severe recessions. How does global growth affect national growth? Does the impact of global growth on national growth vary during global recessions and expansions? Do country-specific features affect the sensitivity of national cycles to the global cycle?

RECONSIDERING THE LINKAGES

The 2007–09 financial crisis sparked intensive discussions about our understanding of the linkages between the global and national business cycles. This was a natural outcome of the significant variation in growth between different groups of countries during the global recession and the ensuing recovery.[1] Emerging market economies were surprisingly resilient during the worst of the financial crisis and rapidly returned to growth. In contrast, advanced economies experienced deep contractions and a disappointingly slow recovery.

The 2009 global recession shifted the focus from the dependence of emerging market and developing economies on advanced economies to the relationship between the global business cycle and national business cycles.

These discussions have taken place against the backdrop of a rich research program on various aspects of global and national business cycles. Most of the studies on this topic have focused on the dependency of the emerging market and developing economies on the advanced economies.[2] We briefly summarize different channels through which developments in advanced economies affect activity in emerging market and developing economies in a FOCUS box at the end of this chapter. These studies confirm that the cyclical fortunes of emerging market and developing economies are tightly linked to developments in advanced economies.[3]

This chapter shifts attention to the linkages between the global business cycle and national business cycles. First, we briefly review our main observations about the linkages between global and national cycles in light of lessons from the analysis in the previous chapters.

FROM GLOBAL TO NATIONAL GROWTH

Our analysis of global recessions and recoveries so far points to three broad observations about the linkages between the global cycle and national business cycles.

- The global cycle behaves significantly differently during recessions and recoveries: average growth in world output per capita is about –0.7 percent during global recessions, but 2.3 percent during global recoveries (Figure 11.1).

- The growth performance of different country groups varies considerably over the global cycle. This implies that the sensitivity of national cycles to the global cycle depends on the phase of the global cycle. Advanced economies tend to perform worse than other country groups during global recessions and often experience weaker recoveries. Differential growth outcomes across country groups are also evident in the time series of growth in GDP per capita.

- The fraction of countries in recession increases significantly during a global recession. Specifically, 60 percent of countries, on average, experienced recessions during the four global recessions whereas only about 25 percent did during the full sample period (1960–2012).

NEED A NEW MODEL

In light of these three broad observations, we examine the sensitivity of national cycles to the global cycle over the two different phases of the global cycle. Specifically, we consider the impact of global growth on national growth during global recessions and expansions and study how this impact varies depending on different country characteristics using an econometric assessment of the interactions between the global cycle and national business cycles. Our econometric model explicitly accounts for the linkages between global growth, national growth, and global financial conditions. It also accommodates national and global real factors (often captured by domestic and worldwide productivity shocks) and global financial conditions (often captured by world interest rate shocks) to assess how these affect cyclical growth outcomes.

We focus on the impact of two major global variables on national growth outcomes: rest of the world growth per capita and the world real interest rate. The first variable is similar to the global business cycle measure employed in previous chapters. For each country, it is the purchasing-power-parity-weighted output growth of the remaining countries in the sample minus their population growth. The second variable is based on a widely used measure of the world real interest rate and corresponds to the difference between the

FIGURE 11.1

Growth and Synchronization: The Big Picture

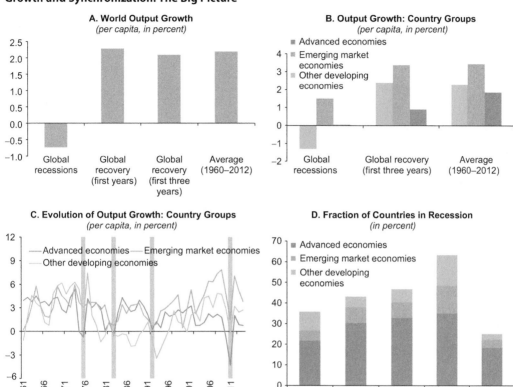

Note: Each bar in panel A corresponds to purchasing-power-parity-weighted average growth rate of GDP per capita of all countries during the indicated periods. Each bar in panel B corresponds to purchasing-power-parity-weighted average growth rate of GDP per capita of respective country groups during the indicated periods. Each line in panel C shows the purchasing-power-parity-weighted GDP per capita growth rate for the respective country group. Each bar in panel D shows the proportion of countries in recession during respective global recessions. The bar "Average (1960–2012)" shows the average proportion of countries in recession during 1960–2012.

three-month U.S. dollar London interbank offered rate (LIBOR) and U.S. inflation. It helps capture the influence of global credit and monetary conditions on national cycles.[4]

In addition, we use standard de facto measures of trade and financial integration in our model: the ratio of the sum of imports and exports to GDP and the ratio of the sum of total assets and liabilities to GDP. We also account for country-specific features (fixed effects) by capturing differences in institutions, structural factors, and initial conditions.

To structure our analysis of the linkages between the national cycles and the global cycle, we ask three basic questions. How does global growth impact national growth? How does its impact vary across country groups? Are country-specific features important? We present a preliminary analysis of these issues. There are obviously many extensions to consider and we provide a discussion of some of these in the last chapter.

HOW DOES GLOBAL GROWTH IMPACT NATIONAL GROWTH?

There is a positive and statistically significant association between national output growth and rest of the world growth, which implies that national cycles tend to move in tandem with the global cycle (Figure 11.2).[5] However, the strength of this relationship varies over the two phases of the global cycle. In particular, national cycles tend to be much more sensitive to the global cycle during recessions than during expansions.

A 1 percentage point increase in global growth is associated with a 0.7 percentage point pickup in national growth rate during global expansions, but it is associated with a 1.4 percentage point rise during global recessions. These findings imply that the impact of the global cycle on national cycles is much more pronounced during global recessions than during expansions.

There appears to be a negative association between national cycles and the world real interest rate, but this relationship differs across the two phases of the global cycle.[6] During global expansions, it is negative and statistically significant, whereas during global recessions it is slightly positive but insignificant (Figure 11.3). A 1 percentage point increase in the world real interest rate during a global expansion is associated with a 0.12 percentage point decrease in the growth rate of these countries. These links, however, weaken substantially during global recessions as lenders retrench their activities, including for international trade.[7]

Why is national growth more sensitive to global growth during global recessions? First, as documented earlier, global recessions often coincide with large shocks that adversely affect many countries. This reduces external demand and leads to a significant decline in international trade flows. This in turn hurts national growth, especially in countries that rely heavily on exports. Second, global recessions are often periods of financial turmoil that coincide with contracting credit and declining asset prices. In a highly integrated world economy, disruptions in global financial markets often translate into slower national growth as international capital flows quickly dry up. Disruptions in global financial markets also affect the financing of exports and imports, aggravating the growth effects of declining international trade flows.

FIGURE 11.2
Linkages between National and Global Cycles *(percent)*

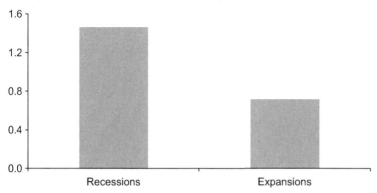

Note: The bars show the impact of a 1 percentage point increase in the rest of the world per capita output growth on the national output growth rate per capita. See table 1 in Appendix J for detailed results.

FIGURE 11.3
National Cycles and the World Interest Rate *(percent)*

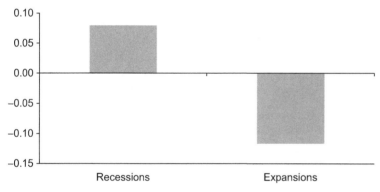

Note: The bars show the impact of a 1 percentage point increase in the world real interest rate on the national output growth rate per capita. See table 1 in Appendix J for detailed results.

HOW DO LINKAGES VARY ACROSS COUNTRY GROUPS?

The nature of linkages between the national and global cycles appears to vary across different country groups (Figure 11.4). In particular, both advanced and emerging market economies are more sensitive to the global business cycle during global recessions than are other developing economies. During global recessions, a 1 percentage point increase in global growth is associated with a 1.5 to 2 percentage point rise in the national growth rate in the emerging market and advanced economies, compared with only a 1 percentage point

FIGURE 11.4

Linkages between National and Global Cycles: Country Groups *(percent)*

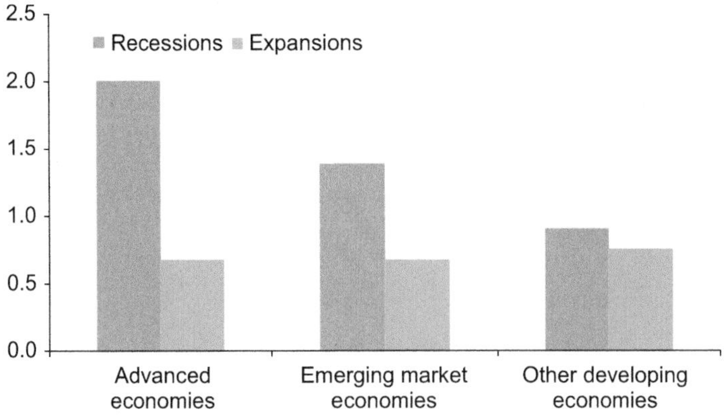

Notes: The bars show the impact of a 1 percentage point increase in the rest of the world per capita output growth on the national per capita output growth rate during recessions and expansions. See Appendix J (J.2) for detailed results.

FIGURE 11.5

National Cycles and the World Interest Rate: Country Groups *(percent)*

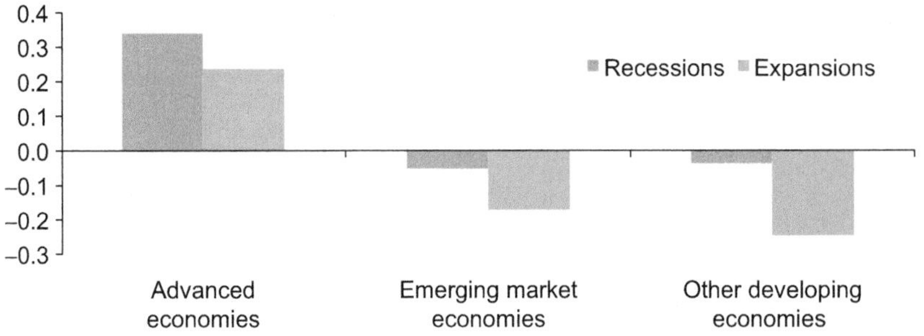

Note: The bars show the impact of a 1 percentage point increase in the world real interest rate on the national output growth rate per capita. See table 2 in Appendix J for detailed results.

pickup in other developing economies. These results are consistent with those from other studies analyzing the importance of global and national factors in explaining business cycles in different country groups.[8]

The sensitivity of national cycles to world interest rates also differs across country groups (Figure 11.5). For advanced economies, national cycles tend to move with the global interest rate cycle given the statistically significant positive association between domestic growth and the world real interest rate. However, for emerging market and other developing economies, national cycles tend to move in the opposite direction of the world interest rate cycle

The impact of global growth on national growth is more pronounced during global recessions.

during global expansions. For example, a 1 percentage point increase in the world real interest rate during a global expansion is associated with a roughly 0.2 percentage point decrease in the national growth rate of the emerging market economies. In contrast, an increase in the world real interest rate during global recessions has a negative, but statistically insignificant, effect on the growth of these countries.

These results likely reflect that movements in interest rates have differential effects on the business cycles of debtor and creditor countries. While there has been a role reversal in recent years, advanced economies were historically creditors and emerging market and other developing economies debtors during most of the period under study. Creditors tend to benefit from increases in interest rates, whereas debtor countries face larger debt-service costs.

ARE COUNTRY-SPECIFIC FEATURES IMPORTANT?

Both trade and financial integration appear to influence the sensitivity of national cycles to the global cycle and to the world interest rate. For instance, national cycles are more sensitive to the global business cycle in countries that are more open to trade flows. The intensity of this empirical relationship, however, varies between the two phases of the global cycle. A 1 percentage point increase in global growth is on average associated with a roughly 0.7 percentage point increase in the national growth rate during a global expansion for a country if its degree of trade openness is equal to the average of countries in our sample (about 70 percent). Likewise, a 1 percentage point reduction in global growth is associated with about a 1.6 percentage point decrease in the national growth rate during a global recession for a country if its degree of trade openness is equal to the average of countries in our data sample.

There is a statistically significant negative association between the national cycle and the global interest rate cycle during global expansions, but this association becomes weaker in countries with stronger international financial linkages. This result probably stems from the fact that countries with stronger financial linkages are able to attract a diverse variety of capital flows, including foreign direct investment and portfolio investment, whereas those with weaker links with the rest of the world often rely on debt flows that are sensitive to movements in world interest rates.

Movements in global interest rates have differential effects on creditor and debtor countries.

The inclusion of variables measuring a country's integration with the global economy to our baseline econometric model does not change the positive association between the global and national cycles. Increased trade integration tends to accentuate the sensitivity of national cycles to the global cycle, whereas increased financial integration helps shield national growth from fluctuations in world interest rates during global expansions.

WHAT DOES IT ALL MEAN?

Our findings collectively portray an intricate relationship between the global business cycle and national cycles. National business cycles are tightly linked to the global cycle, but the sensitivity of national cycles to the global cycle is much higher during global recessions than during expansions. There are significant differences in how countries respond to the global cycle, with advanced economies seemingly more sensitive than developing economies. Moreover, countries tend to be more sensitive to the global cycle the more integrated they are with the global economy.

FOCUS

TRANSMISSION OF CYCLES ACROSS BORDERS

As emerging market and developing economies establish stronger linkages with the world economy, macroeconomic fluctuations in these countries become more sensitive to external developments. Indeed, the 2007–09 financial crisis originated in a small set of advanced economies, but it rapidly spread to a large number of emerging market and developing economies. The cycles in advanced economies can be transmitted to emerging market and developing economies through three channels: trade, finance, and direct sectoral linkages.

During the 2009 global recession, the financial channel played an important role in transmitting the initial shock from advanced to emerging market and developing economies. In addition, the other channels associated with trade and sectoral interdependence significantly affected macroeconomic fluctuations in the latter group.[9]

The Trade Channel

- *Foreign demand shocks.* Business cycles in advanced economies have a significant effect on demand for commodities, intermediate goods, and finished goods produced by emerging market and developing economies. As their trade relationship with the advanced economies has rapidly expanded in recent decades, emerging market and developing economies have become increasingly more affected by aggregate demand conditions in the advanced economies. This is especially true for the many Asian and Latin American countries that have strong trade linkages with advanced economies (Kim 2001; Canova 2005; Akin and Kose 2008; Fidrmuc and Korhonen 2010).[10]

- *Aggregate productivity shocks.* For many emerging market and developing economies, technology transfers occur mainly through imports from advanced economies. Technological spillovers and their effects on macroeconomic fluctuations therefore tend to be larger for countries that have strong trade relations with advanced economies, although this also depends on the nature of products traded (Kose, Prasad, and Terrones 2003a, 2009; Jansen and Stokman 2004).

- *Terms-of-trade fluctuations.* Research indicates that terms-of-trade shocks could account for a substantial fraction of output fluctuations in developing economies. These shocks include variations in commodity prices that are often influenced by cyclical conditions in advanced economies. The volatility of commodity prices tends to have large spillover effects within developing economies that rely on exports of commodities and other primary products for much of their export earnings (and, in some cases, for a significant fraction of their national incomes). In this vein, commodity price shocks have been shown to be important determinants of investment and output fluctuations among commodity-exporting countries (Kose and Riezman 2001; Eicher, Schubert, and Turnovsky 2008; Broda and Tille 2003).[11]

The Financial Channel

- *Private capital flows.* Foreign direct investment and other forms of capital flows from advanced to emerging market and developing economies have expanded considerably in recent decades. The magnitude and volatility of capital flows from advanced economies can significantly influence investment and output in developing economies (Kose, Prasad, and Terrones 2003b, 2006). The effects of capital inflows and their reversal on domestic activity in emerging market and developing economies are well documented (Mendoza 2001; Cardarelli, Elekdag, and Kose 2010). The phenomenon of financial contagion also implies that macroeconomic disturbances in one or a few emerging market and developing economies could be transmitted rapidly to other countries via the financial channel. The rising correlation of stock market fluctuations is another aspect of this phenomenon. As emerging market and developing economies strengthen their linkages to international financial markets, the financial channel is likely to become increasingly important in transmitting fluctuations to these countries.

- *Aid and remittance flows.* The volatility of aid and remittance flows can also affect macroeconomic fluctuations in some emerging market and developing economies. Research finds that while these flows are volatile, they appear to help smooth the home country business cycles (Ratha 2005; Acosta, Lartey, and Mandelman 2009; Durdu and Sayan 2010; Frankel 2011; Mandelman and Zlate 2012).

- *Global financial market conditions.* Changes in world interest rates and investors' appetite for risk, along with perceptions of the riskiness of investments in emerging market and developing economies, are likely to influence the quantity of capital inflows to these economies. The ability of these countries to conduct countercyclical macroeconomic policies could also be constrained by externally generated changes in interest rates and spreads. Evidence suggests that the effects of world real interest rate shocks on output volatility tend to be significant for countries with high external indebtedness (Kose 2002; Neumeyer and Perri 2005).

Sectoral Interdependence

- *Similarities in economic structure.* These similarities imply that sector-specific shocks—including productivity shocks and shocks to the composition of import demand from advanced economies—tend to have similar effects on aggregate fluctuations across national borders. Some studies find that the high degree of business cycle synchronization across the major East Asian economies compared with those in Latin America may be largely attributable to similarities in the sectoral composition of output in these countries (Imbs 2004; Dées and Zorell 2012).

I believe that during the last financial crisis, macroeconomists (and I include myself among them) failed the country, and indeed the world. In September 2008, central bankers were in desperate need of a playbook that offered a systematic plan of attack to deal with fast-evolving circumstances. Macroeconomics should have been able to provide that playbook. It could not.

Narayana Kocherlakota (2010)

The global economy is at a critical juncture. Most economists agree on what is needed to avoid another round of lost growth opportunities, inadequate employment, financial instability, and worsening inequality. Central banks and markets cannot achieve an orderly global rebalancing on their own. As difficult as it may be, politicians need to pursue comprehensive policy responses. The longer they delay, the less effective their efforts will be.

Mohamed El-Erian (2015)

CHAPTER 12

Lessons: Past, Present, and Future

"We live in a global world" is a cliché of our time, but there is no commonly accepted definition of a global recession to tell us when our economic world has gone off track. We have provided definitions of the concepts of global recession and recovery, presented a comprehensive analysis of the main features of these episodes, studied the unique properties of the 2009 global recession and the subsequent recovery, and examined the complex interactions between global and national growth. What can we draw from our analysis? What are the implications for the design of policies? And for future research?

WHAT WAS OUR OBJECTIVE?

This book addresses a critical need: despite the repeated use of "global recession" and "global recovery" since 2006, there are no commonly accepted definitions of these terms. One reason may be that, especially before 2007, the world economy had enjoyed an extended period of stability stretching back to the mid-1980s, the so-called era of Great Moderation. Moreover, the spectacular performance of the world economy during 2002–07 made the concept of a global recession an odd thing to worry about.

The spectacular performance of the world economy during 2002–07 made the concept of a global recession an odd thing to worry about.

Understanding these two terms became increasingly important after the severe 2009 global recession and the fragile ensuing recovery. There has been a lot of confusion over these terms, rooted in the difficulty of decomposing the global business cycle into the well-known phases of national business cycles. While national cycles naturally go through periods of contraction and expansion, the global cycle rarely contracts outright.

This book presents the first comprehensive analysis of global recessions and recoveries. It defines these concepts and documents their main features. We analyzed the specific properties of the latest global recession and recovery in light of the lessons of three previous episodes since 1960 (1975, 1982, 1991). We also examined the interactions between global and national cycles.

WHAT DID WE LEARN?

02:24
The authors summarize their findings.

Getting the concepts right. Our definitions of global recessions and recoveries follow the standard definitions of national cycles. Specifically, we define a global recession as a contraction in world real GDP per capita accompanied by a broad decline in various other measures of global economic activity. A global recovery corresponds to a rebound in worldwide activity in one to three years following a global recession. These definitions lead to natural parallels between the phases of the global business cycle and those of national cycles.

Four global recessions. Since 1960, the world economy experienced four global recessions: 1975, 1982, 1991, and 2009. These four dates constitute clear reference points for comparisons. Although each episode presented unique difficulties for the world economy, they also shared multiple similarities.

Events surrounding the global recessions. After identifying the dates of global recessions, we presented brief descriptions of the relevant events surrounding each episode. Global recessions often occurred under complex circumstances, but each episode was characterized by specific events. For example, the 1975 global recession coincided with a sharp increase in oil prices and left an enduring recognition of the importance of supply shocks. The 1982 global recession also featured gyrations in oil markets but came on the heels of the employment of contractionary monetary policies in the major advanced economies and financial crises in some emerging market economies. The global recessions of 1991 and 2009 took place alongside financial crises in many advanced economies.

Main features of global recessions and recoveries. Global recessions feature synchronized declines in world output per capita, employment, industrial production, trade and capital flows, and oil consumption. The average decline in world output per capita during the four global recessions is about 0.7 percent, roughly 3 percentage points lower than its historical average.

In addition to the four global recession episodes, the world economy experienced two global downturns, in 1998 and 2001. Discussions during each of these downturns centered on the likelihood that a global recession would ensue, reflecting the confusion about the definition of a global recession. In both years, world growth was indeed quite low, some indicators signaled vulnerability, and many countries had indeed entered a recession. That said, world output per capita did not decline, and worldwide activity showed no broad-based weakness.

Global recoveries are often accompanied by a rebound in activity, which is generally driven by a synchronized revival in worldwide consumption, investment, and trade. Most indicators of global activity also recover and start registering growth in the first year of recovery. Specifically, industrial production, trade, and capital flows quickly bounce back during the first year of a global recovery. Credit and asset prices fluctuate sharply during global recessions and recoveries. These results together indicate that there are strong parallels between the main features of the global business cycle and those of national cycles.

The 2009 global recession. The 2009 episode was the most severe and most synchronized global recession of the past half century. In fact, it was the only episode during which world output contracted outright. A collapse in international trade and capital flows accompanied the recession, and global unemployment rose rapidly.

The global recovery since then has been comparable to previous episodes. However, it has followed surprisingly divergent paths in the advanced and emerging market economies: it has been the weakest recovery yet for advanced economies and the strongest for emerging market economies. The latest recovery is similar to the one that followed the 1991 recession in multiple dimensions. In both cases, the ripple effects of a collapse in credit and asset markets in the advanced economies hurt the global economy. Moreover, lingering effects of financial crises and policy challenges in Europe slowed both recoveries.

WHAT ARE THE KEY LESSONS?

Why was the 2009 global recession so deep? Why has the recovery been so sluggish? The severity of the 2009 global recession and the unusually sluggish nature of the ensuing recovery have been the subject of intense debates. We analyzed various explanations: the highly synchronized nature of the global recession; the severity of the financial crisis during 2007–09; unusually high levels of macroeconomic and policy uncertainty during the recovery; and the surprising divergence of macroeconomic policies and their effectiveness after 2010.

The 2009 global recession was the most severe and most synchronized global recession of the past half century. Almost all the advanced economies and roughly half the emerging market and developing economies were in recession in 2009.

An unprecedented degree of synchronization. One of the distinguishing features of the 2009 global recession was the unprecedented degree of synchronization of national recessions. The number of countries in recession was at a historical low during 2006–07. But in a dramatic reversal, almost all the advanced economies and roughly half the emerging market and developing economies were in recession in 2009. The gravity of the global financial crisis and the forces of trade and financial globalization are significant factors in explaining the extraordinary extent of the latest global recession.

Highly synchronized recessions are longer and deeper than other recessions. In parallel, recoveries from synchronous recessions are very slow and tend to be weaker than other recoveries. When highly synchronized recessions occur, a domestic recovery driven by a turnaround in net exports becomes difficult. Indeed, compared with other recessions, exports are typically more sluggish in highly synchronized recessions, and financial markets struggle. The significant narrowing of global imbalances—which had reached their peak the year before the global financial crisis—is the result of the expenditure reduction in deficit economies, which in turn led to a compression in imports.

A financial crisis for the ages. The severity of the 2007–09 financial crisis and the fact that the original crisis was followed by a massive sovereign debt and banking crisis in the euro area also explain why the 2009 global recession was so deep and the ensuing recovery so sluggish. Financial crises can prolong and deepen recessions through a variety of channels as the adverse feedback loops between the real economy and the financial sector are magnified. Firms and households face a significant erosion of wealth and capital as sharp declines in asset prices reduce net worth; this in turn constrains consumption and investment.

Financial crises are also followed by weak recoveries. Specifically, it takes longer to recover from recessions accompanied by financial crises, and such recoveries are generally more sluggish. Consumption typically grows more slowly than during other recoveries, and investment continues to decline even after the end of the recession. Output growth stays weak, and the unemployment rate tends to climb more than usual during recoveries following recessions with financial crises. Moreover, credit and asset markets often experience prolonged busts during recoveries following recessions that coincide with financial crises.

High uncertainty. High uncertainty has been another factor prominently blamed for stifling the recovery—including uncertainty about macroeconomic prospects and economic policies and regulations. Uncertainty can undermine economic growth through multiple channels. When faced with high uncertainty, firms reduce investment demand and delay projects, and consumers reduce consumption of durable goods. In addition, the adverse effects of uncertainty become more pronounced during periods of financial stress.

The evidence we present indicates that uncertainty tends to be detrimental to economic growth. High uncertainty is often associated with a large drop in investment and consumption growth. Recessions accompanied by high uncertainty are often deeper than others and the recoveries weaker. Policy-induced uncertainty is also negatively associated with growth.

Great divergence of policies. Since 2007, a fierce debate has raged about the roles played by fiscal and monetary policies in dampening the impact of the global financial crisis. Some claimed that the depth of the 2009 global recession required a massive policy response, but others disagreed. As these debates became more passionate, the 2009 global recession gradually differentiated itself from previous global recessions: the direction of fiscal and monetary policies, which had been aligned during previous episodes, diverged, mainly in advanced economies.

The direction of fiscal and monetary policies, which had been aligned during previous global recessions, diverged after the 2009 global recession.

Since 2008, monetary policy has clearly served its function by restoring financial sector health and mitigating the adverse effects of the global recession in advanced economies. The major central banks aggressively employed the policy weapons in their arsenals, especially during the initial stages of the financial crisis. They slashed interest rates to almost zero, expanded liquidity facilities, and started purchasing longer-term assets. The combination of near zero interest rates and record expansions of central bank balance sheets was unprecedented.

Although monetary policy in advanced economies remained exceptionally accommodative, fiscal policy followed a different trajectory. During 2008–09, many advanced and emerging market economies responded to the global recession with wide-ranging, expansionary fiscal measures. These policies were helpful in supporting the real economy during the height of the financial crisis. However, many advanced economies started withdrawing fiscal support in 2010 and employed increasingly contractionary fiscal measures to address record-high public debt levels, and market pressures and political constraints forced policymakers to embark on front-loaded fiscal adjustment programs. The change in policies created substantially different paths for government expenditures in advanced economies than during past recoveries, when policy was decisively expansionary.

In addition, the effectiveness of these policies also appears to have diverged in a detrimental fashion. Monetary policy has been supportive of the recovery but has become less potent because of the zero lower bound on interest rates and the massive disruption in channels of financial intermediation. Contractionary fiscal policy has become a more powerful drag on growth because of the same zero lower bound and the extent of slack in advanced economies. The divergence of policies and their effectiveness thus appears to be one factor that has made the ongoing recovery unusually weak.

Which factor is most important? It is natural to ask which of these four factors has played a more important role in driving growth outcomes during the latest recession and ongoing recovery. We think each factor has played a distinctive role. It is very difficult, if not impossible, to perfectly disentangle the impact of one from the others since there have been close interactions among them. For example, policy uncertainty has been naturally related to policies in place. In addition, the extent of financial disruption has inevitably shaped the design of policies. Our broader message is that the regrettable coincidence of these four factors has led to an extraordinarily severe recession and a painfully weak recovery.

Interactions between global growth and national growth. The global cycle behaves significantly differently during recessions and recoveries. In addition, there are substantial differences in national growth outcomes across country groups depending on the phase of the global cycle. These suggest that it is difficult to have a good grasp of global recessions and recoveries without understanding the linkages between the global and national business cycles. While national business cycles are tightly linked to the global business cycle, the strength of this linkage varies significantly over the cycle. In particular, national cycles are more sensitive to developments in the global economy during global recessions than during expansions. There are also significant differences in how various groups of countries respond to the global cycle. Advanced economies appear to be more sensitive to global recessions than emerging market and developing economies. Moreover, countries tend to be more susceptible to the global cycle the more integrated they are with the world economy.

FOUR POLICY MESSAGES

A study of global recessions and recoveries during the past half century can suggest a wide range of policy implications. We focus on four general policy lessons: the importance of having sufficiently large policy space to respond, the significance of policies targeting macro-financial stability, the value of a sustainable growth strategy, and the role of international coordination of policies.

Policy space: the larger the better during global recessions. Having sufficient policy space to counteract adverse shocks is always critical, but it is even more important during a global recession. National growth outcomes become more sensitive to global growth during global recessions. Moreover, a global recession means that an economy can no longer rely on external demand to support domestic activity.

The 2009 global recession clearly demonstrates the importance of policy space. In terms of fiscal policy, because of high levels of debt, many advanced economies rapidly exhausted the policy space they had prior to the global recession and were forced to shift from expansionary to contractionary policies early in the recovery. In the context of monetary policy, a number of advanced economies quickly lost their ability to use interest rates as a policy instrument because of the zero lower bound. In contrast, emerging market economies had more policy room to counteract the global recession, and partly because of the policies they employed, they were quite resilient during the crisis.

Policies for macro-financial stability: be aware of risks. A lesson from the devastation caused by the 2007–09 global financial crisis is that close monitoring of cycles in financial markets should be an integral part of macroeconomic surveillance and policy design. During the 2009 global recession, powerful adverse feedback loops between the real economy and the financial sector pushed many countries into deep recession and resulted in weak recoveries. The multidimensional interactions between financial and business cycles are especially forceful in a highly integrated global economy with sophisticated financial markets. In addition to the traditional linkages between the inflation and business cycles, monetary policymakers should take into account the state of cycles in financial markets when formulating monetary policies.

Close monitoring of cycles in financial markets should be an integral part of macroeconomic surveillance and policy design.

It is also important to account for the interactions among financial cycles when designing regulatory policies to ensure the health of the overall financial system. Again, the 2009 global recession provides a clear policy lesson: because cycles in housing markets and credit tend to enhance each other, if both house prices and credit are rapidly growing, it might be necessary to employ stricter rules and standards for mortgage lending as well as larger countercyclical buffers to moderate fluctuations in banks' capital positions. Moreover, it is imperative to consider the global aspects of financial regulation and surveillance policies since domestic financial cycles are often highly synchronized internationally.

A balanced growth strategy. Global recessions offer painful reminders of the importance of a balanced growth strategy supported by both domestic and external demand. Excessive reliance on external demand creates a host of vulnerabilities to demand shocks originating in trade partners, especially during global recessions. For those countries that rely heavily on exports to generate growth, it is important to balance the risks of greater trade openness by creating a more diversified export base along with a broader set of trading partners. In addition, policy measures to stimulate domestic demand are important.[1] These measures can translate into a more diversified exposure to world export markets.

Policy coordination: essential during global recessions. In the event of an isolated domestic recession stemming from a country-specific shock, a country can respond with various policy measures if it has a sufficient policy buffer. In the event of a global recession, countries often have to cope with a global shock and must respond by coordinating their policies. In a highly integrated world economy, the reach of a global recession is likely to be wider, making policy coordination even more essential to mitigate the adverse effects of global shocks.[2]

The latest global recession spurred an unprecedented degree of policy coordination, especially at the height of the crisis in 2008–09.[3] Specifically, the crisis made the Group of Twenty (G20) a significant forum for dialogue on issues related to global economic and financial stability.[4] The G20 was formally established in September 1999, but the first meeting of the G20 leaders took place at the height of the crisis in November 2008 to formulate policies to respond to the crisis. The G20 was able to successfully coordinate expansionary fiscal and monetary policies in late 2008 and early 2009, which were instrumental in helping the global economy emerge from the global recession.[5] As advanced economies navigate the uncharted waters of policy normalization, it is again critical that they coordinate policies to achieve better growth outcomes while reducing financial market volatility.[6]

FUTURE WORK: WHAT IS NEXT?

Our findings indicate the need to further improve our understanding of global recessions and recoveries. There are a number of potential avenues for future research.

Human and social costs. It is vital to develop a better understanding of the human and social costs of global recessions, which are periods of collapse in the growth of income per capita, but more important, are periods of enormous pain with large human and social costs. The costs include the loss of jobs and income, an increase in poverty and inequality, and the loss of human capital. It is clear that the study of such costs and the design of policies that help reduce them should be a critical component of future research.

Designing policies that help reduce the enormous human and social costs of global recessions should be a critical component of future research.

Macroeconomic models and policies. Global recessions have occasioned a rethinking of macroeconomic theories and policies. The 1975 recession showed the importance of supply shocks, leading to a new generation of models emphasizing the critical role of microeconomic foundations. The 1982 and 1991 episodes led to substantial changes in the design of monetary policy and paved the way for new research on a wide range of critical issues, including linkages between credit markets and the real economy, determinants of exchange rates, and currency unions. The 2009 global recession was a truly tectonic episode for macroeconomics because it starkly exposed the limits of macroeconomic models and policies.

The implications of these observations are clear: research on policies is more urgent than ever. Years after the 2009 global financial crisis, its deep scars remain visible all around. Many advanced economies are still struggling with low growth, large public and private debt, persistently high unemployment rates, and impaired financial systems. Emerging market economies are experiencing what appears to be a synchronized slowdown amid financial market problems. There is consensus that the economics profession needs to develop a richer menu of fiscal, monetary, financial sector, and structural policies.[7]

National and global business cycles. Another natural topic for future research is how various countries are affected by the global business cycle. Specifically, it would be useful to undertake a deeper analysis of the differential effects of global and national shocks, policy responses, and structural features of countries—including their linkages with the global economy through different types of trade and financial flows. For example, the role played by the global business cycle in explaining domestic cycles in different country groups (that is commodity exporters versus manufacturing goods exporters; debtor countries versus creditor countries) is a promising topic.

Macro-financial linkages. Another key area of future research involves a better understanding of the linkages between financial cycles and macroeconomic outcomes. This research program has become all the more important because we now have a better appreciation of the critical role played by problems in financial markets as motivating factors for macroprudential policy. However, the conceptual frameworks underpinning the problems and associated policy proposals are not well understood. There still remains a vigorous debate on the effectiveness of regulatory measures to cope with large fluctuations in asset and credit markets. More research on macro-financial linkages can improve our grasp of these complex issues and help guide the design of macroprudential policies.

Determinants of global financial flows. Global financial flows declined substantially in the latest global recession. Moreover, worrisome signs point to a significant slowing of the pace of financial globalization since 2008.[8] For example, after growing at about 8 percent a year during 1990–2007, global financial assets have increased by roughly 2 percent annually since the global financial crisis. In addition, there has been a substantial decline in cross-border bank lending, and the process of financial development in emerging market economies appears to be stagnating. It is important to understand the sources of these financial trends and their implications for economic growth and macroeconomic stability.

Regional cycles. Our discussion of regional cycles around the episodes of global recessions and recoveries was limited to a set of basic stylized facts. It would be useful to extend this analysis and study channels through which regional cycles are affected by the global cycle, especially during periods of recession and recovery. This is particularly important in the context of regional surveillance efforts.

Recessions and downturns. It is important to present an extensive comparison between global recessions and global downturns. We just documented the basic features of these episodes here, but a more detailed study that provides a better characterization of the behavior of the global economy during global recessions and global recoveries could improve our understanding of how some downturns turn into global recessions while others have relatively mild effects. This could also enhance our ability to forecast the turning points in the global business cycle.

COLLAPSE AND REVIVAL: THE ENDURING REALITY

Considering the large and long-lasting macroeconomic, financial, human, and social costs associated with global recessions, it is natural that each episode creates fears of impending economic catastrophe. After each global recession, however, the world economy has been able to go through a period of revival and eventually recover. For advanced economies, however, the latest episode has played out quite differently so far. Most of these economies have been struggling with lackluster growth and experiencing unprecedented policy challenges since the end of the 2009 global recession.

There have been occasional pronouncements that the business cycle has been eliminated, especially during periods of prolonged stability and prosperity.[9] In the 1960s, for example, there was such a discussion as the global economy enjoyed a long expansion. At the end of the 1980s, some observers argued that the business cycle was disappearing as the world economy had experienced an extended period of uninterrupted growth. During

03:37
In October 2012, IMF Managing Director Christine Lagarde said the top priority was for the world to restore sufficient growth to generate jobs for the millions of unemployed.

the late 1990s, the idea was popular again as some commentators bravely declared the end of the business cycle because of the forces of globalization and changes in technology and finance. Such claims have been proven false time and again. The business cycle, national as well as global, is alive and well.

Our main message is that collapse and revival are unavoidable features of the global business cycle. If there is one recurring lesson, it is our fundamental need to develop better policy tools to mitigate the costs associated with collapses and accelerate revivals.

Notes

CHAPTER 2 GLOBAL CYCLES: TOWARD A BETTER UNDERSTANDING

1. Gross domestic product (GDP) is the total value of output (that is, all goods and services) produced within a country during a given period. GDP per capita is the average income of a citizen in a country and is often used as a measure of a country's standard of living (Callen 2008). Coyle 2014 provides a detailed history of the concept of GDP and discusses its strengths and weaknesses. We use "output" and "GDP" interchangeably. Appendix A includes a glossary of acronyms and abbreviations used in the book.

2. The definition of the national business cycle goes back to the seminal study conducted by Arthur Burns and Wesley Mitchell in the 1940s. Arthur Burns served as the chairman of the U.S. Council of Economic Advisers (1953–1956), chairman of the U.S. Federal Reserve (1970–1978), and ambassador to West Germany (1981–1985, see the *New York Times*, 1987). Wesley Mitchell was one of the founders of the National Bureau of Economic Research—NBER (Burns 1952). The book by Burns and Mitchell *Measuring Business Cycles* was published in 1947 and became the seminal study describing the statistical methods of business cycle analysis employed by the NBER.

3. Economists have studied a wide range of real and financial factors that can drive national business cycle fluctuations: technological developments (productivity shocks), policies (shocks associated with fiscal, monetary, financial, and structural policies), movements in factors of production (labor and capital), disturbances in financial markets, fluctuations in commodity prices, political developments, news, changes in consumer confidence, and uncertainty. In a similar fashion, these same factors can play important roles in driving global business cycles because national shocks transmit across borders. We survey different branches of the literature on the global business cycles in a FOCUS box later in this chapter, the linkages between globalization and business cycle synchronization in Chapter 7, and the transmission of business cycles in Chapter 11.

4. Prior to the global financial crisis, there was fierce debate about whether business cycles in emerging market economies could "decouple" from advanced economies and keep global growth at a reasonable rate. This debate led to a number of studies about the growth potential of emerging market economies and their dependence on advanced economies (Kose and Prasad 2010; King 2010; Magnus 2011; Spence 2011; World Bank 2011; O'Neill 2011; Sharma 2012).

5. Rather than analyze the evolution and implications of the global financial crisis, we consider a broader topic here and study the global recessions and recoveries since 1960. The 2007–09 global financial crisis has been studied from different vantage points (Bosworth and Flaaen 2009; Swagel 2009; Krugman 2009a; Wessel 2010; Lewis 2010; Paulson 2011; Rajan 2011; Roubini and Mihm 2011; Sorkin 2011; Gorton 2012; Obstfeld, Cho, and Mason 2012; Blinder 2013; Bernanke 2013; Obstfeld 2013; Geithner 2014; Claessens and others 2014). Lo (2012) reviews a set of 21 books on the global financial crisis. Swagel (2013) also presents a short survey of a selected list of books on the financial crisis.

6. Understanding the similarities of business cycle fluctuations across countries has long been a subject of interest to macroeconomists. See Hirata, Kose, and Otrok 2013 for a review of recent studies and Zarnovitz 1992 for a survey of the earlier research program. Leamer (2009) presents a nice description of the U.S. business cycles.

7. Stock and Watson 2005; Canova, Ciccarelli, and Ortega 2007; Mumtaz, Simonelli, and Surico 2011; Kose, Otrok, and Whiteman 2003, 2008; and Kose, Otrok, and Prasad 2012 analyze the importance of global factors in explaining business cycles. Other studies consider the role of international business cycle linkages using a variety of approaches (Gerlach 1988; Norrbin and Schlagenhauf 1996; Gregory, Head, and Raynauld 1997; Gregory and Head 1999; Lumsdaine and Prasad 2003; Yilmaz 2010; Diebold and Yilmaz 2014).

8. Ambler, Cardia, and Zimmermann 2004; Imbs 2004; Bordo and Helbling 2004; Baxter and Kouparitsas 2005; and Kose, Prasad, and Terrones 2003a, 2009a document the highly correlated nature of national business cycles.

9. For a detailed analysis of these findings and a review of the literature on regional cycles, see Hirata, Kose, and Otrok 2013. For research on European business cycles, see de Haan, Inklaar, and Jong-A-Pin 2008. For research on the North American, Latin American, and Central American cycles, see Bergman, Bordo, and Jonung 1998; Kose, Meredith, and Towe 2005; Kose and Rebucci 2005; and Aiolfi, Catão, and Timmermann 2011. For research on the Asian business cycles, see Moneta and Rüffer 2009 and He and Liao 2012; and on the African cycles, see Tapsoba 2009 and Ncube, Brixiova, and Meng 2014.

CHAPTER 3 TOOLS OF THE TRADE

1. We emphasize the global nature of our database since most of the earlier studies focus only on a smaller set of countries when they consider global business cycles. In fact, our study is the first to include such a large number of countries and a rich collection of variables.

2. A number of studies analyze the similarities and differences between the 2009 global recession and the Great Depression, such as Eichengreen and O'Rourke 2009; Romer 2009a; Helbling 2009; and Eichengreen 2015. These studies draw attention to the surprising similarities between the two episodes, especially during the early stages of the Great Recession.

3. The emerging market economies in our sample roughly correspond to those in the MSCI Emerging Markets Index. The main differences between our sample and that of the MSCI are that, due to the data limitations, we drop some countries, while we include other, relatively more "mature" emerging market economies since the sample starts in 1960. Emerging market economies on average had higher incomes per capita and experienced faster growth rates than other developing economies over the last two decades. In addition, the trade openness ratio for emerging market economies has risen rapidly over the past two decades (Kose and Prasad 2010).

4. The IMF often uses this measure of world growth in its *World Economic Outlook*. It is possible to consider alternative measures using different types of weighting schemes, but those generally portray qualitatively similar dynamics to the one we have here. One could also directly construct a series of world GDP (in purchasing-power-parity or market exchange rates), but it would be difficult to relate such a series to the growth rates of national GDP. Our measure is intuitively appealing because it provides a natural parallel between national and global growth.

5. We present the decadal averages of these weights for each country group in Appendix C. The temporal evolution of the weights shows the rising role of emerging market economies in the world economy, and this is especially pronounced for purchasing-power-parity weights. Callen 2007 explains the implications of purchasing-power-parity- and market-rates-based measures of GDP.

6. Bry and Boschan (1971) first introduced this method. Harding and Pagan (2002) extended it to identify the turning points in quarterly series. This dating algorithm is widely used in the cross-country context (Artis, Kontolemis, and Osborn 1997; Artis, Marcellino, and Proietti 2003; Cotis and Coppel 2005; Hall and McDermott 2007; and Claessens, Kose, and Terrones 2008a, 2009, 2012). The algorithm is also used in the analysis of cycles in credit and asset prices (Claessens, Kose, and Terrones 2008b, 2011a, 2011b; Pagan and Sossounov 2003). It is possible to employ a different algorithm, such as a Markov Switching (MS) model (Hamilton 1989), to date the turning points. Harding and Pagan (2002) compare this method with their algorithm and conclude that their algorithm is preferable because the MS model depends on the validity of the underlying statistical framework. Hamilton (2003) also presents a discussion of this issue.

7. Other methodologies consider how a variable fluctuates around its trend and then identify the cycles (or output gaps) as deviations from this trend. The addition of new data, however, can affect the estimated trend, and thus the identification of a cycle in these methodologies. Many studies have also documented that the features of growth cycles can depend on the detrending method used (Canova 1998). In addition, it is difficult to determine the deviation from trend (the output gap) in real time. Blanchard and Fischer (1989) explain the benefits of the Burns-Mitchell approach: "Much of the recent work has proceeded, instead, under the assumption that variables follow linear stochastic processes with constant coefficients . . . this has had the advantage of allowing for better integration of macroeconomic theory and econometrics. In return for this integration and for well-understood statistical properties, some of the richness of the Burns-Mitchell analysis, such as its focus on asymmetries between recession, and expansions or its notion of business cycle time (as opposed to calendar time) may well have been lost."

8. We also employ this statistical method when we consider the dates of business cycles in the quarterly frequency in some of the chapters. We provide additional information on this whenever we discuss these results.

9. The NBER (2013) notes that its Business Cycle Dating Committee does not accept the two-quarter definition because "The committee's procedure for identifying turning points differs from the two-quarter rule in a number of ways. First, we do not identify economic activity solely with real GDP and real GDI (gross disposable income), but use a range of other indicators as well. Second, we place considerable emphasis on monthly indicators in arriving at a monthly chronology. Third, we consider the depth of the decline in economic activity. Recall that our definition includes the phrase, 'a significant decline in activity.' Fourth, in examining the behavior of domestic production, we consider not only the conventional product-side GDP estimates, but also the conceptually equivalent income-side GDI estimates. The differences between these two sets of estimates were particularly evident in the recessions of 2001 and 2007–2009."

10. The NBER (2003) defines a recession as "a significant decline in activity spread across the economy, lasting more than a few months, visible in industrial production, employment, real income, and wholesale-retail trade. A recession begins just after the economy reaches a peak of activity and ends as the economy reaches its trough." The CEPR (2003) employs similar language: "a significant

decline in the level of economic activity, spread across the economy of the euro area, usually visible in two or more consecutive quarters of negative growth in GDP, employment and other measures of aggregate economic activity for the euro area as a whole; and reflecting similar developments in most countries."

11. The simple rule of "two consecutive quarters of decline in real GDP" at the national level follows the definition by Julius Shiskin in the *New York Times* in 1974 (Abberger and Nierhaus 2008). Claessens and Kose (2009) present a detailed explanation of national recessions. Blanchard (2001) briefly analyzes different types of recessions and argues that "Three types of recessions exist. The first type are those caused by major shocks, say an outbreak of war or a sudden, sharp increase in the price of petroleum. Recall that the OPEC [Organization of the Petroleum Exporting Countries] oil shocks of the 1970's incited two world recessions. The second category of recessions arises by chance, for example when consumer confidence dips, or businesses become uneasy and cut back on investment and/or inventory. This was the cause of America's recession in the early 1990's. The third type of recession occurs when imbalances in an economy build up to unsustainable levels before exploding. This form of recession is sometimes characterized by vast increases in debt (corporate or consumer), or by dizzying stock market or capital asset speculations that eventually come crashing down. The 'popping' of such an asset bubble is what happened in Japan 10 years ago, an event from which that country has not yet recovered. Recessions of the first type are, almost by definition, largely unpredictable. Those of the second type are minor and relatively easy to repair if not to avoid. All that they usually require is a reduction in interest rates or a bit of reflation. Recessions of the third kind are the most worrying." Lucas (2012) presents a simpler view about the sources of recessions: "I now believe that the evidence on post-war recessions (up to but not including the one we are now in) overwhelmingly supports the dominant importance of real shocks. But I remain convinced of the importance of financial shocks in the 1930s and the years after 2008. Of course, this means I have to renounce the view that business cycles are all alike!"

12. In the context of national cycles, a number of studies examine the dynamics of recoveries (Eckstein and Sinai 1986; Balke and Wynne 1995; Mussa 2009; Terrones, Scott, and Kannan 2009; Claessens, Kose, and Terrones 2012). Some define the recovery as the time it takes for output to rebound from the trough to the peak level before the recession. Others associate recovery with the growth achieved after a certain period, such as four or six quarters, following the trough (Sichel 1994).

13. See Rogoff, Robinson, and Bayoumi 2002 for the study. Rogoff (2002a) announced the findings of their study at the *World Economic Outlook* press conference.

14. Kose, Loungani, and Terrones (2009, 2012) extend the study by Rogoff, Robinson, and Bayoumi (2002) and provide a framework for analyzing global recessions and recoveries. Kose and Terrones (forthcoming) build on these earlier studies and summarize the main features of global recessions and recoveries.

CHAPTER 4 DATES AND EVENTS: WHAT HAPPENED WHEN?

1. See Claessens, Kose, and Terrones 2012.

2. Some have employed the definition of global recession that relied on a simple threshold over the years. For example, *The Economist* (2001b) noted that "there is no precise definition of 'world recession' (global output has risen every year since the 1930s), but it is generally taken to be

growth of less than 2–2.5 percent." There was confusion about the definition of global recession used by the IMF, as *The Economist* (2008a) noted: "according to the IMF's most recent *World Economic Outlook*, published on October 8th, the world economy is 'entering a major downturn' in the face of 'the most dangerous shock' to rich-country financial markets since the 1930s. The Fund expects global growth, measured on the basis of purchasing power parity, to come down to 3 percent in 2009, the slowest pace since 2002 and on the verge of what it considers to be a global recession. (The IMF's definition of global recession takes many factors into account, including the rate of population growth.)"

3. Those 14 years include the following episodes: 1974–75, 1980–83, 1991–93, 1998, 2001–02, and 2008–09. If one uses market weights, the list includes 1974–75, 1980–83, 1990–93, 1995, 1998, 2001–03, 2008–09, and 2011–13.

4. With purchasing-power-parity weights and a 1 percent threshold, the list of global recessions includes 1974–75, 1980–82, 1991–93, and 2009. With market weights and a 1 percent threshold, the list contains 1974–75, 1980–82, 1991–93, 1998, 2001–02, and 2008–09. *The Economist* (2008b) notes the difficulty of identifying global recessions with a single threshold tied to global GDP growth: "When tracking such diverse economies, it does make much more sense to define a global recession not as an absolute fall in GDP, but as when growth falls significantly below its potential rate. This can cause anomalies, however. Using the IMF's definition (i.e., growth below 3 percent), the world economy has been in recession for no fewer than 11 out of 28 years. This sits oddly with the fact that America, the world's biggest economy, has been in recession for only 38 months during that time, according to the National Bureau of Economic Research (the country's official arbiter of recessions), which defines a recession as a decline in economic activity. It is confusing to have different definitions of recession in rich and poor economies." It is important to note that the IMF does not have an institutional definition of global recession endorsed by its Executive Board. Although the IMF's *World Economic Outlook* has occasionally studied the topic, the publication reflects the views of the IMF staff and, hence, should not be attributed to IMF executive directors or their national authorities.

5. In our sample, growth of world GDP was positive in all years except 2009. During the 2009 global recession, a market observer, Philip Suttle, correctly noted that "We have got the world economy contracting by just under a half percentage point, which really does not sound like very much . . . But it is really, really important to recognize the world economy basically never contracts. Somewhere in the world economy there is always enough [growth] to offset recessions even in the major industrial countries" (Voice of America 2009).

6. Blanchard (2008) argued that "it is not useful to use the word 'recession' when the world is growing at 3 percent. In the normal definition of things, recession is a negative number, and that is not the case. This being said, 3 percent is a very low number for world growth, and in the past, indeed, this might have been defined as on the borderline of a global recession. I think the words, 'global downturn with still positive growth,' are a better description of what we are facing."

7. Rogoff, Robinson, and Bayoumi (2002) also concluded that a global recession took place in 1975, 1982, and 1991. Rogoff (2002a) announced the findings of their study at the *World Economic Outlook* press conference: ". . . we looked closely at the question of what constitutes a global recession, and concluded—looking at per capita output growth as well as many other variables such as world trade and industrial production—that the years 1975, 1982, and 1991 did, officially, constitute global recessions."

8. According to the National Bureau of Economic Research (NBER) chronology, since 1960, the United States experienced eight recessions: 1960:Q2–1961:Q1, 1969:Q4–1970:Q4, 1973:Q4–1975:Q1, 1980:Q1–1980:Q3, 1981:Q3–1982:Q4, 1990:Q3–1991:Q1, 2001:Q1–2001:Q4, and 2007:Q4–2009:Q2.

9. Knoop 2004, Reinhart and Rogoff 2009, and Allen 2010 discuss the events during these episodes. For a detailed analysis of the surrounding macroeconomic and financial developments, see the IMF's *World Economic Outlook*, Organisation for Economic Co-operation and Development's (OECD's) *Global Economic Outlook*, and World Bank's *Global Economic Prospects* published in the years of the global recessions.

10. We list the countries that experienced financial crises around global recessions and downturns in Appendix D.

11. The 1975 episode was also compared with the Great Depression. *The Economist* (1974b) noted that "As in 1929, collapses have come first in precisely the sectors where it was thought during the boom that it was easiest for any idiot to become a millionaire. In early 1972, it would have been thought ridiculous to say that bankruptcy would hit first at beef barons, property speculators, stockbrokers, whizz-kids' new sorts of banks. But stock market crashes have now already gone further than those in 1929. Property prices have collapsed, transmitting strain to the financial system through the fringe banks and towards banks within the fringe . . . Paradoxically the most important difference produced the greatest similarity. Inflation is doing to the world economy of 1970s what falling prices did in the 1930s—causing unemployment and company failures . . . One big difference *between* 1929 is that this slump has been signaled well in advance, and still a real crash has not come . . . Remember that in 1929 the federal government's purchases of goods and services amounted to a tiny 1.25 percent of America's (gross national product), so that a big Keynesian fiscal restimulation was not easy then. But in a slump accompanied by huge price inflation big fiscal restimulation is not going to be easy either."

12. During the stagflation era of the 1970s, debates raged about the likelihood of a deep recession. As it is now, "depression" was a sensitive term then and led to a humorous search to replace it with an attractive alternative, as described by *Time* (1978): "Maverick Economist Alfred Kahn has a penchant for candor that is both refreshing and dangerous in Washington. When he said that there is the possibility of a 'deep, deep depression' if inflation continues to soar, the President was furious. Kahn responded by purging the word depression from his vocabulary and instead using 'banana.' So he now says: 'We're in danger of having the worst banana in 45 years.'" Kahn was an economist who worked in the Carter Administration as chairman of the Civil Aeronautics Board and chairman of the Council on Wage and Price Stability (Lang 2010). Golden (1975) and Shabecoff (1975) discuss whether the 1975 episode was a recession or a depression. Mullaney (1977) documents the debates about the weak recovery following the 1975 global recession.

13. Hamilton (2009a) claims that oil prices increased prior to all global recessions, including the latest. Hamilton (2009b) examines the role played by oil price increases before the last recession in the United States. Blinder and Rudd (2012) present evidence that supply shocks stemming from significant movements in oil and food prices during 1973–74 and 1978–80 played important roles in driving inflation in the United States (and the recessions associated with these episodes). Barsky and Kilian (2004) and Hamilton (2011) present surveys of the history of oil shocks and the downturns that followed these shocks. Baffes and others (2015) analyze the sharp decline in oil prices over the period June 2014-January 2015 and compare the latest episode with the earlier ones.

14. Even before its start, media articles compared the 1982 global recession with the Great Depression: "This month sees the fiftieth anniversary of the international economic crisis of September, 1931, when the world suddenly threw away its main safeguard against long-term inflation and its principal previous weapon against short-term slump. There may not be full recovery from 1981's slumpflation until this safeguard and weapon are in some degree reestablished, so it is awkward that most of today's statesmen do not remember what they were" (*The Economist* 1981a).

15. In the United States, the implementation of contractionary monetary policies was led by Paul Volcker, who became the chairman of the Federal Reserve Board in August 1979 (Meltzer 2010). The Volcker disinflation reduced annual inflation from 9 percent in 1979 to 5 percent by the end of 1983. The United States experienced two consecutive recessions with large declines in output and employment during the same period (Goodfriend and King 2005). Kenen (1983) links the debt crisis to the high-interest-rate policies of the advanced economies.

16. Kuczynski (1982) presents a nice narrative of the events leading up to the Latin American debt crisis: "The music has stopped. In August, Mexico, the largest single recipient of Eurocurrency bank credits in recent years, announced that it could not for the time being meet its scheduled repayments of principal on the external debt of the public sector. Service on the Mexican private sector and banking system debt is sporadic or interrupted because of the shortage of foreign exchange. Argentina has in effect been unable to meet its scheduled debt service since the time of the South Atlantic conflict. And, since mid-1982, international bank lending to Latin American countries has all but ground to a halt. As a result, Brazil may find it very difficult to meet its scheduled debt service, since, like the other countries in the area, it needs a constant inflow of funds to pay off old debt."

17. The following Latin American countries experienced financial crises around the 1982 global recession: Argentina, Bolivia, Brazil, Chile, Costa Rica, the Dominican Republic, Ecuador, Guyana, Honduras, Mexico, Nicaragua, Panama, Paraguay, Uruguay, and Venezuela. Dornbusch, Johnson, and Krueger 1988 and Edwards 1995 provide reviews of the Latin American debt crisis. Since many developing economies in other regions also experienced crises, some observers called this episode the Less Developed Country Debt Crisis.

18. In 1991, some speculated that the recession would be a milder one because of the differential growth prospects across countries. "Similarly, the so-called 'desynchronization' of the big economies, which has helped to prevent global recession, may now moderate the recovery. As America and Britain sank into recession last year, Japan and Germany continued to boom, helping to prop up world demand. But, as America and Britain start to recover, the former locomotives are losing steam. With growth in both Germany and Japan in 1991 likely to be barely half that in 1990, this will trim the growth in their imports from the rest of the world" (*The Economist* 1991). Fuerbringer (1991) discusses the implications of the U.S. recession for the global economy. The impact of the global recession was indeed felt across Europe in 1992, with a number of countries falling into recessions because of the European Exchange Rate Mechanism (ERM) crisis.

19. For detailed discussions of the savings and loan crisis in the United States, see FDIC 1997; Curry and Shibut 2000; and Barth, Trimbath, and Yago 2004.

20. Bernanke and Lown (1991) provide a careful study of the evolution of credit markets during this episode. For a discussion of the importance of household debt during this episode, see Altig, Byrne, and Samolyk 1992. Walsh 1993; Blanchard 1993; Hall 1993; and Hansen and Prescott 1993 analyze the sources of the 1990:Q3–1991:Q1 recession in the United States. Mian and Sufi

(2014) analyze how the accumulation of large household debt followed by a sharp drop in household spending led to a deep global recession in 2009.

21. The ERM was established in 1979 by eight members of the European Economic Community (Belgium, Denmark, France, Germany, Ireland, Italy, Luxembourg, Netherlands) to minimize exchange rate fluctuations within a band by fixing their exchange rates relative to one another and floating jointly against the U.S. dollar. Spain, Portugal, and the United Kingdom joined the ERM later. The ERM was designed as an intermediate step before the introduction of the euro. Higgins (1993) and Buiter, Corsetti, and Pesenti (1998) analyze the sources and implications of the ERM crisis.

22. Fischer, Sahay, and Végh 1996; IMF 2000; and Orlowski 2001 present detailed accounts of the many challenges the transition economies experienced in the early 1990s.

23. In late 1992, amid intense debate about growth forecasts, comparisons with the Great Depression were back in the headlines: "Needless to say, all this may turn out to be—like most forecasts during the past year—too optimistic. But that is still very far from saying that a depression like the one in the 1930s may be on the way. For a slowdown to become a slump, extra things need to go badly wrong—and governments can make this unlikely. Lessons from the Depression have been learnt, as the response to the global stock market crash of October 19th, 1987 showed. First and foremost, today's central bankers understand their duties as lenders of last resort. That makes a contagious financial collapse of the sort that preceded the depression of the 1930s much less likely . . . Moreover, today's governments account for a far bigger share of their countries' national incomes than they did 60 years ago. A trend that is in many ways regrettable should console those inclined to slit their wrists just in case: these days much more of the economy is slump-proof. Thanks to the welfare state when output falls and unemployment rises, the victims (and the economy at large) are cushioned. In the 1930s, some governments raised taxes and cut public spending as the Depression grew worse. That is a mistake which is unlikely to be repeated, less because no government would try to do it than because their electorates would not let them . . . A third lesson from the 1930s, though familiar, demands the undivided attention of governments in the coming days and weeks: perhaps the best way to turn a recession into something far worse is to arrange an outbreak of protectionism. Off and on for months, the governments have seemed likely to do just that . . . If, despite everything, governments let the Uruguay round slip through their fingers, they will be helping to make the world's worst economic nightmare come needlessly true" (*The Economist* 1992b).

24. Claessens, Kose, and Terrones (2010) and Mendoza and Terrones (2012) discuss the evolution of financial markets during the last episode.

25. Even in late 2008, discussions about the severity of the coming global recession started appearing in the media: "Where does that leave us today? America's GDP may have fallen by an annualized 6 percent in the fourth quarter of 2008, but most economists dismiss the likelihood of a 1930s-style depression or a repeat of Japan in the 1990s, because policy makers are unlikely to repeat the mistakes of the past. In the Great Depression, the Fed let hundreds of banks fail and the money supply shrink by one-third, while the government tried to balance its budget by cutting spending and raising taxes. America's monetary and fiscal easing this time has been more aggressive than Japan's in the 1990s. However, these reassurances come from many of the same economists who said that a nationwide fall in American house prices was impossible and that financial innovation had made the financial system more resilient. Hopefully, they will be right this time.

But this crisis was caused by the largest asset-price and credit bubble in history—even bigger than that in Japan in the late 1980s or America in the late 1920s. Policymakers will not make the same mistakes as in the 1930s, but they may make new ones (*The Economist* 2008b).

26. Many articles documented the spread of the recession in early 2009: "Manufacturing deteriorated around the world in December, signaling a worsening global recession . . . The euro-area's gauge fell to a record low, while industry in China contracted for a fifth month. Indicators for the U.K., Sweden, Hong Kong and Australia also showed factories in decline. The ISM's (Institute of Supply Management's) gauge of new orders dropped to the lowest level since records began in 1948" (Chandra 2009).

27. The latest episode was also compared with the Great Depression, and a number of similarities were documented, especially for the early stages of these two episodes. For example, Eichengreen and O'Rourke (2009) note that "the world is currently undergoing an economic shock every bit as big as the Great Depression shock of 1929–30." For an extended discussion of similarities and differences between the episodes, see Almunia and others 2010 and Bordo 2012b. For more information on the Great Depression, see Temin 1991 and Eichengreen 1996. Solomou (1998) discusses economic cycles since 1870 and lists many studies on various aspects of the Great Depression.

28. Rowen (1974) nicely articulates this observation in the *Washington Post*: "In the immediate future, the policy makers will have to be worrying not about demand and how to sustain it or moderate it, but also shortages of supply. It is much more difficult to shape policies that deal with a recession produced not because people fail to buy goods—but because the factories cannot get enough fuel to keep things going."

29. Lucas and Sargent (1978) provide a perceptive critique of Keynesian economics in light of the events of the 1970s and explain the fundamentals of the "rational expectations revolution" in macroeconomics that became influential during the late 1970s. Miller (1994) presents a rich list of essays that describe the origins and growth of this revolution. Romer and Romer (2002) and Sargent (2002) examine the evolution of stabilization policies over the past 50 years. Federal Reserve Bank of Kansas City 2002 provides a set of insightful papers on the design, objectives, and implications of fiscal and monetary policies. Blanchard (2009a) presents a brief summary of the major changes in macroeconomics during the 1970s.

30. Rotemberg (2013) notes that the 1960s and 1970s were often called the "Great Inflation" period because of the Federal Reserve's inflation tolerance. He argues that this period ended with the famous Volcker disinflation of 1979–1982. The period that followed, 1982–2007, was a period of inflation intolerance.

31. Economists extensively debated the sources of the decline in the volatility of macroeconomic fluctuations in a number of advanced economies (Blanchard and Simon 2001; Ahmed, Levin, and Wilson 2004; Bernanke 2004; Davis and Kahn 2008).

32. There has been vigorous debate over the past seven years about macroeconomists' inability to predict the global financial crisis and develop the necessary policy measures to mitigate its adverse effects. Krugman (2009b) criticizes the macroeconomics literature for its failure to recognize the strong linkages between the financial sector and the real economy: "During the golden years, financial economists came to believe that markets were inherently stable—indeed, that stocks and other assets were always priced just right . . . Meanwhile, macroeconomists were divided in their views . . . Unfortunately, this romanticized and sanitized vision of the economy led most economists

to ignore all the things that can go wrong. They [economists] turned a blind eye to the limitations of human rationality that often lead to bubbles and busts; to the problems of institutions that run amok; to the imperfections of markets—especially financial markets—that can cause the economy's operating system to undergo sudden, unpredictable crashes." Cochrane (2009a) provides a critical response to Krugman's views: "First, he [Krugman] argues for a future of economics that 'recognizes flaws and frictions,' and incorporates alternative assumptions about behavior, especially towards risk-taking. To which I say, 'Hello, Paul, where have you been for the last 30 years?' . . . Pretty much all we have been doing for 30 years is introducing flaws, frictions and new behaviors, especially new models of attitudes to risk, and comparing the resulting models, quantitatively, to data. The long literature on financial crises and banking . . . has also been doing exactly the same." Rodrik (2015) emphasizes the importance of selecting the "correct model" to analyze the question at hand and notes that "the profession's internal critics are wrong to claim that the discipline has gone wrong because economists have yet to reach consensus on the "correct" models (their preferred ones of course). Let us cherish economics in all its diversity – rational and behavioral, Keynesian and Classical, first-best and second-best, orthodox and heterodox – and devote our energy to becoming wiser at picking which framework to apply when." Caballero 2010, Woodford 2010, and other papers in the fall 2010 issue of the *Journal of Economic Perspectives* analyze how the recent crisis may affect research on the intersection between macroeconomics and finance. Gordon 2009; Kocherlakota 2010; Turner 2012; Blanchard, Dell'Ariccia, and Mauro 2010, 2013; and Blanchard and others 2012 discuss in detail the impact of the financial crisis on the design of macroeconomic policies. Claessens and Kose (2014a, 2014b) analyze the linkages between the financial sector and real economy in light of the debates after the global financial crisis.

33. For extensive discussions of the similarities and differences between the last and earlier crises, see Claessens, Kose, and Terrones 2010. Blanchard 2009b; Brunnermeier 2009; Calomiris 2009; Cecchetti 2009; Reinhart and Rogoff 2008; Shin 2009; Mankiw 2012; Gourinchas and Obstfeld 2012; and Calomiris and Haber 2014 analyze the evolution of the crisis from various angles. Claessens and Kose 2014c present a synthesis of the sources and implications of various types of crisis.

CHAPTER 5 GLOBAL RECESSIONS: SAD STORIES OF COLLAPSE

1. Other names were also given to the latest episode: Krugman (2011a) called it the "Lesser Depression," DeLong (2011a) the "Little Depression," and Reinhart and Rogoff (2009) the "Second Great Contraction."

2. The relatively low rate of global unemployment prior to the 1974 episode is mostly due to very low unemployment in advanced economies.

3. Baldwin and Evenett 2009; Bussière and others 2010; Henn and McDonald 2011; and Bown 2011 study various aspects of protectionist measures introduced during the 2009 global recession.

4. The collapse of trade (relative to output) during the global recession is puzzling, in that it was much larger than predicted by the standard business cycle models. For potential explanations of the trade collapse, see Levchenko, Lewis, and Tesar 2010; Bems, Johnson, and Yi 2010; Chor and Manova 2012; Alessandria, Kaboski, and Midrigan 2010; Amiti and Weinstein 2011; Freund 2009; and Bussière and others 2013. Gourinchas and Kose 2010, 2011; and Bems, Johnson, and Yi 2012 summarize these explanations.

5. Milesi-Ferretti and Tille (2011) and Lane (2012) study the links between declines in flows and country-specific features during the global financial crisis. Forbes and Warnock (2012) analyze the sources of large fluctuations in international financial flows.

6. For the evolution of global and national labor markets since the global recession, see International Labour Organization 2013, 2014.

7. A number of recent studies have examined the reasons for cross-country differences in the impact of the 2009 global recession (Berkmen and others 2009; Blanchard, Faruqee, and Das 2010; Lane and Milesi-Ferretti 2011; Giannone, Lenza, and Reichlin 2011; Rose and Spiegel 2011; De Gregorio 2014). Kose and Prasad (2010) provide a detailed account of these reasons and surveys the relevant literature.

8. Jeanne 2007; Durdu, Mendoza, and Terrones 2009; and Independent Evaluation Office of the IMF 2012 discuss the sources and implications of reserve accumulation in emerging market economies.

9. For a narrative of events that took place around these two downturns, see IMF 1998a, 1998b, 2001a, 2001b, 2001c; and Fischer 1998.

10. Some declared that all evidence pointed to a looming global recession in 1998: "Is the world headed for recession? Look at the evidence, and it's difficult to draw any other conclusion. Asia is under water, Russia has collapsed, Latin America is shaky, and the United States and Britain look weaker than expected. When financial panic begins to spread—as it has in recent months, now hitting U.S. shocks—little can be done to stop it. The only tool available to governments is a cut in interest rates to try to stoke the economy. Central banks in the United States and Europe should be ready to take that step if things get much worse" (*Journal of Commerce* 1998).

11. In August 2001, *The Economist* (2001a) claimed that the global economy was already experiencing a recession: "The world economy is probably already in recession. How bad might it get? One by one, economies around the world are stumbling. By cutting interest rates again this week—for the seventh time this year—the Federal Reserve hopes it can keep America out of recession. But in an increasing number of economies, from Japan and Taiwan to Mexico and Brazil, GDP is already shrinking. Global industrial production fell at an annual rate of 6% in the first half of 2001 . . . The picture may soon look even worse. Early estimates suggest that gross world product, as a whole, may have contracted in the second quarter, for possibly the first time in two decades. Welcome to the first global recession of the 21st century."

12. See Rogoff, Robinson, and Bayoumi 2002. Rogoff (2002b) presents a nice narrative of the mood of financial market participants and policymakers in early 2002: "Amid increasing signs of recovery, there seems to be a growing denial that the global economy was ever in any real danger. Many private forecasters have stopped asking when the US economy is going to pick up and started asking when it is going to slow down. A popular refrain is that 'it's the recession that wasn't.' Europeans congratulate themselves that the eurozone only barely experienced negative growth in one quarter. Meanwhile, some in Japan still seem to believe that their country's third recession in a decade is just a passing phase that can be forgotten as soon as US-led export growth picks up. The reality is that the sharp downturn of the past year was almost a global recession."

13. It is difficult to predict the exact date of the beginning of national recessions. Mankiw (2007) notes that "The economy is teetering on the edge. Many economists, as well as online betting sites, put the risk of recession next year at about 50 percent. Once we get the final numbers, we might even learn that a recession has already begun."

CHAPTER 6 GLOBAL RECOVERIES: TALES OF REVIVAL

1. The graphs showing the behavior of the macroeconomic and financial variables during global recessions and recoveries in Figures 5.1–5.3 and Figures 6.1–6.3 emphasize the differences in the evolutions of these variables around these episodes. We focus on the period prior to recessions in Figures 5.1–5.3 and the postrecession recoveries in Figures 6.1–6.3. The year prior to the recession is the reference point in the former; in the latter, this is the global recession year.

2. Specifically, we study the elasticities of world consumption per capita, investment, and trade to world output by estimating a basic regression of the growth rate of each of these variables on the growth rate of world GDP per capita. We report the results of these regressions in Appendix G. Our findings with respect to trade elasticity are consistent with those in Freund 2009.

3. The first year of the ongoing recovery was strong, but it has since been subject to various headwinds, nicely illustrated by the evolving narrative in the IMF's *World Economic Outlook*: "The global recovery is off to a stronger start than anticipated earlier but is proceeding at different speeds in the various regions" (IMF 2010a). "The two-speed recovery continues. In advanced economies, activity has moderated less than expected, but growth remains subdued . . . In many emerging economies, activity remains buoyant" (IMF 2011a). "The global recovery is threatened by intensifying strains in the euro area and fragilities elsewhere" (IMF 2012a). "Policy action is needed to secure the fragile global recovery" (IMF 2013a). "Global growth is still weak, its underlying dynamics are changing, and the risks to the forecast remain to the downside" (IMF 2013a). "Global activity strengthened during the second half of 2013. . . But downward revisions to growth forecasts in some economies highlight continued fragilities, and downside risks remain" (IMF 2014a). "Global activity has broadly strengthened and is expected to improve further in 2014–15 with much of the impetus for growth coming from advanced economies. Although downside risks have diminished overall, lower-than-expected inflation poses risks for advanced economies, there is increased financial volatility in emerging market economies, and increases in the cost of capital will likely dampen investment and weigh on growth" (IMF 2014b). "Global growth in 2014 was a modest 3.4 percent, reflecting a pickup in growth in advanced economies relative to the previous year and a slowdown in emerging market and developing economies. Medium-term prospects have become less optimistic for advanced economies, and especially for emerging markets, in which activity has been slowing since 2010. At the same time, the distribution of risks to global growth is now more balanced relative to the October 2014 WEO, but is still tilted to the downside" (IMF 2015a). "Global growth is projected at 3.3 percent in 2015, marginally lower than in 2014, with a gradual pickup in advanced economies and a slowdown in emerging market and developing economies. In 2016, growth is expected to strengthen to 3.8 percent . . . The distribution of risks to global economic activity is still tilted to the downside. Near-term risks include increased financial market volatility and disruptive asset price shifts, while lower potential output growth remains an important medium-term risk in both advanced and emerging market economies. Lower commodity prices also pose risks to the outlook in low-income developing economies after many years of strong growth" (IMF 2015b).

4. Kose, Otrok, and Prasad (2012) present a detailed account of the many differences in cyclical performance between advanced and emerging market economies over the past two decades.

5. For discussions of different aspects of the ongoing weak recovery, see Sachs 2008; Boskin 2009; Shiller 2009; Blanchard 2010; Calvo and Loo-Kung 2010; Wolf 2010b; Feldstein 2010; Davies 2011; DeLong 2011b; Rogoff 2011; Lagarde 2011; Samuelson 2012, 2014; and Fischer 2014.

6. In other words, Okun's law, which describes an empirical relationship between GDP growth and changes in the unemployment rate, appears to hold quite well (Ball, Leigh, and Loungani 2013). Industry-by-county-level data on employment in the United States also suggest that the drop in aggregate demand (and income) driven by shocks to household balance sheets was a key factor driving the rise in unemployment during 2007–09 (Mian and Sufi 2012). The global recession had a profound impact on the U.S. labor market as it led to the highest level of long-term unemployment in the postwar period. Elsby, Hobijn, and Sahin (2010) and Elsby and Valletta (2011) describe the evolution of the U.S. labor market during the global recession. Rothstein (2012) argues that cyclical factors, such as shortfalls in aggregate demand for labor, rather than structural factors play an important role in explaining the weak performance of the U.S. labor market during the latest recovery. Daly and others (2013) document how the global financial crisis changed the relationship between unemployment and output in advanced economies. Blanchard, Jaumotte, and Loungani (2013) provide a summary of labor market policies in advanced economies during the latest global recession and recovery. Gourinchas and Kose (2013a, 2013b) provide summaries of a series of studies on the dynamics of labor markets during the global financial crisis and its aftermath. Katz and others (2014) analyze how the long-term unemployment dynamics have changed in the aftermath of the Great Recession.

7. Prior to both the 2009 global financial crisis and the European Exchange Rate Mechanism (ERM) crisis of the early 1990s, many advanced economies experienced highly synchronized credit booms (Mendoza and Terrones 2012).

8. Thirteen advanced European economies experienced recessions during this period: Austria, 1992:Q3–1993:Q1; Belgium, 1992:Q2–1993:Q; Denmark, 1992:Q3–1993:Q2; Finland, 1990:Q1–1993:Q2; France, 1992:Q1–1993:Q3; Germany, 1992:Q1–1993:Q1; Greece, 1992:Q2–1993:Q1; Italy, 1992:Q1–1993:Q3; Portugal, 1992:Q2–1993:Q3; Spain, 1992:Q1–1993:Q2; Sweden, 1990:Q1–1993:Q1; Switzerland, 1990:Q2–1991:Q2 and 1991:Q4–1993:Q1; and the United Kingdom, 1990:Q2–1991:Q3.

9. During the 2009 global financial crisis, 18 advanced European economies experienced recessions. Many of these economies went through double-dip recessions during 2011–13. For recent developments in the euro area business cycle, see CEPR 2012 and 2014.

10. See Draghi 2012.

11. For a summary of the human costs of recessions, see Dao and Loungani 2010; for the social costs of financial crises, see van Dijk 2013 and Otker-Robe and Podpiera 2013; and for the implications of recessions for social cohesion, see Giuliano and Spilimbergo 2009. World Bank 2010 considers the implications of the crisis for poverty reduction in developing economies. World Bank 2013 analyzes the jobs crisis triggered by the 2007–09 financial crisis.

12. The International Labour Organization (2013, 2014) describes the evolution of global and national labor markets since the global recession. For a discussion of the jobs crisis following the 2009 global recession, see OECD 2009, 2012a; Dao and Loungani 2010; Loungani 2012; and World Bank 2013. Atkinson, Luttrell, and Rosenblum (2013) find that because of the 2007–09 financial crisis, the U.S. economy lost at least 40 to 90 percent of its annual output. However, they also consider other cost factors and conclude that "given our range of estimates, the tepid economic recovery, and the litany of other adverse effects stemming from the Second Great Contraction, we suggest that the total domestic cost is likely greater than the equivalent of an entire year's output."

13. It is not a subject we discuss here but one can debate about the logic of having only two business cycle phases. Leamer (2008) argues that "One reason we need a clear definition is that the media focus intensely on two questions: Is it a bear market? Are we in recession? If the answer is 'yes, we are in recession,' it seems useful to me if both speaker and listener understand what is being said. The focus on recession is not nearly as silly as the focus on bear markets. It is only somewhat misleading to describe the economy as having two states: healthy and ill."

14. For discussions about the information technology revolution, see OECD 2002, 2012b; and Byrne, Oliner, and Sichel 2013.

CHAPTER 7 SYNCHRONIZATION OF RECESSIONS

1. Recent studies examine the sources of the highly synchronized nature of national recessions during the latest global recession. Perri and Quadrini (2011) emphasize the problems in credit markets as the main source of synchronization. Bacchetta and van Wincoop 2013 argue that national business cycles can become highly synchronized when the world economy is hit by a "global panic" shock. Kamin and DeMarco (2012) and Rose and Spiegel (2010) study this issue using empirical approaches. The former study concludes that "The U.S. subprime crisis, rather than being a fundamental driver of the global crisis, may have been merely a trigger for a global bank run and for disillusionment with a risky business model that already had spread around the world." The latter one reports that "while countries with higher income seemed to suffer worse crises, we find few clear reliable indicators in the pre-crisis data of the incidence of the Great Recession."

2. Imbs (2010), using monthly industrial production data, concludes that the degree of cross-country business cycle correlations during the latest crisis was the highest over the past three decades. Dua and Banerji (2010) use a wide range of measures to analyze the degree of synchronization of recessions and report that "the 2009 global recession was possibly the most concerted in the post world war period." Recent research indicates that shocks originating in credit markets have been influential in driving global activity during global recessions (Helbling and others 2011).

3. We employed the statistical method to identify the dates of the turning points of cycles in the quarterly data. The algorithm is the same as the one applied to the annual data in Chapter 3, but it requires the duration of a complete cycle and for each phase to be at least five quarters and two quarters, respectively. For details of the methodology with the quarterly data and data set of advanced economies, see Claessens, Kose, and Terrones 2012.

4. A number of studies examine the behavior of macroeconomic and financial variables around recessions and recoveries. For additional information on this literature, see Claessens, Kose, and Terrones 2009, 2012; and Terrones, Scott, and Kannan 2009. In related research, Diebold and Yilmaz (2009) examine "return spillovers" and "volatility spillovers" of equities during crisis and noncrisis periods.

5. Appendix D provides a list of countries that experienced financial crises around global recessions.

6. Recent studies examine the degree of synchronization of cycles using a so-called concordance index, which measures the percentage of time that two financial variables are in the same phase of their respective cycles (Claessens, Kose, and Terrones 2012). Credit and equity cycles display the highest degree of synchronization across countries. These cycles tend to be in the same phase about 80 percent of the time. Although housing is a nontradable asset, the extent of synchronization of housing cycles across countries is still high at about 60 percent (Hirata and others 2012).

This partly reflects the important roles played by global factors, including world interest rates, the global business cycle, and commodity prices in explaining house price movements around the world. The degree of synchronization in housing and equity markets has increased over time, probably due to the expansion of cross-border trade and financial flows.

7. Bluedorn, Decressin, and Terrones (2013) provide evidence that asset price drops are significantly associated with the beginning of recessions in the Group of Seven countries.

8. See Forbes and Rigobon 2002. The implications of the coincidence of financial cycles have provided fertile ground for recent research. Claessens, Kose, and Terrones (2011a, 2011b) show the presence of strong interactions—between credit and housing markets, for example. Credit downturns overlapping with house price busts are longer and deeper than other credit downturns. Similarly, when credit upturns coincide with housing booms, they tend to be longer and stronger. For example, a typical credit upturn becomes 25 percent longer and 40 percent stronger when it coincides with a housing boom.

9. For discussions on the theoretical implications of globalization for synchronization, see Kose, Prasad, and Terrones 2003a; and Hirata, Kose, and Otrok 2013.

CHAPTER 8 DOUBLE WHAMMY: CRISIS AND RECESSION

1. Beauchemin 2011; Bernanke 2012b; Council of Economic Advisers 2009, 2010, 2012; Reinhart and Rogoff 2012a, 2012b; Krugman 2012a; Bordo and Haubrich 2012; Taylor 2012; Hassett and Hubbard 2012; and Wynne 2011 provide arguments for different sides of this debate.

2. Reinhart and Rogoff 2009; Papell and Prodan 2011; Queralto 2013; Claessens, Kose, and Terrones 2009, 2012; and Terrones, Scott, and Kannan 2009 present detailed analyses of the implications of financial disruptions for macroeconomic outcomes during recessions and recoveries. This chapter builds on the last two studies.

3. Bordo and Haubrich 2012; and Howard, Martin, and Wilson 2011 argue that recessions and recoveries associated with financial disruptions are no different than other episodes. The conflicting conclusions across studies on the issue stem from differences in the definition of financial crises, the sample of countries, and the definition of recovery. There were also some speeches given by policymakers on the issue prior to the crisis. For example, Roger W. Ferguson (Vice Chairman of the Federal Reserve Board) argued that "recessions that follow swings in asset prices are not necessarily longer, deeper, and associated with a greater fall in output and investment than other recessions" in a speech he gave in January 2005 (Ferguson 2005).

4. Our sample includes recessions that took place during 1960:Q1–2007:Q4 (Claessens, Kose, and Terrones 2009). Recessions associated with the 15 financial crises include Australia (1990:Q2–1991:Q2), Denmark (1987:Q1–1988:Q2), Finland (1990:Q2–1993:Q2), France (1992:Q2–1993:Q3), Germany (1980:Q2–1980:Q4), Greece (1992:Q2–1993:Q1), Italy (1992:Q2–1993:Q3), Japan (1993:Q2–1993:Q4), Japan (1997:Q2–1999:Q1), New Zealand (1986:Q4–1987:Q4), Norway (1988:Q2–1988:Q4), Spain (1978:Q3–1979:Q1), Sweden (1990:Q2–1993:Q1), United Kingdom (1973:Q3–1974:Q1), and United Kingdom (1990:Q3–1991:Q3).

5. Recessions associated with the Big Five financial crises (identified by Reinhart and Rogoff 2009) include Finland (1990:Q2–1993:Q2), Japan (1993:Q2–1993:Q4), Norway (1988:Q2–1988:Q4), Spain (1978:Q3–1979:Q1), and Sweden (1990:Q2–1993:Q1).

6. Mendoza and Terrones (2012) study the likelihood of crises around credit booms. They report that the probability of having a financial crisis is more than 75 percent over the seven-year period around a credit boom. The likelihood of a financial crisis is 45 percent at the peak of a boom or after the boom. Credit booms have frequently followed financial deregulation. For example, almost all of the 15 financial crises considered here followed deregulation in the mortgage market. Claessens and others (2014) provide a wide range of studies analyzing the consequences of asset price and credit booms, busts and financial crises, and policy responses to these episodes.

7. Abiad and others (2009) study the medium-term output dynamics after 88 banking crises in a large number of countries. Cecchetti, Kohler, and Upper 2009; Reinhart and Reinhart 2010; Haltmaier 2012; and Furceri and Zdzienicka 2012 also document significant medium-term output losses associated with different types of financial crises. Ball (2014) estimates that the loss in potential output following the 2009 global recession ranges from almost nothing in Australia and Switzerland to more than 30 percent in Greece, Hungary, and Ireland with the weighted average loss of 23 OECD economies is 8.4 percent. IMF 2015c documents that potential output growth in advanced economies is likely to increase slightly from current rates as some crisis-related effects wear off but will likely remain below precrisis rates in the medium term.

8. This stylized fact is consistent with the finding that productivity is procyclical. Basu and Fernald (2000) argue that the procyclical nature of productivity is mainly explained by two forces—the variable utilization of inputs over the cycle and the reallocation of resources.

9. Their recent research also supports the sluggish nature of recoveries following financial crises. Reinhart and Rogoff (2014) report that, after systemic banking crises, it takes, on average, about eight years to reach the precrisis level of income; the median is about 6.5 years.

10. Mohammed El-Erian is a former chief executive officer and co–chief investment officer of PIMCO and Bill Gross is founder and former co–chief investment officer of PIMCO.

11. See El-Erian 2009, 2011; and Gross 2009. Gross (2009) claims that "we are heading into what we call the New Normal, which is a period of time in which economies grow very slowly as opposed to growing like weeds, the way children do; in which profits are relatively static; in which the government plays a significant role in terms of deficits and reregulation and control of the economy; in which the consumer stops shopping until he drops and begins, as they do in Japan (to be a little ghoulish), starts saving to the grave." Roubini (2011) argues that "there are good reasons to believe that we are experiencing a more persistent slump."

12. IMF 2013b and 2014b present these growth forecasts and an analysis of the evolutions of global real interest rates.

13. Summers (2013, 2014) presents the basic arguments describing secular stagnation. Summers (2013) notes that "There are many a priori reasons why the level of spending at any given set of interest rates is likely to have declined. Investment demand may have been reduced due to slower growth of the labor force and perhaps slower productivity growth. Consumption may be lower due to a sharp increase in the share of income held by the very wealthy and the rising share of income accruing to capital. Risk aversion has risen as a consequence of the crisis and as saving—by both states and consumers—has risen. The crisis increased the costs of financial intermediation and left major debt overhangs. Declines in the cost of durable goods, especially those associated with information technology, mean that the same level of saving purchases more capital every year." Krugman (2013c, 2014c) and Cassidy (2014) also support the notion of secular stagnation for the United States. Samuelson (2013) considers the possible causes of secular stagnation and

notes that "The problem might not be a dearth of investments so much as a surplus of risk aversion. For that, candidates abound: the traumatic impact of the Great Recession on confidence; a backlash against globalization, reduced cross-border investments by multinational firms; uncertain government policies; aging societies burdened by diminishing innovation and costly welfare states. Whatever the cause, we are in unfamiliar territory." Baily and Bosworth (2013) examine the sources of the weak recovery in the United States and conclude that "the unresolved problems suggest a long period of slow growth and higher than normal unemployment." Bernanke (2015a, 2015b, 2015c, 2015d) states that low interest rates are not a short-term aberration, but part of a long-term trend. He notes that global trade imbalances and unequal financial flows contribute to low global interest rates. OECD 2014 argues that "a global slowdown in productivity and the risk of higher structural unemployment threaten to usher in a new era of low economic growth" (Hutchens and Martin 2014). Gordon 2012 and 2014 present a broader discussion of a growth slowdown in the United States due to a variety of structural reasons. Alvin Hansen (1939), the president of the American Economic Association, advanced the idea of "secular stagnation" in 1939. His idea was that the Great Depression could lead to a prolonged period of stagnation and high unemployment because of the decline in the birth rate and excessive savings that constrain aggregate demand (Eggertsson and Mehrotra 2014). Foster, Grim, and Haltiwanger (2014) report that during the Great Recession, the intensity of reallocation across producers fell rather than rose and the reallocation that did occur was less productivity enhancing than in prior recessions. Hamilton and others (2015) conclude that the secular stagnation hypothesis confuses a delayed recovery with chronically weak aggregate demand.

14. Hoshi and Kashyap (2013) study the implications of the Japanese experience during its banking crisis in the 1990s for the United States and Europe. They focus on the delay in bank recapitalization and the lack of structural reforms in Japan, arguing that these two policy choices were responsible for stagnant postcrisis growth. They conclude that "In France, Italy, and Spain bank recapitalization has been delayed and the structural reforms have been slow. Without drastic changes, they are likely to follow Japan's path to long economic stagnation. The situation in Germany looks somewhat better mainly because the structural reform was already advanced before the crisis. Although the recovery has been slow in the U.S. as well, the problems are at least different from those faced by Japan then and many European countries now." Buiter, Rahbari, and Seydl (2014) report that "the risk of 'secular stagnation' through a failure to adopt appropriate policy measures is absent in emerging markets, low in the US and UK, somewhat higher in Japan and highest in the euro area." Another view, though, is that the global economy has enormous potential to generate a healthy dose of growth in the coming decades (see Mokyr 2014). Innovations, well-designed policies and vibrant emerging market and frontier economies can help realize that potential.

15. Taylor (2014b) and Rogoff (2013) present detailed arguments. George Osborne (2014), Chancellor of the Exchequer in the United Kingdom, claims that the pickup in economic growth in the United States and the United Kingdom in 2014 repudiates the secular stagnation argument. Fernald (2014) argues that it would be unreasonable to expect the U.S. productivity growth would reach its level over the 1973–95 period.

16. Rodrik (2013) argues that "developing countries will face stronger headwinds in the decades ahead, both because the global economy is likely to be significantly less buoyant than in recent decades and because technological changes are rendering manufacturing more capital and skill

intensive." Dervis (2013) provides an alternative view and claims that "With weak demand in advanced countries now impeding growth in emerging economies, including major players in Asia and Latin America, many are arguing that the era of income convergence has come to an end. Nothing could be further from the truth." Spence (2014) is also optimistic about future growth in emerging market economies as he writes, "The most likely scenario is that most major emerging markets, including China, will experience a transitional growth slowdown but will not be derailed by shifts in monetary policy in the West, with high growth rates returning in the course of the coming year. There are internal and external downside risks in each country that cannot and should not be dismissed, and volatility in international capital flows is complicating the adjustment. The problem today is that the downside risks are becoming the consensus forecast. That seems to me to be misguided – and a poor basis for investment and policy decisions."

17. For example, the 1975 episode led to such predictions as *The Economist* (1975c) notes that "Economic growth over the next 10 years will be slower than the world is accustomed to, unless politicians dare sharply to increase the rewards for risk taking. The danger ahead is (a) that the world economy will experience more violent fluctuations in demand and activity over the decade to 1985 than it experienced during the three decades to 1975; (b) that these fluctuations will be about a much slower growth trend; and that (c) the only countries that get decent growth will be those that are willing to give much higher rewards for risk-bearing—that are ready to see a substantial shift in the share of GNP away from personal consumption and government spending towards company profits. Political considerations in Britain, and some other countries, do not seem likely to favor this." Tylecote (1992) argues that "the period of downswing—slow growth or worse—lasts some 25 years. But after about 1982, the United States and Britain led a sustained recovery among the wealthy nations of the North. The outlook seemed rosy. Those of us who never shared the optimism can now say, 'We told you so.' I, for one, said the world depression never went away, for the world economy also includes the poor East, and the poorer South. For them, the 1980s were a nightmare. Their foreign debts were higher than ever and the real prices of their exports lower—the latter the main cause of the rise in living standards in the North. Beggars make bad customers. Yes, for now—just as the American New Deal would have been in 1930. That is why this Long Wave downswing still has about a decade to run." Kose and Ozturk (2014, 2015) provide a summary of some of the major changes the global economy has experienced over the past 50 years and conclude that no one could have accurately predicted these changes.

18. Gertler 1988; Sinai 1992, 2010; and Bernanke 1993 review some of the early literature. Claessens and Kose 2014a, 2014b broadly survey the topic. Gourinchas and Kose 2014, 2015 present summaries of recent studies analyzing the implications of various types of crises.

19. These frictions often stem from information asymmetries and enforcement problems (Claessens and Kose 2014b).

20. Aoki, Proudman, and Vlieghe 2004; and Iacoviello 2005 provide models with these features. Using a New Keynesian model, Christiano, Eichenbaum, and Trabandt (2014) find that the vast bulk of the movements in aggregate real economic activity during the recent global recession was due to financial frictions interacting with the zero lower bound.

21. For example, Carroll, Otsuka, and Slacalek (2006) report that the propensity to consume from a $1 increase in housing wealth ranges between 2 cents (short term) and 9 cents (long term), twice that for equity wealth. Kishor (2007) reports that while 98 percent of the change in housing

wealth is permanent, only 55 percent of the change in financial wealth is. Case, Quigley, and Shiller (2013) also report that a collapse in house prices tends to be followed by a sharp decline in household spending.

CHAPTER 9 UNCERTAINTY: HOW BAD IS IT?

1. For a more detailed discussion of this, see Friedman 1964, 1993.

2. Bloom 2009, 2013 and Baker, Bloom, and Davis 2013 provide details on the measurement of uncertainty, discuss interactions between uncertainty and activity, and present a detailed evaluation of the implications of uncertainty. Krugman 2012b and 2013b present a critical perspective on the relevance of policy uncertainty. Davis 2013 provides a response to Krugman's criticisms. FOMC 2008, 2009; Blanchard 2009b; Summers 2009; and Romer 2009b also mention the negative impact of uncertainty on demand. Chinn 2011; Zandi 2013; and Stone 2013 analyze various aspects of policy uncertainty and their impact on activity. Lee 2014 considers the impact of uncertainty on global investment. Baker and others 2014 analyze the causes of the strong upward drift in policy-related economic uncertainty since 1960. This chapter builds on Kose and Terrones 2012 and Bloom, Kose, and Terrones 2013.

3. For a description of survey findings, see National Association for Business Economics 2014.

4. The National Association for Business Economics—NABE (2014b) reports that "A majority of the NABE Policy Survey panel feels that uncertainty about fiscal policy is holding back economic recovery, although the share that holds this opinion is smaller than that which held this view in the August 2013 survey." Baker and others (2014) report that policy-related economic uncertainty has risen in the United States since 1960. They argue that the secular increase in policy uncertainty can be explained by two factors: growth in government spending, taxes, and regulation and a rise in political polarization and its implications for the policy-making process and policy choices.

5. Bloom and others (2012) document this observation.

6. Bachmann and Moscarini (2011) find that the direction of causality runs from recessions to uncertainty. Cesa-Bianchi, Peseran, and Rebucci (2014) also report that uncertainty is not a driver of business cycles since there is a significant impact of future output growth on current volatility (uncertainty) but exogenous changes in volatility have no effect on business cycles. Bachmann and Bayer (2013, 2014) find that the impact of uncertainty on growth is quite small in the context of general equilibrium models. In contrast, Baker and Bloom (2013) offer evidence, using disaster data as instruments, that the causality runs from uncertainty to recessions, and Bloom and others (2012) report that growth does not cause uncertainty. Predictions of theory and findings from empirical studies collectively indicate that uncertainty can play a dual role over the business cycle; that is, it can be an impulse as well as a propagation mechanism.

7. Bernanke (1983) and Dixit and Pindyck (1994) provide analytical models showing the impact of uncertainty on investment.

8. Gilchrist, Sim, and Zakrajsek (2010) and Arellano, Bai, and Kehoe (2012) provide models illustrating these interactions.

9. Carrière-Swallow and Céspedes (2013) present an empirical analysis of the impact of uncertainty in advanced economies on emerging market economies.

10. The growth rate of output is negatively correlated with macroeconomic uncertainty. Appendix I presents detailed results of this.

11. Empirical evidence based on vector autoregressive models points to a significant negative impact of uncertainty shocks on output and employment (Bloom 2009; Hirata and others 2012). These results also echo findings in a broader area of research on the negative impact of macroeconomic and policy volatility on economic growth (Ramey and Ramey 1995; Kose, Prasad, and Terrones 2005 and 2006; Fatas and Mihov 2013).

12. Figure 9.5 is based on the study by Baker, Bloom, and Davis 2012. Bloom and others (2012) and Baker and Bloom (2013) analyze the effects of uncertainty shocks on business cycle movements. For additional evidence on the impact of uncertainty, see Bloom 2009, 2013; and Hirata and others 2012.

13. Stock and Watson (2012) study the evolution of the Great Recession in the United States using a dynamic factor model. They report that many of the events during this episode were unprecedented and led to macroeconomic shocks that were larger than those previously experienced. They also find that while oil price shocks played a role in the initial slowdown, shocks stemming from financial market turbulence and heightened uncertainty were the major driving forces of the recession.

CHAPTER 10 THE GREAT DIVERGENCE OF POLICIES

1. Krugman (2013a) and Romer (2013) support the use of more aggressive expansionary policies to help economic recovery and argue that continued austerity could lead to an intensification of economic malaise, as happened in 1937. For a discussion of the use of a higher inflation target, see Rogoff 2008; Blanchard, Dell'Ariccia, and Mauro 2010; and Krugman 2014b, 2014d. Some argue that monetary policy, by stopping adverse feedback loops, can play a significant role during a financial crisis (Mishkin 2009). Bernanke (2012a); English, Lopez-Salido, and Tetlow (2013); and Reifschneider, Wascher, and Wilcox (2013) take stock of the diverse monetary policy actions, conventional and unconventional, taken by the Federal Reserve since late 2007. Yellen (2013a) discusses the difficulties the Federal Reserve faced in achieving its dual mandate of price stability and maximum employment after interest rates hit the zero lower bound.

2. Some argue that the severity of the recent recession reflects the aggressive use of fiscal and structural policies (that is, subsidies, taxes, and regulations) implemented after 2007 as these policies reduced incentives for firms to hire and for people to work (Mulligan 2012). Similarly, others state that the weak recovery has been the result of the adverse effects of policies and regulations on growth (Ohanian, Taylor, and Wright 2012; Cogan and Taylor 2012c; Taylor 2013, 2014a).

3. In particular, some claim that central banks might have exercised too much policy discretion with unknown medium- to long-term implications. For instance, Meltzer (2012) notes that many of the actions taken by the Federal Reserve since late 2007 have been inappropriate for an independent central bank, as they have distorted credit markets and focused on the near term.

4. Kose, Loungani, and Terrones (2013a) document how policies diverged during the latest global recovery and compare their paths with the average behavior of policies during previous episodes.

5. Other indicators, such as the ratio of government deficits to GDP and short-term real interest rates, often lead to noisy signals about the stance of policies over the business cycle (Kaminsky, Reinhart, and Végh 2005).

6. For a discussion of fiscal policies early in the crisis, see Spilimbergo and others 2008; Freedman and others 2009; Mankiw 2009a; Wolf 2009, 2010c, 2013a, 2013b; and the U.S. Department of

the Treasury 2013. There have been intense debates on the effectiveness of the large fiscal stimulus implemented by the United States early in the crisis. Matthews (2011) provides a brief evaluation of nine studies on the subject (see also Cochrane 2009b; Frankel 2013; Council of Economic Advisers 2014a; Furman 2014; Krugman 2014a; Davies 2014; and Luce 2014). Coenen and others (2012) evaluate the effectiveness of discretionary fiscal policy in the euro area during the crisis. Végh and Vuletin (2013) analyze fiscal policy responses during the Latin American crisis and the euro area crisis. They conclude that procyclical fiscal policy has aggravated the duration and intensity of the crisis in both cases. Chari and Henry (2013) compare policy responses during the Asian crisis and the global financial crisis. They document that the fiscal adjustment in Asia was far more modest than is commonly known and that the switch from stimulus to austerity in Europe was quite abrupt. They conclude that the difference in fiscal stance helps explain the difference in the postcrisis paths of output and employment in the two regions. Davies (2012) draws some lessons from the Asian crisis for Europe. Wolf (2010a) considers the Japanese experience and draws parallels with the current episode. Wolf (2014) analyzes the experience of the economies that experienced credit cycles. Kollman, Roeger, and Veld (2012) examine government support programs to the financial sector during the crisis. Laeven and Valencia (2011) evaluate the implications of financial sector interventions for the real economy during the crisis. Claessens and others (2014) include several studies about various macroeconomic and structural policy measures that can help mitigate the adverse effects of financial crises.

7. The change in the direction of fiscal policy in the United States has also been a subject of intense debates. For example, Krugman (2014a) argues that "So, let me make the obvious point, just in case anyone missed it: the "pivot" of 2010—when all the Very Serious People decided that the danger from debt trumped any and all concern for job creation—was an utter disaster, economic and human. It was even a disaster in fiscal terms, because a permanently depressed economy will cost far more in revenue than was saved by slashing the deficit by a few percent of GDP in the short term." On the opposite side, Sachs (2015) argues that although we need larger government spending relative to GDP, we should pay for this through higher taxes on the wealthy since there is nothing progressive about large budget deficits and a rising debt-to-GDP ratio. Similarly, Cochrane (2014) notes that "by Keynesian logic, fraud is good; thieves have notoriously high marginal propensity to consume. That's a hard sell, so stimulus is routinely dressed in 'infrastructure' clothes. In the context of the United Kingdom, there was also a passionate debate about the direction of fiscal policy. Wolf (2013b) claims that "Austerity has failed. It turned a nascent recovery into stagnation. That imposes huge and unnecessary costs, not just in the short run, but also in the long term: the costs of investments unmade, of businesses not started, of skills atrophied, and of hopes destroyed." George Osborne (2014), Chancellor of the Exchequer of the United Kingdom, defends the fiscal policy his government implemented: "Our economy has grown faster than any other in the G-7 over the past year and is now forecast by the International Monetary Fund to do the same in 2014. This is despite warnings from some that our determined pursuit of our economic plan made that impossible. At the same time, job creation has been better than anyone expected: three times faster than any previous U.K. recovery, with more than four new jobs in the private sector for every job lost in the public sector. All of this demonstrates that fiscal consolidation and economic recovery go together, and it undermines the pessimistic prognosis that only further fiscal stimulus can drive sustainable growth. Indeed, that is precisely the wrong prescription."

8. In 2012, fiscal deficits declined to 6 percent of GDP in the advanced economies and 2 percent of GDP in the emerging market economies (IMF 2013b).

9. After Herndon, Ash, and Pollin (2013) point out some problems in a study by Reinhart and Rogoff (2010a), the debate on the impact of public debt on economic growth has become even more intense. Although other studies also document a negative correlation between public debt and economic growth, there is no conclusive evidence suggesting a causal relationship running from debt to growth (IMF 2012b; Panizza and Presbitero 2013).

10. In December 2013, the Federal Reserve decided to start reducing the pace of its asset purchases beginning in January 2014 (FOMC 2013).

11. In addition, IMF 2014c notes that "in most advanced economies, the pace of fiscal consolidation will slow in 2014 as average gross debt stabilizes and the focus shifts appropriately toward ensuring that the composition of adjustment supports the still uneven recovery."

12. For a discussion of how the financial crisis has affected the design of macroeconomic policies, see Blanchard, Dell'Ariccia, and Mauro 2010, 2013; Blanchard and others 2012; and Taylor 2014a.

13. See, for instance, Blanchard and Perotti 2002; DeLong and Summers 2012; Blanchard and Leigh 2013b; Christiano, Eichenbaum, and Rebelo 2011; Ramey 2011; Auerbach and Gorodnichenko 2012; and Chinn 2014. One limitation of these studies is the difficulty in identifying truly exogenous policy changes (Alesina 2012; Alesina and Giavazzi 2013). This issue is complicated by the fact that fiscal and monetary policy changes are often simultaneous. Romer (2013) argues that one of the lessons from the Great Depression is that fiscal policy is a very effective tool to spur recovery. Alesina and Ardagna (2010) report that fiscal consolidation (particularly that based on spending cuts as opposed to tax increases) can be expansionary. More recent evidence, however, suggests that expansionary austerity is very rare (Perotti 2012) and, when properly measured, fiscal consolidation is indeed contractionary (Guajardo, Leigh, and Pescatori 2011). Mankiw (2009a) also provides a discussion of this issue.

14. Sargent and Wallace (1975) provide a discussion of this idea. See also Barro 1981 and Lucas 1975, 1977. Lucas (1995) argues that the distinction between anticipated and unanticipated money shocks is one of the main findings of research on monetary policy. While the anticipated monetary expansions affect nominal variables (that is, interest rates and inflation tax effects), the unanticipated monetary expansions can temporarily influence production and employment.

15. For the effectiveness of monetary policies under these circumstances, see Eggertsson and Woodford 2003; Krishnamurthy and Vissing-Jorgensen 2011; Carvalho, Eusipe, and Grisse 2012; Woodford 2012; Bauer and Rudebusch 2012; Baumeister and Benati 2010; Chen, Cúrdia, and Ferrero 2012; and Swanson and Williams 2013, among others.

16. Williamson (2013) makes this point and examines how the changes in the size and composition of central bank balance sheets can affect monetary policy. Gagnon and Sack (2014) discuss the implications of a large balance sheet and substantial amount of liquidity in the financial system.

17. There is broad agreement that unconventional monetary policies (based on liquidity provision and private asset purchases) at the early stages of the crisis were also effective in restoring the functioning of financial markets (IMF 2013c).

18. These findings have been partially confirmed by other studies in the United States and United Kingdom employing different methodologies (see, for instance, Krishnamurthy and Vissing-Jorgensen 2011, 2013; Gagnon and others 2011; Joyce and others 2010). Fischer 2015 notes that asset purchases have helped make financial conditions overall more accommodative and have provided significant stimulus for the broader economy.

19. Some of these risks or costs are also discussed in Bernanke 2012a. Yellen (2013b) argues that financial stability risks in the United States are being carefully monitored and that currently there is no pervasive evidence of excessive credit growth, a buildup of leverage, or asset bubbles. However, she admits that the financial stability concern is the most important potential cost of the monetary policy stance since the global financial crisis. A prolonged period of monetary accommodation in the advanced economies could weaken the resolve to repair and reform financial entities, encourage excessive risk taking by economic agents, and promote large capital flows to emerging market economies (Caruana 2013, Feldstein 2013, IMF 2013c, Stein 2013).

CHAPTER 11 A COMPLEX AFFAIR: GLOBAL AND NATIONAL CYCLES

1. The IMF provided descriptions of the differential performance across various regions during the global recession and recovery. For example, IMF 2009b mentions the challenges of the Middle East and Central Asia region and notes that "The global crisis is now affecting the countries in the Middle East and Central Asia region, and economic and financial vulnerabilities are rising. In the Middle East and North Africa, good economic fundamentals, appropriate policy responses, and sizable currency reserves are helping mitigate the impact of the shock. In the Caucasus and Central Asia, lower commodity prices and adverse economic developments in Russia have hit hard." IMF 2010b observes the strong performance of Asian economies: "Asia has entered the second year of the global economic expansion still firmly in the lead of the recovery. Growth in the first half of 2010 proceeded well above trend in almost all regional economies, as global manufacturing continued to rebound and fueled exports and investment in the region." IMF 2010c discusses the rapid growth in the Latin America and Caribbean region: "A multispeed global recovery is under way, with some emerging markets in the lead and the major advanced economies growing more slowly. This macroeconomic setting has brought a return to easy global financial conditions and high commodity prices—a situation likely to be sustained for some time but unlikely to be permanent. Against that external backdrop, the recovery in the Latin America and Caribbean region overall is advancing faster than anticipated, but moving at different speeds across countries." These themes are also discussed in IMF 2015a and IMF 2015b.
2. Goldstein and Khan 1982; Dornbusch 1985; Hoffmaister, Pradhan, and Samiei 1998; Frankel and Roubini 2001; IMF 2001d; and Calvo and others 2001 analyze the linkages between advanced and emerging market economies. Currie and Vines 1988 and Chui and others 2002 present surveys of studies focusing on trade and growth in the context of North-South interactions. Another branch of this research program examines the role of trading partners' economic performance in driving the dynamics of domestic growth (see Akin and Kose 2008 for a summary).
3. Lewis (1980) makes this observation. Akin and Kose (2008) examine the extent of growth spillovers from the advanced economies to the emerging market economies and concludes that the impact of the former group on the growth dynamics of the latter has declined over time.
4. LIBOR is an index of the interest rates at which banks are willing to offer to lend unsecured funds to other banks in the London wholesale money market. We provide the details of our model and present an extensive discussion of our findings in Kose, Loungani, and Terrones 2013b.
5. Appendix J presents the details of regression results.
6. A number of papers study these types of asymmetric effects of interest rates on output during recessions and expansions (Garcia and Schaller 2002; Sensier, Osborn, and Ocal 2002; Karras 1996).

7. Forbes and Warnock (2012) find evidence that global factors are key drivers of waves of international capital flows. These factors become especially important during global recessions (as we saw during the latest episode) because foreign investors can rapidly reduce their bank and equity flows. Milesi-Ferretti and Tille (2011) report that countries with large precrisis debt positions indeed witnessed much larger outflows of capital at the height of the 2009 global recession.

8. Kose, Otrok, and Prasad (2012) provide details about the roles played by global and national factors in driving cycles in advanced, emerging market, and other developing economies.

9. Gourinchas and Kose (2010, 2011) present summaries of recent studies analyzing the transmission of the global financial crisis across borders through trade and financial linkages.

10. For example, Arora and Vamvakidis (2004) find that advanced economies benefit from trading with rapidly growing emerging market economies, while developing economies benefit from trading with the relatively high-income advanced economies. Helbling and others (2007) find that spillovers from the United States to other economies have increased with greater trade and financial integration.

11. These types of terms-of-trade shocks tend to play a more important role in countries connected to each other through vertical linkages involving multinational production chains. Research indicates that vertical linkages appear to amplify transmission of business cycles across borders (Kose and Yi 2001, 2006; Burstein, Kurz, and Tesar 2008; di Giovanni and Levchenko 2010; Chinn, 2013).

CHAPTER 12 LESSONS: PAST, PRESENT, AND FUTURE

1. Blanchard and Milesi-Ferretti (2009, 2012) discuss the implications of global imbalances and policies to adjust them.

2. An extensive research program has analyzed the benefits and costs of policy coordination. Most studies suggest that given the costs of reaching a consensus among countries with different objectives, the benefits of policy coordination are quite small (Oudiz and Sachs 1985; Obstfeld and Rogoff 2002; Williamson 2005; Stiglitz 2009; Angeloni and Pisani-Ferry 2012; Taylor 2013a). Analyzing the implications of fiscal policy coordination at the zero lower bound, Gomes and others (2015) show that international coordination is helpful but it does not necessarily play a major role.

3. The importance of policy coordination was also emphasized in previous global recessions. For example, Nossiter (1974) describes the expectations of the international organizations during the 1975 episode: "The International Monetary Fund notes that it has appealed for global coordination in the past 'but never with greater urgency than at the present time.' The IMF calls the unbalanced accounts created by the oil states a 'disequilibrium wholly unprecedented in size and character.' A failure to redistribute these funds, it warns, 'could seriously damage the world economy.' In the same vein, the Organization for Economic Coordination and Development, a grouping of the wealthiest nations, declares: 'Cooperation and consultation between governments have never been more necessary than they are today, given the unaccustomed and troubled waters on which the world economy is now embarked.'" In 1983, *The Economist* ran a piece by Helmut Schmidt, ex-chancellor of Germany, about the necessary policy measures to head off a global recession. He noted that "The world's economic interdependence has never been greater than it is this decade. It has never been more necessary to make sure that economic policies complement each other and are internationally compatible. Never has co-operation been as necessary as today. Just

as democracies cannot keep going without a general consensus about the rules, the world economy cannot survive without agreement on the rules of the game and the distribution of roles" (*The Economist* 1983). In 1992, the U.S. Treasury noted that "Since the mid-1980s, the Group of Seven (G7) has worked intensively to achieve consistent and compatible policies and performance necessary for sustained growth with price stability, reduced external imbalances and greater stability of exchange markets. The economic policy coordination process grew directly out of each country's growing recognition that, in an interdependent world, economic performance at home depends in large part on economic developments in the rest of the world, and particularly in the major industrial economies. As recent experience has once again demonstrated, the formulation of economic policies—especially fiscal and monetary policies—by individual G7 countries has a major impact on the economies of the others. Moreover, no individual G7 member acting alone can overcome economic difficulties which affect all of the G7 economies" (Department of the Treasury 1992). Uchitelle (1991) explains how the international policy coordination effort failed during the G7 meeting in April 1991.

4. The G20 web page states that "the G20 is the premier forum for international cooperation on the most important issues of the global economic and financial agenda. The objectives of the G20 refer to: (i) policy coordination between its members in order to achieve global economic stability and sustainable growth; (ii) promoting financial regulations that reduce risks and prevent future financial crises; and (iii) modernizing international financial architecture."

5. Despite its initial success, the effectiveness of the G20 has become a topic of debate, especially after 2010 (Angeloni and Pisani-Ferry 2012; Faruqee and Srinivasan 2012). O'Neill and Terzi (2014) make predictions about the world economy in 2020 and conclude that "If our projections to 2020 are broadly right, then many established frameworks for the running of the world economy and its governance are not going to be fit for purpose, and will need to change. The global monetary system itself, and global organizations such as the IMF, G7 and G20 will have to adapt considerably if they want to remain legitimate representatives of the world order. The alternative is their relegation to irrelevance."

6. There has been an intense debate on the feasibility and benefits of international monetary policy coordination in light of the developments in financial markets in emerging market economies following the announcements of tapering of bond purchases by the U.S. Federal Reserve in mid-2013. Raghuram Rajan, governor of the Reserve Bank of India, made a strong case for coordination: "Hence, my call is for more coordination in monetary policy because I think it would be an immense improvement over the current international non-system. International monetary policy coordination, of course, is unpopular among central bankers, and I therefore have to say why I reiterate the call and what I mean by it. I do not mean that central bankers sit around a table and make policy collectively, nor do I mean that they call each other regularly and coordinate actions. In its strong form, I propose that large country central banks, both in advanced countries and emerging markets, internalize more of the spillovers from their policies in their mandate, and are forced by new conventions on the 'rules of the game' to avoid unconventional policies with large adverse spillovers and questionable domestic benefits" (Rajan 2014). Harding (2014) notes that "Janet Yellen has turned a cold shoulder to the pleas of emerging markets by signaling that only a domestic slowdown will influence US monetary policy, in comments that suggest there will be no relief for those countries being battered by the Fed's reduction of its asset purchases." William F. Dudley, president of the Federal Reserve Bank of New York, argues that "Moreover, it

is far from clear that explicitly coordinated policy would produce better outcomes for the global economy generally, or the EMEs (emerging market economies) specifically. Central banks have challenges enough in tailoring policies to their domestic circumstances. I believe that it would be taking on too much to attempt to collectively fashion policy in reference to global conditions. Moreover, our last system of explicit coordination—the system of fixed exchange rates under Bretton Woods—broke down for a reason. Monetary policy meant to suit everybody is likely in the end to suit nobody" (Dudley 2014). Prasad (2014) emphasizes the importance of addressing domestic vulnerabilities in emerging market economies and notes that "Rather than fulminating about other countries' monetary policies, national leaders ought to put their own houses in order. Monetary authorities should focus on delivering low inflation and financial stability. If central bankers wage proxy battles on behalf of their feckless political leaders, they risk damaging their own hard-won credibility, independence and effectiveness." Christine Lagarde, managing director of the IMF, often emphasizes the importance of policy coordination: "Getting beyond the crisis still requires a sustained and substantial policy effort, coordination, and the right policy mix" (Lagarde 2014).

7. Blanchard (2013) discusses the importance of advancing research on policies.

8. McKinsey Global Institute (2013) analyzes the evolution of financial flows in recent years. Kose and others (2010) present a review of the literature on the implications of financial flows for macroeconomic stability and long-term growth.

9. For a discussion about the end of the business cycles in the 1960s, see Bronfenbrenner 1969 and Gordon 1970. *The Economist* (1989) noted that "thousands of economists have studied the business cycle—the regular swings in economic activity between boom and bust. But just as they thought they understood its causes and consequences, it seems to be disappearing." Weber (1997) discusses the end of the cycle in light of developments during the late 1990s. *The Economist* (1998) noted that "History is, indeed, littered with premature obituaries of the business cycle. In the late 1920s, on the eve of the Depression, there was talk of a new industrial era of rapid, everlasting growth. In the late 1960s, Arthur Okun, an economic adviser to Presidents Kennedy and Johnson, proclaimed that the business cycle was 'obsolete'—and the Commerce Department was so confident that it decided to change the name of one of its publications from *Business Cycle Developments* to *Business Conditions Digest*. A recession began a year later." *Businessweek*, in a cover story in early 2000, claimed that we lived in an era of a new economy: "It seems almost too good to be true. With the information technology sector leading the way, the U.S. has enjoyed almost 4% growth since 1994. Unemployment has fallen from 6 percent to about 4 percent, and inflation just keeps getting lower and lower . . . consumer inflation in 1999 was only 1.9 percent, the smallest increase in 34 years. This spectacular boom was not built on smoke and mirrors . . . The result is the so-called New Economy: faster growth and lower inflation" (*Businessweek* 2000).

APPENDICES

List of Appendices

A. Abbreviations
B. Database
    1. Definitions and Sources of Variables
        a. Activity Variables
        b. Financial Variables
        c. Commodity Prices
        d. Weights Used to Compute Aggregate and per Capita Variables
        e. Measures of Uncertainty
        f. Macroeconomic Policy Variables
        g. Variables Used in Regressions in Chapter 11
    2. List of Countries: Functional Groups (163 Countries)
    3. List of Countries: Regional Groups (128 Countries)
    4. List of Countries Used in Regressions in Chapter 11 (97 Countries)
C. Evolution of Purchasing Power Parity and Market Weights
D. Crises around Global Recessions and Global Downturns
    1. Banking Crises
    2. Currency Crises
    3. Debt Crises
E. Timeline: Selected Events around Global Recessions and Recoveries
F. Global Recessions: Regional Country Groups
G. Sensitivity of Global Activity Variables
H. Global Recoveries: Regional Country Groups
I. Uncertainty, Business Cycles, and Growth
    1. Uncertainty over the Business Cycle
    2. Uncertainty and Growth
J. Linkages between the Global Cycle and National Cycles
    1. Linkages between Global and National Cycles: All Countries
    2. Linkages between Global and National Cycles: Country Groups
    3. Linkages between Global and National Cycles: Roles of Trade and Financial Integration

Appendix A. Abbreviations

CEO	Chief executive officer
CIO	Chief information officer
CEPR	Centre for Economic Policy Research
CPI	Consumer price index
CIS	Commonwealth of Independent States
Datastream	Thomson Reuters financial and economic data
DX Databases	Financial and economic databases produced by EconData Pty Ltd., CEIC Data Ltd., and Emerging Markets Economic Data Ltd. (EMED)
ECB	European Central Bank
ERM	European Exchange Rate Mechanism
G20	Group of Twenty major advanced and emerging market economies
GDI	Gross domestic income
GDP	Gross domestic product
GDS	IMF Global data source
GFD	Global financial data
GNP	Gross national product
GPG	*Global Property Guide*
IFS	IMF International Financial Statistics
ILO	International Labour Organization
IMF	International Monetary Fund
LIBOR	London interbank offered rate
MS	Markov Switching
MSCI	Morgan Stanley Country Index
MW	Market-exchange-rate-weighted average
NBER	National Bureau of Economic Research
OECD	Organisation for Economic Co-operation and Development
OMT	Outright Monetary Transactions
PFMHD	IMF Public Finance in Modern History Database
PIMCO	Pacific Investment Management Company, LLC.
PPP	Purchasing power parity
PW	PPP-exchange-rate-weighted average
PWT	Penn World Tables
QE	Quantitative easing
S&P	Standard & Poor's
VAR	Vector autoregression
VXO	Chicago Board Options Volatility Index
WDI	World Development Indicators
WEO	IMF *World Economic Outlook*
ZLB	Zero lower bound

Appendix B. Database

1. DEFINITIONS AND SOURCES OF VARIABLES

a. Activity Variables

Variable	Definition	Source
Output	Gross domestic product (GDP), constant prices. Before 1968, the series are spliced using data from the Organisation for Economic Co-operation and Development (OECD).	IMF *World Economic Outlook* (WEO)
Trade Flows	Exports + imports. World trade flows growth is the sum of the trade weights multiplied by trade flows growth. Trade weights are the sum of exports and imports of each country over the sum of exports and imports of all countries.	WEO
Capital Flows over GDP	Total capital flows = (|outflows| + |inflows|) / GDP in U.S. dollars. Outflows = direct assets + portfolio assets + other assets. Inflows = direct liabilities + portfolio liabilities + other liabilities. World capital flows over GDP growth is the difference from the previous year of the sum of total capital flows of all countries.	WEO
Oil Consumption	World aggregate oil consumption.	British Petroleum, WEO
Unemployment	Unemployment rate = (labor force − employment)/labor force. Labor weight = labor force/total labor force of all countries. The change in the world unemployment rate is the difference from the previous year of the sum of the labor-weighted unemployment rate of all countries.	
Industrial Production	Industrial production (if not available, manufacturing production) index. Data are in quarterly frequency, and year-over-year growth rates are annualized as the average of four quarters. Data for advanced countries are from the OECD, and whenever series are not available in the OECD, they are spliced using the growth rates of series from the IMF Global Data Source (GDS). Data for emerging market economies are from the IMF International Financial Statistics (IFS) and GDS.	OECD, GDS, IFS
Consumption	Private consumption expenditure, constant prices. World consumption growth is the sum of weighted consumption growth.	WEO
Investment	Gross fixed capital formation, constant prices. World investment growth is the sum of weighted investment growth.	WEO
Residential Investment	Private residential fixed capital formation volume.	OECD

b. Financial Variables

Variable	Definition	Source
Credit	Nominal credit deflated using the consumer price index (CPI). Data are in quarterly frequency, and year-over-year growth rates are annualized as the average of four quarters. Nominal credit from IFS is generally titled as "Claims on Private Sector." Growth of world credit is the weighted sum of the year-over-year growth rate of credit of each country annualized as the average of four quarters. Weights are in annual frequency, and for each quarter the weight is equal to the weight in the corresponding year.	IFS, Datastream
Equity Prices	Share price (index) deflated using the CPI. World equity price growth is the weighted sum of the year-over-year growth rate of stock prices of each country annualized as the average of four quarters. Weights are in annual frequency, and for each quarter the weight is equal to the weight in the corresponding year.	IFS, Datastream, Global Financial Database
House Prices	National house prices deflated using the CPI. World house price growth is the weighted sum of the year-over-year growth rate of house prices of each country annualized as the average of four quarters. Weights are in annual frequency, and for each quarter the weight is equal to the weight in the corresponding year.	Global Property Guide, OECD
Inflation Rate	Percentage change in CPI. Growth in world inflation is the weighted sum of the year-over-year difference of each country's inflation rate. Weights are in annual frequency, and for each quarter the weight is equal to the weight in the corresponding year.	IFS
Short-Term Interest Rates	Treasury bill rates or short-term interest rates. Real short-term interest rate is the difference between nominal short-term interest rate and inflation. Growth in short-term interest rate is the weighted year-over-year difference annualized as the average of four quarters.	IFS, Datastream, Haver Analytics, GDS, DXTime
LIBOR Overnight/ 3 Month	Overnight (3-month) U.S. dollar deposits in London. Growth in London interbank offered rate (LIBOR) is the year-over-year difference and is annualized as the average of four quarters.	IFS

c. Commodity Prices

Variable	Definition	Source
Oil Prices	Three spot price index. Real oil prices are nominal oil prices deflated by world CPI.	IFS
Food Prices	Real food prices are nominal food prices deflated by world CPI.	IFS
Gold Prices	Gold London Average Second Fix. Real gold prices are nominal gold prices deflated by world CPI.	IFS

d. Weights Used to Compute Aggregate and per Capita Variables

Variable	Definition	Source
Purchasing-Power-Parity (PPP) Weights	PPP weight of a country is the ratio of GDP in PPP terms over the sum of GDP in PPP terms of all countries. For series prior to 1970, PPP weights are generated using PPP-weighted per capita GDP and population data from the Penn World Tables (PWT), version 7.	WEO, PWT
Market Weights	The market weight of a country is the nominal GDP in U.S. dollar terms of that country over the sum of nominal GDP in U.S. dollar terms of all countries. This is used for weights of output and industrial production. Consumption (investment) in U.S. dollar terms is calculated by multiplying GDP in U.S. dollar terms by real consumption (investment) over real GDP in local currency. Market weight for consumption (investment) is consumption (investment) in U.S. dollar terms over sum of consumption (investment) in U.S. dollar terms of all countries.	WEO
Per Capita Growth Variables	World population is the sum of population of all countries. World population growth is the annual percentage change in the world population. The per capita growth rate of a variable is the difference between the growth rate of the variable and the population growth of the group. If data for the variable of interest are not available for a particular country, then the group population does not include the population of that country. When there is a jump in the population growth due to inclusion of a country in a year, then this jump is smoothed using the average growth rate of population one year before and one year after.	WEO

e. Measures of Uncertainty

Variable	Definition	Source
Macroeconomic Uncertainty	Macroeconomic uncertainty refers to the monthly standard deviation of daily stock returns in each country. Daily returns are calculated using each country's stock price index; time coverage varies across economies. Global uncertainty is the dynamic common factor of country-specific uncertainty of the three major advanced economies with the longest data available. Uncertainty in the United States is the Chicago Board Options Exchange (CBOE) Volatility Index, which is calculated from Standard and Poor's (S&P) 100 calls and puts.	Baker, Bloom, and Davis (2012); Kose and Terrones (2012); and CBOE
Economic Policy Uncertainty	Economic policy uncertainty is an index of policy uncertainty for the United States and the euro area from Baker, Bloom, and Davis (2012). It refers to the weighted average of three indicators, including the frequency of the appearance of terms like "economic policy" and "uncertainty" in the media, the number of tax provisions that will expire in the coming years, and the dispersion of forecasts of future government outlays and inflation.	Baker, Bloom, and Davis (2012)

f. Macroeconomic Policy Variables

Variable	Definition	Source
Government Expenditures	Primary government expenditure = expenditure − interest expense from WEO for 2006 onward and spliced back using data from Public Finances in Modern History Database (PFMHD). Series is a mix of general and central government data for some countries.	WEO, PFMHD
Short-Term Interest Rates	Policy rates from GDS or policy/discount rates from IFS depending on the length of the data. If three- or four-month Treasury bill rate series are longer, they are used as proxies. Observations are dropped in instances where inflation is greater than 50 percent from the previous year.	GDS, Haver Analytics, IFS
Central Bank Assets	Total Central Bank Assets. Principal series are from Haver Analytics and spliced backward using growth rates from IFS. Series were deflated with WEO consumer price index (CPI). Euro area countries data were converted to euros using exchange rates from Eurostat. Foreign assets are from IFS and calculated as a percentage of the total. Series were deflated using WEO CPI and are expressed as a percent of real GDP for the year prior to the crisis.	Haver Analytics, Bank of England, IFS
Public Debt-to-GDP Ratio	Gross Government Debt from WEO (for 2006 onward) and spliced backward using PFMHD data. Data were deflated using WEO CPI. Series is a mix of general and central government data for some countries.	WEO, PFMHD
Overall Balance	Defined as the difference between revenue and total expenditure, using the 2001 edition of the IMF's *Government Finance Statistics Manual* (GFSM 2001).	*Fiscal Monitor*
Net Debt	Gross debt minus financial assets, including those held by the broader public sector; for example, social security funds held by the relevant component of the public sector, in some cases.	*Fiscal Monitor*
Gross Domestic Debt	All liabilities that require future payment of interest and/or principal by the debtor to the creditor. The term "public debt" is used in the *Fiscal Monitor*, for simplicity, as synonymous with gross debt of the general government, unless specified otherwise. (Strictly speaking, public debt refers to the debt of the public sector as a whole, which includes financial and nonfinancial public enterprises and the central bank.)	*Fiscal Monitor*

g. Variables Used in Regressions in Chapter 11

Variable	Definition	Source
Rest of the World per Capita Output Growth	For each country it is the PPP-weighted output growth of the remaining countries in the sample minus their population growth.	
World Real Interest Rate	Difference between the three-month U.S. dollar LIBOR interest rate and U.S. inflation.	
Trade Openness	Ratio of the sum of exports and imports to GDP.	World Development Indicators
Financial Openness	Ratio of the sum of total assets and liabilities to GDP.	Lane and Milesi-Ferretti (2007)
External Leverage	Ratio of a country's total assets to its gross equity liabilities (domestic and foreign).	

2. LIST OF COUNTRIES: FUNCTIONAL GROUPS (163 COUNTRIES)

Advanced Economies (24)

Australia*	Denmark *	Iceland	Netherlands*	Sweden*
Austria*	Finland*	Ireland*	New Zealand*	Switzerland*
Belgium*	France*	Italy*	Norway*	United Kingdom*
Canada*	Germany*	Japan*	Portugal*	United States*
Cyprus	Greece*	Luxembourg	Spain*	

Emerging Markets (30)

Argentina*	Costa Rica*	Israel*	Pakistan	South Africa*
Brazil*	Czech Republic	Jordan	Peru*	Taiwan Province of China*
Chile*	Egypt	Korea*	Philippines*	Thailand*
China: Mainland*	Hungary	Malaysia*	Poland	Turkey*
Hong Kong SAR*	India*	Mexico*	Russia	Ukraine
Colombia*	Indonesia*	Morocco	Singapore*	Venezuela*

Note: All data series are in annual frequency. For countries denoted with *, we also use data in quarterly frequency in Chapters 5, 6, 7, 8, and 9.

Other Developing Economies (109)

Afghanistan	Cameroon	Guatemala
Algeria	Cape Verde	Guinea
Antigua and Barbuda	Central African Republic	Guinea-Bissau
Armenia	Democratic Republic of the Congo	Guyana
Azerbaijan	Republic of Congo	Haiti
The Bahamas	Croatia	Honduras
Bahrain	Côte d'Ivoire	Iran, Islamic Rep. of
Bangladesh	Djibouti	Jamaica
Barbados	Dominica	Kazakhstan
Belarus	Dominican Republic	Kenya
Benin	Ecuador*	Kiribati
Bhutan	El Salvador	Kyrgyz Republic
Bolivia	Eritrea	Lao P.D.R.
Bosnia and Herzegovina	Estonia	Latvia
Botswana	Ethiopia	Lesotho
Brunei Darussalam	Fiji	Liberia
Bulgaria	Gabon	Libya
Burkina Faso	Georgia	Lithuania
Burundi	Ghana	Macedonia, former Yugoslav Republic of
Cambodia	Grenada	

Other Developing Economies (109) (*continued*)		
Madagascar	Qatar	São Tomé and Príncipe
Malawi	Romania	Tajikistan
Maldives	Rwanda	Tanzania
Mali	St. Kitts and Nevis	Timor-Leste
Malta	St. Lucia	Tonga
Mauritius	St. Vincent and the Grenadines	Trinidad and Tobago
Moldova	Samoa	Tunisia
Montenegro	Saudi Arabia	Turkmenistan
Mozambique	Senegal	United Arab Emirates
Myanmar	Serbia	Uruguay*
Namibia	Seychelles	Uzbekistan
Nicaragua	Slovak Republic	Vanuatu
Niger	Slovenia	Vietnam
Nigeria	Sri Lanka	Yemen
Oman	Sudan	Zambia
Papua New Guinea	Suriname	Zimbabwe
Paraguay	Syria	

3. LIST OF COUNTRIES: REGIONAL GROUPS (128)

Emerging Asia (10)	
China: Mainland	Malaysia
Hong Kong SAR	Philippines
India	Singapore
Indonesia	Taiwan Province of China
Korea	Thailand

Developing Asia (15)		
Bangladesh	Lao P.D.R.	Samoa
Bhutan	Maldives	Sri Lanka
Cambodia	Myanmar	Tonga
Fiji	Pakistan	Vanuatu
Kiribati	Papua New Guinea	Vietnam

Latin America and the Caribbean (30)		
Antigua and Barbuda	Dominican Republic	Nicaragua
Argentina	Ecuador	Paraguay
The Bahamas	El Salvador	Peru
Barbados	Grenada	St. Kitts and Nevis
Bolivia	Guatemala	St. Lucia
Brazil	Guyana	St. Vincent and the Grenadines
Chile	Haiti	Suriname
Colombia	Honduras	Trinidad and Tobago
Costa Rica	Jamaica	Uruguay
Dominica	Mexico	Venezuela

3. LIST OF COUNTRIES: REGIONAL GROUPS (128) (CONTINUED)

Middle East and North Africa (14)

Algeria	Libya	Syria
Bahrain	Morocco	Tunisia
Egypt	Oman	United Arab Emirates
Iran, Islamic Rep. of	Qatar	Yemen
Jordan	Saudi Arabia	

Emerging Europe and Commonwealth of Independent States (24)

Armenia	Estonia	Lithuania	Russia
Azerbaijan	Georgia	Macedonia, former Yugoslav Republic of	Slovak Republic
Belarus	Hungary	Malta	Tajikistan
Bulgaria	Kazakhstan	Moldova	Turkey
Croatia	Kyrgyz Republic	Poland	Turkmenistan
Czech Republic	Latvia	Romania	Uzbekistan

Sub-Saharan Africa (35)

Benin	Democratic Republic of the Congo	Guinea	Mauritius	Seychelles
Botswana	Republic of Congo	Guinea-Bissau	Mozambique	South Africa
Burkina Faso	Côte d'Ivoire	Kenya	Namibia	Sudan
Burundi	Djibouti	Lesotho	Niger	Tanzania
Cameroon	Ethiopia	Madagascar	Nigeria	Tunisia
Cabo Verde	Gabon	Malawi	Rwanda	Zambia
Central African Republic	Ghana	Mali	Senegal	Zimbabwe

4. LIST OF COUNTRIES USED IN REGRESSIONS IN CHAPTER 11 (97 COUNTRIES)

Advanced Economies (21)

Australia	Finland	Ireland	New Zealand	Sweden
Austria	France	Italy	Norway	Switzerland
Belgium	Germany	Japan	Portugal	United Kingdom
Canada	Greece	Netherlands	Spain	United States
Denmark				

Emerging Markets (30)

Argentina	Czech Republic	Israel	Pakistan	South Africa
Brazil	Egypt	Jordan	Peru	Taiwan Province of China
Chile	Hong Kong SAR	Korea	Philippines	Thailand
China: Mainland	Hungary	Malaysia	Poland	Turkey
Colombia	India	Mexico	Russia	Ukraine
Costa Rica	Indonesia	Morocco	Singapore	Venezuela

Other Developing Economies (46)		
Bangladesh	Jamaica	Niger
Belarus	Kazakhstan	Papua New Guinea
Benin	Kenya	Paraguay
Bolivia	Kyrgyz Republic	Romania
Bulgaria	Latvia	Saudi Arabia
Burkina Faso	Lesotho	Senegal
Cameroon	Liberia	Slovak Republic
Central African Republic	Lithuania	Slovenia
Republic of Congo	Macedonia, former Yugoslav Republic of	Sri Lanka
Dominican Republic	Madagascar	Tanzania
Ecuador	Malawi	Trinidad and Tobago
El Salvador	Mali	Tunisia
Estonia	Mauritius	Uruguay
Ghana	Mozambique	Uzbekistan
Guatemala	Namibia	Vietnam
Honduras		

Appendix C. Evolution of Purchasing Power Parity and Market Weights

Evolution of Purchasing Power Parity and Market Weights *(in percent)*

	1960s	1970s	1980s	1990s	2000s	**Full Sample**
Market weights						
Advanced economies	87.53	67.63	70.75	76.74	70.92	74.25
Emerging market economies	10.55	23.32	21.67	19.35	24.28	20.27
Other developing economies	1.91	9.05	7.58	3.91	4.80	5.48
Purchasing-power-parity weights						
Advanced economies	72.39	64.20	61.01	60.03	52.88	61.37
Emerging market economies	22.51	26.74	30.11	32.24	38.71	30.71
Other developing economies	5.10	9.06	8.88	7.72	8.41	7.92

Note: Market weights (purchasing-power-parity weights) are the ratio of total gross domestic product (GDP) in U.S. dollars (GDP in purchasing power parity) of countries in each group to the total GDP in U.S. dollars (GDP in purchasing power parity) of all countries in the sample.

Appendix D. Crises around Global Recessions and Global Downturns

1. Banking Crises

1975	1982	1991	2009	1998	2001
Central African Rep. (1976)	Argentina (1980)	Argentina (1989)	United Kingdom (2007)	Bulgaria (1996)	Turkey (2000)
Chile (1976)	Morocco (1980)	Jordan (1989)	United States (2007)	Czech Republic (1996)	Argentina (2001)
Israel (1977)	Chile (1981)	Sri Lanka (1989)	Austria (2008)	Jamaica (1996)	Uruguay (2002)
Spain (1977)	Mexico (1981)	Algeria (1990)	Belgium (2008)	Yemen (1996)	
Mexico (1977)	Uruguay (1981)	Brazil (1990)	Denmark (2008)	Indonesia (1997)	
	Colombia (1982)	Romania (1990)	France (2008)	Japan (1997)	
	Ecuador (1982)	Lebanon (1990)	Greece (2008)	Korea (1997)	
	Ghana (1982)	Nicaragua (1990)	Hungary (2008)	Malaysia (1997)	
	Turkey (1982)	Sierra Leone (1990)	Iceland (2008)	Philippines (1997)	
	Chad (1983)	Dem. Rep. of Congo (1991)	Ireland (2008)	Thailand (1997)	
	Dem. Rep. of Congo (1983)	Finland (1991)	Italy (2008)	Vietnam (1997)	
	Nigeria (1983)	Georgia (1991)	Latvia (2008)	China (1998)	
	Peru (1983)	Hungary (1991)	Luxembourg (2008)	Colombia (1998)	
	Philippines (1983)	Liberia (1991)	Kazakhstan (2008)	Croatia (1998)	
	Thailand (1983)	Norway (1991)	Mongolia (2008)	Ecuador (1998)	
		Sweden (1991)	Netherlands (2008)	Slovak Republic (1998)	
		Tunisia (1991)	Portugal (2008)	Ukraine (1998)	
		Bosnia and Herzegovina (1992)	Russia (2008)		
		Chad (1992)	Slovenia (2008)		
		Estonia (1992)	Spain (2008)		
		Kenya (1992)	Sweden (2008)		
		Poland (1992)	Switzerland (2008)		
		Rep. of Congo (1992)	Ukraine (2008)		
		São Tomé and Príncipe (1992)	Nigeria (2009)		
		Slovenia (1992)			
		Guinea (1993)			
		India (1993)			
		Guyana (1993)			
		Togo (1993)			
		Macedonia FYR (1993)			

Note: Global recessions: 1975, 1982, 1991, 2009; global downturns: 1998, 2001.

2. Currency Crises

1975	1982	1991	2009	1998	2001
Bolivia (1973)	Israel (1980)	Dem. Rep. of	Iceland (2008)	Bulgaria (1996)	Belarus (1999)
Argentina (1975)	Guinea-Bissau	Congo (1989)	Venezuela	Romania (1996)	Brazil (1999)
Iceland (1975)	(1980)	Iceland (1989)	(2010)	Turkey (1996)	Dem. Rep. of
Israel (1975)	Argentina (1981)	Jordan (1989)		Kyrgyz Republic	Congo (1999)
Maldives (1975)	Bolivia (1981)	Paraguay (1989)		(1997)	Georgia (1999)
Myanmar (1975)	Costa Rica (1981)	Venezuela		Lao P.D.R. (1997)	Hong Kong SAR
Brazil (1976)	Iceland (1981)	(1989)		Mongolia (1997)	(1999)
Bangladesh	Italy (1981)	Dominican Rep.		Nigeria (1997)	Kazakhstan (1999)
(1976)	Morocco (1981)	(1990)		São Tomé and	Tajikistan (1999)
Dem. Rep. of	Peru (1981)	Honduras		Príncipe (1997)	Ghana (2000)
Congo (1976)	Brazil (1982)	(1990)		Fiji (1998)	Serbia (2000)
Peru (1976)	Chile (1982)	Lebanon (1990)		Indonesia (1998)	Myanmar (2001)
Mexico (1977)	Ecuador (1982)	Mongolia (1990)		Malaysia (1998)	Suriname (2001)
	Guinea (1982)	Myanmar (1990)		Philippines	Argentina (2002)
	Mexico (1982)	Nicaragua		(1998)	Libya (2002)
	Dem. Rep. of	(1990)		Sierra	Paraguay (2002)
	Congo (1983)	Suriname (1990)		Leone (1998)	Uruguay (2002)
	Ghana (1983)	Tanzania (1990)			Venezuela (2002)
	Greece (1983)	Uruguay (1990)			Dominican Rep.
	Nigeria (1983)	Angola (1991)			(2003)
	Philippines (1983)	Costa Rica			Haiti (2003)
	Portugal (1983)	(1991)			The Gambia (2004)
	Spain (1983)	Jamaica (1991)			
	Sierra	Rwanda (1991)			
	Leone (1983)	Brazil (1992)			
	Uruguay (1983)	Cambodia			
	Botswana (1984)	(1992)			
	Lebanon (1984)	Estonia (1992)			
	Madagascar	Georgia (1992)			
	(1984)	Haiti (1992)			
	Namibia (1984)	Latvia (1992)			
	Nepal (1984)	Lithuania (1992)			
	New Zealand	Nepal (1992)			
	(1984)	São Tomé and			
	Paraguay (1984)	Príncipe			
	South Africa	(1992)			
	(1984)	Cape			
	Turkey (1984)	Verde (1993)			
	Venezuela (1984)	Ethiopia (1993)			
		Finland (1993)			
		Ghana (1993)			
		Mauritania			
		(1993)			
		Iran, Islamic			
		Rep. of (1993)			
		Sweden (1993)			

3. Debt Crises

1975	1982	1991	2009	1998	2001
Dem. Rep. of Congo (1976)	Bolivia (1980)	Cameroon (1989)	Hong Kong SAR (2008)	Russia (1998)	Hong Kong SAR (1999)
Sierra Leone (1977)	Liberia (1980)	Jordan (1989)	Ireland (2008)		Indonesia (1999)
	Nicaragua (1980)	Trinidad and Tobago (1989)	Greece (2009)		Argentina (2001)
	Costa Rica (1981)	Albania (1990)	Spain (2010)		Côte d'Ivoire (2001)
	Madagascar (1981)	Bulgaria (1990)	Portugal (2011)		Dominica (2002)
	Honduras (1981)	Iran, Islamic Rep. of (1992)	Cyprus (2012)		Gabon (2002)
	Poland (1981)				Moldova (2002)
	Uganda (1981)				Uruguay (2002)
	Argentina (1982)				Dominican Rep. (2003)
	Dominican Rep. (1982)				
	Ecuador (1982)				
	Guyana (1982)				
	Malawi (1982)				
	Mexico (1982)				
	Paraguay (1982)				
	Romania (1982)				
	Venezuela (1982)				
	Brazil (1983)				
	Chile (1983)				
	Morocco (1983)				
	Niger (1983)				
	Nigeria (1983)				
	Panama (1983)				
	Philippines (1983)				
	Uruguay (1983)				
	Yugoslavia (1983)				
	Zambia (1983)				
	Côte d'Ivoire (1984)				
	Mozambique (1984)				
	Tanzania (1984)				

Note: Crises that are three years before and after the global recessions and downturns are reported. The crises dates are from Laeven and Valencia (2008, 2012).

Appendix E. Timeline: Selected Events around Global Recessions and Recoveries

1975 GLOBAL RECESSION

A. End of the Gold Standard

1971

- August 15: Exit of the United States from the Bretton Woods gold standard system; suspension of the convertibility of dollars into gold; end of the system of fixed bilateral exchange rates established at Bretton Woods in 1944 (*The Economist* 1971)

B. 1973–74 Oil Embargo

1973

- October 6–26: Yom Kippur/Ramadan war between a coalition of Arab states and Israel (BBC News 1973)
- October 16: Start of an oil embargo by the Arab members of the Organization of the Petroleum Exporting Countries against countries siding with Israel during the war; the price of oil quadruples, adversely affecting oil importers; massive oil exporter windfall profits and flow of most of the windfall into the U.S. banking system (*The Guardian* 1973)

1974

- January 1: Tripling of oil prices in one month; imposition of U.K. Prime Minister Edward Heath's "three-day-week," a measure to reduce electricity consumption in the United Kingdom (*The Economist* 1974c)
- March 17: End of the oil embargo, following the resolution of the Arab-Israeli war (*The Economist* 1974d)

C. Synchronized Recessions in Advanced Economies

1974

- Recessions in Austria, Belgium, Denmark, France, Germany, Greece, Italy, Portugal, Spain, Switzerland, United States, and United Kingdom

D. Stagflation

1973–75

- Period of "stagflation" in a number of advanced economies during 1973–75 (*The Economist* 1973)

1982 GLOBAL RECESSION

A. 1978–80 Second Oil Crisis

1978

- August–December: Strikes and demonstrations in the Islamic Republic of Iran; spread of the strikes to the oil sector and reduction of oil production; increase in oil production by Saudi Arabia and other countries to partly offset the lost Iranian production (*The Economist* 1978a, 1978b)

1979

- January 16: Change in the political regime in the Islamic Republic of Iran (*The Economist* 1979a)
- Further decline in oil production by the Islamic Republic of Iran; more than tripling of oil prices between August 1978 and November 1979 (*The Economist* 1979b)

1980

- September 22: Beginning of the Iran-Iraq war; adverse effects of the war on oil production and increase in oil prices (*The Economist* 1980a)
- Inflation at new highs in several advanced economies—13.5 percent in the United States and 17 percent in the United Kingdom in 1980 (*The Economist* 1980b)

B. Tight Monetary Policies

1979

- October: Introduction of explicit targeting of money supply by the Federal Reserve and application of measures to limit credit expansion to fight inflation expectations; discount rate rises to 12 percent (*The Economist* 1979c)

1981

- Federal funds rate is raised to about 18–20 percent to curb inflation in the United States (*The Economist* 1981b)

1980–82

- Introduction of measures to deregulate the thrift industry (which includes institutions that accept deposits); deposit insurance coverage per account raised from $40,000 to $100,000; phaseout of Regulation Q deposit rate ceilings; deregulation of U.S. savings and loan associations to allow commercial lending; banks permitted to offer adjustable rate mortgages (Robinson 2013)

C. Double-Dip Recession in the United States

1980

- January: Beginning of the U.S. recession following contractionary monetary policies and high oil prices (*The Economist* 2010)

1981

- July: Beginning of the second U.S. recession; previous recession ended in July 1980 (NBER 2010)

D. Synchronized Recessions in Advanced Economies

1980–82

- Recessions in Australia, Austria, Belgium, Canada, Denmark, Finland, France, Germany, Greece, Ireland, Italy, Netherlands, New Zealand, Norway, Portugal, Spain, Sweden, Switzerland, United States, and United Kingdom

E. Less-Developed-Countries (LDC) Debt Crisis

1982

- Accumulation of $327 billion in Latin American debt by U.S. commercial banks (FDIC 1997)
- Financial crises in Argentina, Bolivia, Chile, Costa Rica, Dominican Republic, Ecuador, Guyana, Honduras, Mexico, Nicaragua, Panama, Paraguay, Uruguay, and Venezuela (Laeven and Valencia 2008, 2013)
- August 12: Mexican default on sovereign debt (following falling world oil prices, rising world interest rates, and a reversal of capital flows); rescheduled debt by 16 Latin American and 11 other countries (Rabobank 2013; Sims 2013)

1983–89

- Restructuring of LDC sovereign debt; increase in banks' loan-loss reserves and recognition of losses on their LDC loans; introduction of the Brady Plan in 1989, leading to permanent reduction in loan principal and debt-service obligations of the debtor countries, which agreed to reform their economies and strengthen their debt-service capacity (Sims 2013)

1991 GLOBAL RECESSION

A. Asset Price Busts

1987

- October 19 (Black Monday): Sharp declines in stock markets around the world beginning in Hong Kong SAR and spreading to Australia, Canada, New Zealand, Spain, United Kingdom, and United States (Carlson 2006; Goodley 2012)

1990–92

- End of the commercial real estate construction boom in the United States (*The Economist* 1990)
- Sharp fall in Japanese stock markets starting in 1990 and collapse by 1992; severe drop in land prices (Kanaya and Woo 2000)

B. Banking Crises

1986–95

- Savings and loan crisis: The number of federally insured thrift institutions (savings and loan associations that accept savings deposits and offer mortgages and other loans) in the United States declines from 3,234 to 1,645, with total asset failure of more than $500 billion (Curry and Shibut 2000)

Late 1980s–early 1990s

- Nordic crises: Banking crises in Finland, Norway, and Sweden starting in 1991; currency crises in Finland and Sweden starting in 1993 and in Iceland starting in 1989; the first systemic crisis in advanced economies since the 1930s (Laeven and Valencia 2008)

C. European Exchange Rate Mechanism (ERM) Crisis

1990

- Expansionary fiscal policies by the German government following the reunification of East and West Germany; tightening monetary policy by the Bundesbank in an attempt to control runaway inflation (Bayer and others 2009)

1992

- September 13: Devaluation of the Italian lira by 7 percent against other currencies in participating ERM countries (Mitchener 1992)
- September 16 (Black Wednesday): Speculative attack on the British pound; increase of interest rates to 12 percent by the Bank of England and extensive use of foreign currency reserves to prop up the pound; fall of the pound below its minimum level in the ERM; exit of the United Kingdom from the ERM (BBC News 1992)
- September 16: Exit of Italy from the ERM; devaluation of the Spanish peseta by 5 percent within the ERM; defense of the Irish pound by the Central Bank of Ireland through overnight interest rate increase to 300 percent (Buiter, Corsetti, and Pesenti 1998)
- September 23: Speculative attacks on the French franc; despite successful containment of the attack by the Banque de France, loss of 80 billion francs in reserves and increase in the French repo rate to 13 percent; heavy Bundesbank interventions in support of the franc (Buiter, Corsetti, and Pesenti 1998)

1993

- ERM aftershocks: Resumption of speculation against the franc in late June and July 1993; attacks against the Belgian franc and Austrian shilling; widening of ERM bands from 4.5 percent to plus or minus 15 percent to end the new speculative attacks (Buiter, Corsetti, and Pesenti 1998)

D. Synchronized Recessions in Advanced Economies

1990–92

- Recessions in Australia, Austria, Belgium, Canada, Denmark, Finland, France, Germany, Greece, Italy, New Zealand, Portugal, Spain, Sweden, Switzerland, United Kingdom, and United States

E. Persian Gulf War

1990

- August 2: Invasion of Kuwait by Iraq; international quarantine of Iraq in mid-August for its conquest of Kuwait (BBC News 1990; *New York Times* 1990)
- November 29: Authorization by United Nations Security Council of use of force against Iraq barring withdrawal from Kuwait by January 15, 1991 (United Nations 1990)

1991

- January 17–February 28: Defeat of Iraqi forces after war between the coalition and Iraqi forces; liberation of Kuwait (*USA Today* 1996)
- Rise in oil prices by more than 35 percent between July 1990 and February 1991

F. Transition of Eastern European Economies

1989–92

- November 9, 1989: Fall of the Berlin Wall (BBC News 1989)
- Beginning of transition process: Construction of democratic institutions and market-oriented economies in eastern European countries after dissolution of the Soviet Union (Office of the Historian 2013)

2009 GLOBAL RECESSION

A. Financial Sector Problems

2007

- August 9: Freeze of three investment funds of France's largest bank, BNP Paribas, following problems calculating the value of their holdings of subprime loans (*New York Times* 2007)
- September 14: Bank run on one of largest U.K. mortgage lenders, Northern Rock, and liquidity support from the Bank of England (Wallop 2007; Shin 2009)

2008

- February 17: Nationalization of Northern Rock by the U.K. Treasury (Desai and Jones 2008)
- March 14–24: Sale of Bear Stearns to JPMorgan with the backing of the Federal Reserve (Goldstein 2008)
- Increase in oil prices to $133 a barrel in July from $53 a barrel in January 2007
- September 7: Bailout by the U.S. Treasury of Fannie Mae and Freddie Mac, the two largest mortgage financing companies in the United States (Sommerville 2008)
- September 15: Chapter 12 bankruptcy protection filing by U.S. securities firm Lehman Brothers, under severe liquidity pressure; sale of Merrill Lynch, another large investment bank with liquidity problems, to Bank of America (Mollenkamp and others 2008)
- September 16: Bailout of American International Group (AIG), the world's largest insurance company, by the Federal Reserve (Karnitschnig and others 2008)

- September 17: Acquisition of HBOS, the U.K.'s largest mortgage lender, by Lloyds TSB (Cimilluca, Macdonald, and Munoz 2008)
- September 21: End of investment banking as Federal Reserve approves designation of Goldman Sachs and JPMorgan Chase as bank holding companies (*New York Times* 2008)
- September 25: Seizure of Washington Mutual (WaMu) by federal regulators and its sale to JPMorgan Chase (Sidel, Enrich, and Fitzpatrick 2008)
- October 3: Passage of the Emergency Economic Stabilization Act of 2008, establishing the $700 billion Troubled Asset Relief Program (TARP), by the U.S. Congress (Sahadi 2008)
- October 7–8: Failure of three major banks in Iceland with a combined balance sheet equal to several times Iceland's GDP
- October 13: Bailout of several banks, including the Royal Bank of Scotland, Lloyds TSB, and HBOS, by the U.K. government (Wearden 2008)
- November 25: Announcement of the Quantitative Easing operations by the Federal Reserve
- December 11: Announcement by the Business Cycle Dating Committee of the National Bureau of Economic Research (NBER) that the United States had been in a recession since December 2007 (NBER 2011)
- December 16: Announcement of the target range for the federal funds rate of zero to ¼ percent and start of qualitative forward guidance about future policy rates (Board of Governers of the Federal Reserve System 2008)

B. Synchronized Recessions in Advanced Economies

2007–09

- Recessions in Austria, Belgium, Canada, Denmark, Finland, France, Germany, Greece, Ireland, Italy, Japan, New Zealand, Portugal, Spain, Sweden, Switzerland, United Kingdom, and United States
- February 2009: Passage of the American Recovery and Reinvestment Act in the United States, which introduced a fiscal stimulus package of more than $780 billion in spending increases and tax relief (*New York Times* 2009)
- April 2009: Announcement of the G20 global stimulus package of $1 trillion to curb the global financial crisis (CNN 2009)
- 2008:Q1: Start of the recession in euro area (CEPR 2009)
- 2009:Q2: End of the recession in euro area (CEPR 2010)
- June 2009: End of the recession in the United States (NBER 2010)

C. Euro Area Crisis

2010

- April 27: Standard & Poor's downgrade of Greek credit rating to junk status (Reuters 2010)
- May 2: Announcement of a series of austerity measures by the Greek government to secure a multiyear loan from the European Union and the IMF (BBC News 2010a)
- November 28: Bailout of Ireland with a loan from the European Union; the IMF; and Denmark, Sweden, and the United Kingdom (BBC News 2010b)

2011

- May 5: Financial rescue package for Portugal from the European Union and the IMF (Kowsmann 2011)

- July 21: Second bailout package for Greece from the European Union, the IMF, and banks and private investors (BBC News 2011; IMF 2011b)

- August 5: Downgrade of U.S. sovereign debt by Standard & Poor's (Paletta and Phillips 2011)

- August 7: Announcement by the European Central Bank (ECB) of purchase of Italian and Spanish government bonds (Carrell 2011)

- 2011:Q3: Start of the recession in euro area (CEPR 2012)

- October 4–18: Downgrades of credit ratings of Italy and Spain by the three main rating agencies (Totaro and Ross-Thomas 2011)

2012

- June 25: Bailout request by Cyprus, making it the fifth euro area country to seek international help (Reuters 2012)

- July 26: Speech by Mario Draghi, president of the ECB, on the ECB's readiness to do whatever is needed to preserve the euro (Bloomberg News 2012)

- Recessions in Austria, Belgium, Cyprus, Estonia, Finland, France, Germany, Greece, Ireland, Italy, Malta, Netherlands, Portugal, Slovenia, Spain, and United Kingdom

D. A Brief List of Events during 2013–15

2013

- February 1: Dow Jones Industrial Average rises above 14,000 for the first time since October 2007.

- April 5: The Bank of Japan announces policies aimed at increasing inflation to 2 percent within two years.

- May 21: After the Federal Reserve Chairman says the Fed could stop its bond-buying program (known as QE) over the next two Federal Open Market Committee meetings if economic conditions continued to improve, global financial markets react sharply. Several emerging market economies saw their currencies depreciate, equity markets drop, and capital flows reverse.

- December 18: The Federal Reserve announces it will end its QE program in 2014.

2014

- June 5: European Central Bank launches bold measures including negative interest rate to boost euro area growth and inflation.

- June 19: Brent oil price reaches $115 a barrel for the first time since September 2013.

- October 29: The Federal Reserve ends its QE program.

- October 31: The Bank of Japan increases its annual asset purchases target by between 15 and 33 percent.

- November 17: Japan's economy slips back into recession.

- November 27: Morgan Stanley Country Index (MSCI) demotes Greece to emerging market status.
- November 27: The Organization of the Petroleum Exporting Countries (OPEC) decides to maintain its production target of 30 million barrels a day, established in December 2011, unchanged despite the sharp drop in oil prices.
- December 23: U.S. economy posts strongest growth in more than a decade.

2015

- January 12: Brent crude oil prices fall below $50 a barrel, a six-year low (almost a 60 percent drop since oil prices started to fall in June 2014 (Baffes and others 2015).
- January 15: The Swiss National Bank abandons its policy instituted in 2011 of capping the Swiss franc vis-à-vis the euro (at Sfr 1.20 to the euro).
- January 22: The European Central Bank announces an aggressive quantitative easing plan. The bank plans to buy up bonds worth up to 60 billion euros a month for at least 19 months.
- January 25: Elections in Greece bring a radical left party (Syriza) to power. The new government announces plans to renegotiate the bailout program with its creditors, increase the minimum wage, hire additional government employees, cancel privatization plans, and provide free food and electricity to the poor.
- February 20: The new government of Greece and its creditors agree on an extension of the second bailout program to the end of June.
- March 2: The Nasdaq tops the 5,000 level for the first time in 15 years.
- March 9: The European Central Bank starts its bond-buying (QE) program.
- March 21: The U.S. dollar rises 22 percent over the past year (its fastest climb in decades) against a basket of widely used currencies.
- April 27: Fitch downgrades Japan's credit rating over fiscal concerns.
- May 8: U.S. unemployment rate falls to 5.4 percent in April, a seven-year low.
- May 12: Greece makes IMF debt payment after using its own emergency account in the Fund.
- July 12: The Chinese stock markets plunge by more than 1/3 from their peaks in mid-June.
- July 14: IMF report finds that Greece's public debt is unsustainable.
- August 14: Europe agrees on new bailout terms for Greece.
- August 24: China has its own "Black Monday": the Shanghai Composite Index closes down 8.5 percent and is followed by significant losses in global stock markets.
- August 28: Brazil enters recession after activity contracts 1.9 percent in the second quarter.
- September 4: The U.S. unemployment rate falls to 5.1 percent in August, a seven year low.
- September 9: Standard & Poor's downgrades Brazil's sovereign credit rating to "junk" status.
- September 17: The Federal Reserve keeps its policy interest rate close to zero citing concerns about global economic and financial developments.

Appendix F. Global Recessions: Regional Country Groups

Global Recessions: Regional Country Groups

	Average 1972–74	1975	Average 1979–81	1982	Average 1988–90	1991	Average 2006–08	2009	Average All Global Recessions	Average Non-Recession Years 1960–2012	Average 1960–2012	Average Three Years Before
Emerging Asia												
Total output (PW)	5.75	7.14	5.50	5.68	7.35	6.76	9.20	6.18	6.44	6.73	6.71	6.95
Total output (MW)	5.54	7.08	5.69	5.72	7.41	7.04	8.66	5.66	6.38	6.80	6.77	6.83
Per capita output (PW)	3.42	5.05	3.68	3.77	5.60	5.12	8.21	5.23	4.79	5.04	5.02	5.23
Per capita output (MW)	3.22	4.99	3.87	3.80	5.66	5.40	7.67	4.71	4.73	5.12	5.09	5.10
Developing Asia												
Total output (PW)	2.97	3.63	5.14	5.55	4.79	5.01	6.56	3.79	4.50	5.00	4.96	4.86
Total output (MW)	2.63	3.48	4.61	5.71	4.29	4.63	6.44	3.75	4.39	4.83	4.80	4.49
Per capita output (PW)	0.32	1.61	1.65	3.36	2.52	2.94	5.05	1.51	2.35	1.47	1.54	2.39
Per capita output (MW)	−0.02	1.46	1.11	3.51	2.02	2.56	4.93	1.46	2.25	1.30	1.37	2.01
Latin America and the Caribbean												
Total output (PW)	7.90	3.45	4.78	−0.66	1.03	3.83	5.20	−1.56	1.27	4.19	3.96	4.73
Total output (MW)	7.03	2.63	4.32	−1.11	0.55	3.68	5.08	−1.65	0.89	4.00	3.76	4.24
Per capita output (PW)	5.28	0.44	2.78	−2.86	−0.92	1.98	3.91	−2.90	−0.84	2.10	1.87	2.76
Per capita output (MW)	4.41	−0.39	2.32	−3.31	−1.40	1.83	3.78	−2.99	−1.21	1.92	1.68	2.28

Note: All variables are in annual frequency. The "Average Three Years Before" column reflects the average of the three years before global recessions. PW denotes that a variable is the purchasing-power-parity-weighted average of the same variable of each country and MW denotes that a variable is the market-weighted average of the same variable of each country. The 1991 recession lasted until 1993 with market weights; all other recessions lasted one year. See Appendix B for the list of countries in each region. Regional aggregates are the weighted sum of the respective variables of the countries in each region.

Global Recessions: Regional Country Groups (continued)

	Average 1972–74	1975	Average 1979–81	1982	Average 1988–90	1991	Average 2006–08	2009	Average All Global Recessions	Average Non-Recession Years 1960–2012	Average 1960–2012	Average Three Years Before
Middle East and North Africa												
Total output (PW)	11.38	5.16	0.85	2.63	4.72	7.59	5.27	3.00	4.60	5.06	5.02	5.55
Total output (MW)	10.11	5.44	0.67	0.70	4.39	6.73	5.44	2.38	3.81	4.31	4.27	5.15
Per capita output (PW)	8.53	2.39	−2.22	−0.67	2.27	4.80	3.14	0.81	1.83	2.32	2.28	2.93
Per capita output (MW)	7.26	2.66	−2.40	−2.60	1.95	3.94	3.31	0.18	1.05	1.58	1.54	2.53
Sub-Saharan Africa												
Total output (PW)	4.96	2.05	5.37	0.53	3.45	0.35	5.72	2.79	1.43	4.06	3.86	4.88
Total output (MW)	4.75	1.58	5.25	0.05	2.81	0.09	5.35	2.56	1.07	3.71	3.51	4.54
Per capita output (PW)	2.44	−0.76	2.83	−2.52	−0.01	−2.61	3.28	0.29	−1.40	1.25	1.05	2.13
Per capita output (MW)	2.22	−1.22	2.70	−3.00	−0.66	−2.86	2.91	0.06	−1.76	0.90	0.70	1.79
Emerging Europe and CIS												
Total output (PW)	5.90	5.37	2.21	2.76	2.32	−6.14	6.52	−4.76	−0.69	3.89	3.54	4.24
Total output (MW)	5.69	5.13	2.54	3.19	2.64	−5.85	6.24	−5.02	−0.64	3.66	3.33	4.28
Per capita output (PW)	4.80	4.20	1.56	1.92	1.78	−6.84	6.16	−5.29	−1.50	3.07	2.72	3.58
Per capita output (MW)	4.59	3.96	1.90	2.35	2.10	−6.55	5.88	−5.55	−1.45	2.83	2.50	3.62

Note: All variables are in annual frequency. The "Average Three Years Before" column reflects the average of the three years before global recessions. PW denotes that a variable is the purchasing-power-parity-weighted average of the same variable for each country and MW denotes that a variable is the market-weighted average of the same variable for each country. The 1991 recession lasted until 1993 with market weights; all other recessions lasted one year. See Appendix B for the list of countries in each region. Regional aggregates are the weighted sum of the respective variables of the countries in each region.

Appendix G. Sensitivity of Global Activity Variables

Sensitivity of Global Activity Variables

	Consumption	Investment	Industrial Production	Trade
Purchasing-power-parity-weighted per capita output	0.777 [0.076]	2.228 [0.139]	2.440 [0.202]	2.454 [0.261]
Market-weighted per capita output	0.771 [0.079]	1.985 [0.144]	2.479 [0.203]	2.440 [0.251]

Note: Each cell represents the sensitivity of the respective activity variable to changes in global output. The sensitivities of world consumption per capita, investment, industrial production, and trade to changes in global output are computed by estimating a basic regression of the growth rates of each of these variables on the growth rate of world GDP per capita (measured in purchasing-power-parity and market-weighted terms). All coefficients are statistically significant at the 1 percent level.

Appendix H. Global Recoveries: Regional Country Groups

Global Recoveries: Regional Country Groups *(percent change unless otherwise noted)*

	1976	Average 1976–78	1983	Average 1983–85	1992	Average 1992–94	2010	Average 2010–12	Average of First Years	Average 1960–2012 Non-Recession Years	Average 1960–2012
Emerging Asia											
Total output (PW)	4.45	6.68	7.77	7.62	8.53	8.98	9.80	7.69	7.64	7.74	6.71
Total output (MW)	3.82	6.50	7.89	7.92	8.02	8.54	9.72	7.66	7.36	7.66	6.77
Per capita output (PW)	2.77	4.87	6.00	5.84	6.97	7.42	8.82	6.73	6.14	6.22	5.02
Per capita output (MW)	2.13	4.69	6.12	6.14	6.46	6.99	8.75	6.70	5.87	6.13	5.09
Developing Asia											
Total output (PW)	4.90	5.28	5.69	5.67	7.16	5.46	5.32	5.22	5.76	5.41	4.96
Total output (MW)	6.14	5.87	5.71	5.74	6.93	5.24	5.31	5.24	6.03	5.52	4.80
Per capita output (PW)	2.58	2.89	3.29	3.28	4.84	3.14	3.76	3.68	3.62	3.25	1.54
Per capita output (MW)	3.83	3.48	3.31	3.35	4.62	2.92	3.75	3.71	3.88	3.36	1.37
Latin America and the Caribbean											
Total output (PW)	5.64	4.95	−2.50	1.45	3.30	4.05	6.15	4.51	3.15	3.74	3.96
Total output (MW)	4.33	4.36	−2.19	1.05	3.42	4.21	6.08	4.28	2.91	3.47	3.76
Per capita output (PW)	3.13	2.51	−4.67	−0.65	1.52	2.32	4.92	3.30	1.22	1.87	1.87
Per capita output (MW)	1.81	1.92	−4.36	−1.04	1.64	2.48	4.85	3.07	0.99	1.61	1.68

Note: The "Average of First Years" column reflects the average of the first year following the global recession. PW denotes that a variable is the purchasing-power-parity-weighted average of the same variable for each country and MW denotes that a variable is the market-weighted average of the same variable for each country. See Appendix B for the list of countries in each region. Regional aggregates are the weighted sum of the respective variables of the countries in each region.

Global Recoveries: Regional Country Groups *(percent change unless otherwise noted) (continued)*

	1976	Average 1976–78	1983	Average 1983–85	1992	Average 1992–94	2010	Average 2010–12	Average of First Years	Average 1960–2012 Non-Recession Years	Average 1960–2012
Middle East and North Africa											
Total output (PW)	12.24	7.08	2.31	2.38	3.53	1.91	5.32	4.45	5.85	3.95	5.02
Total output (MW)	12.39	7.16	0.96	1.51	3.33	1.91	5.21	4.58	5.47	3.79	4.27
Per capita output (PW)	9.88	4.15	−1.05	−1.01	−1.27	−0.96	3.33	4.58	2.72	1.69	2.28
Per capita output (MW)	10.03	4.23	−2.41	−1.88	−1.47	−0.97	3.22	4.72	2.34	1.53	1.54
Sub-Saharan Africa											
Total output (PW)	6.03	2.08	−1.09	1.25	−0.88	0.99	5.13	4.62	2.30	2.23	3.86
Total output (MW)	4.94	1.71	−1.52	1.02	−1.15	0.86	4.98	4.42	1.81	2.00	3.51
Per capita output (PW)	3.27	−0.77	−4.07	−1.75	−3.73	−1.70	2.68	2.48	−0.46	−0.43	1.05
Per capita output (MW)	2.18	−1.14	−4.51	−1.98	−4.00	−1.83	2.53	2.28	−0.95	−0.67	0.70
Emerging Europe and Commonwealth of Independent States											
Total output (PW)	6.55	5.64	4.12	3.15	−8.77	−6.20	4.71	4.08	1.65	1.67	3.54
Total output (MW)	6.47	5.52	4.19	3.15	−8.34	−4.66	4.72	4.13	1.76	2.03	3.33
Per capita output (PW)	5.48	4.57	2.73	2.08	−9.15	−6.35	3.99	3.55	0.76	0.96	2.72
Per capita output (MW)	5.40	4.45	2.80	2.08	−8.72	−4.80	4.00	3.60	0.87	1.33	2.50

Note: The "Average of First Years" column reflects the average of the first year following the global recession. PW denotes that a variable is the purchasing-power-parity-weighted average of the same variable for each country and MW denotes that a variable is the market-weighted average of the same variable for each country. See Appendix B for the list of countries in each region. Regional aggregates are the weighted sum of the respective variables of the countries in each region.

Appendix I. Uncertainty, Business Cycles, and Growth

1. Uncertainty over the Business Cycle

	Country-Specific Uncertainty	Uncertainty in the United States	Economic Policy Uncertainty	Global Uncertainty
Recession	1.29***	24.12***	134.59***	1.61***
	[0.08]	[0.50]	[2.78]	[0.18]
Expansion	0.93***	19.03***	100.56***	−0.24***
	[0.03]	[0.06]	[0.51]	[0.02]
Number of observations	3,138	4,158	2,268	4,347
Number of economies	21	21	21	21
R^2 adjusted	0.77	0.89	0.92	0.07
Test (P values)				
h0: Recession coefficient = Expansion coefficient	0.00	0.00	0.00	0.00

Note: The dependent variable is the level of uncertainty. Recessions and expansions in regressions refer to dummy variables taking the values of 1 and 0 when the economy is in recession and expansion, respectively. The periods of recession and expansion are defined following Claessens, Kose, and Terrones 2012. Country-specific uncertainty refers to the monthly standard deviation of daily stock returns in each country. Uncertainty in the United States refers to the Chicago Board Options Exchange VXO index, which is calculated from S&P 100 calls and puts. The policy uncertainty measure is an index of economic policy uncertainty for the United States from Baker, Bloom, and Davis 2012. Global uncertainty is the estimated dynamic common factor of the first measure using the series for Italy, Japan, and the United States (these countries have series of stock market indices since 1960). These regressions test whether the levels of uncertainty observed during recession periods are different than those during expansions. For all measures of uncertainty, there is evidence that uncertainty levels are higher during recessions than during expansions. Moreover, these differences are statistically significant. The last row of the table suggests that the null hypothesis, which postulates that there is no difference in the levels of uncertainty during the two phases of the cycle, can be rejected at a 1 percent level. *** denotes that the coefficients are statistically significant at the 1 percent level.

2. Uncertainty and Growth

	Output				Consumption				Investment			
	(1)	(2)	(3)	(4)	(1)	(2)	(3)	(4)	(1)	(2)	(3)	(4)
Country-specific uncertainty	-0.65* [0.37]				-0.23 [0.38]				-1.18 [0.99]			
Uncertainty in the United States		-0.18*** [0.01]				-0.12*** [0.01]				-0.41*** [0.06]		
Economic policy uncertainty			-0.01*** [0.00]				-0.01** [0.00]				-0.02** [0.01]	
Global uncertainty				-0.46*** [0.03]				-0.31*** [0.04]				-0.87*** [0.164]
Number of observations	3,117	4,157	2,267	4,283	3,115	4,155	2,265	4,281	3,111	4,041	2,265	4,123
Number of economies	21	21	21	21	21	21	21	21	21	21	21	21
R^2 adjusted	0.42	0.38	0.44	0.38	0.09	0.13	0.06	0.13	0.31	0.25	0.35	0.25

Note: Dependent variable is the year-over-year growth of the respective macroeconomic aggregates. All specifications include country and time fixed effects. See notes to table 1 in this appendix for explanations of uncertainty measures. *, **, *** denote significance at the 10 percent, 5 percent, and 1 percent levels, respectively.

Appendix J. Linkages between the Global Cycle and National Cycles

1. Linkages between Global and National Cycles: All Countries

	Global Recessions			Global Expansions			Full Sample				
	(1)	(2)	(3)	(4)	(5)	(6)	(7)	(8)	(9)	(10)	(11)
Output growth (lagged)	0.395***	0.370***	0.411***	0.285***	0.291***	0.282***	0.289***	0.293***	0.286***	0.286***	0.287***
	[0.071]	[0.075]	[0.077]	[0.039]	[0.040]	[0.039]	[0.037]	[0.038]	[0.037]	[0.037]	[0.037]
Rest of the world output growth	1.373***		1.463***	0.728***		0.717***	0.725***		0.717***	0.735***	0.714***
	[0.232]		[0.248]	[0.060]		[0.061]	[0.060]		[0.060]	[0.061]	[0.060]
Rest of the world output growth × Global recession dummy							0.507**		0.422*		0.557**
							[0.236]		[0.233]		[0.244]
Real LIBOR rate		−0.005	0.081		−0.135***	−0.117***		−0.135***	−0.091***	−0.117***	−0.117***
		[0.063]	[0.067]		[0.033]	[0.034]		[0.033]	[0.032]	[0.034]	[0.034]
Real LIBOR rate × Global recession dummy								0.113*		0.131**	0.159***
								[0.057]		[0.058]	[0.060]
Global recession dummy							0.089	−2.864***	−0.022	−0.527*	−0.231
							[0.315]	[0.279]	[0.312]	[0.274]	[0.312]
Constant	−0.002	−0.970***	−0.112	−0.013	2.065***	0.262	−0.016	2.060***	0.2	0.21	0.258
	[0.173]	[0.204]	[0.209]	[0.187]	[0.114]	[0.205]	[0.178]	[0.105]	[0.200]	[0.200]	[0.196]
Number of observations	382	382	382	4,197	4,197	4,197	4,579	4,579	4,579	4,579	4,579
Number of economies	97	97	97	97	97	97	97	97	97	97	97
R^2 adjusted	0.15	0.096	0.152	0.133	0.101	0.136	0.16	0.13	0.16	0.16	0.16

Note: The dependent variable is the growth rate of per capita real GDP in each country. LIBOR = London interbank offered rate. Robust and clustered standard errors in brackets. All regressions include fixed effects. ***, **, * denote significance at the 1 percent, 5 percent, and 10 percent levels, respectively.

2. Linkages between Global and National Cycles: Country Groups

	Advanced Economies					Emerging Market Economies						Other Developing Economies			
	(1)	(2)	(3)	(4)	(5)	(6)	(7)	(8)	(9)	(10)	(11)	(12)	(13)	(14)	(15)
Output growth (lagged)	0.291*** [0.077]	0.269*** [0.078]	0.258*** [0.077]	0.270*** [0.077]	0.260*** [0.077]	0.276*** [0.043]	0.275*** [0.041]	0.271*** [0.043]	0.270*** [0.043]	0.271*** [0.043]	0.292*** [0.057]	0.291*** [0.058]	0.281*** [0.057]	0.282*** [0.056]	0.282*** [0.057]
Rest of the world output growth	0.660*** [0.068]		0.683*** [0.067]	0.724*** [0.073]	0.681*** [0.067]	0.693*** [0.089]		0.684*** [0.088]	0.709*** [0.093]	0.682*** [0.088]	0.778*** [0.109]		0.759*** [0.110]	0.760*** [0.110]	0.755*** [0.110]
Rest of the world output growth × Global recession dummy	0.925*** [0.304]		1.232*** [0.313]		1.328*** [0.326]	0.730* [0.393]		0.602 [0.385]		0.691 [0.411]	0.187 [0.430]		-0.028 [0.421]		0.156 [0.435]
Real LIBOR rate		0.213*** [0.025]	0.252*** [0.028]	0.234*** [0.027]	0.235*** [0.027]		-0.185*** [0.052]	-0.153*** [0.046]	-0.172*** [0.052]	-0.173*** [0.052]		-0.267*** [0.046]	-0.212*** [0.046]	-0.246*** [0.047]	-0.247*** [0.047]
Real LIBOR rate × Global recession dummy		0.012 [0.100]		0.032 [0.103]	0.103 [0.107]		0.066 [0.100]		0.087 [0.101]	0.12 [0.106]		0.188** [0.091]		0.203** [0.091]	0.211** [0.094]
Global recession dummy	-0.525 [0.566]	-3.300*** [0.429]	-0.223 [0.575]	-0.996* [0.512]	-0.354 [0.612]	0.365 [0.594]	-2.628*** [0.474]	0.193 [0.593]	-0.357 [0.501]	0.03 [0.568]	0.21 [0.479]	-2.825*** [0.476]	-0.052 [0.475]	-0.41 [0.424]	-0.327 [0.475]
Constant	0.197 [0.246]	1.464*** [0.164]	-0.315 [0.240]	-0.41 [0.238]	-0.28 [0.236]	0.614** [0.236]	2.729*** [0.182]	0.975*** [0.263]	0.955*** [0.268]	1.018*** [0.262]	-0.530* [0.290]	1.944*** [0.133]	-0.029 [0.342]	0.037 [0.337]	0.051 [0.333]
Number of observations	1,050	1,050	1,050	1,050	1,050	1,432	1,432	1,432	1,432	1,432	2,097	2,097	2,097	2,097	2,097
Number of economies	21	21	21	21	21	30	30	30	30	30	46	46	46	46	46
R^2 adjusted	0.306	0.257	0.344	0.336	0.344	0.148	0.121	0.154	0.153	0.154	0.141	0.124	0.149	0.15	0.15

Note: The dependent variable is the growth rate of per capita real GDP in each country. LIBOR = London interbank offered rate. Robust and clustered standard errors in brackets. All regressions include fixed effects. ***, **, * denote significance at the 1 percent, 5 percent, and 10 percent levels, respectively.

3. Linkages between Global and National Business Cycles: Roles of Trade and Financial Integration

	(1)	(2)	(3)	(4)	(5)	(6)
Output growth (lagged)	0.265***	0.265***	0.266***	0.264***	0.265***	0.265***
	[0.0367]	[0.0366]	[0.0367]	[0.0368]	[0.0369]	[0.0368]
Rest of the world output growth	0.774***	0.567***	0.520***	0.772***	0.659***	0.512***
	[0.0565]	[0.0792]	[0.0748]	[0.0568]	[0.0569]	[0.0752]
Real LIBOR rate	−0.123***	−0.123***	−0.142***	−0.159***	−0.192***	−0.191***
	[0.0351]	[0.0351]	[0.0359]	[0.0417]	[0.0436]	[0.0433]
Trade openness (lagged)	1.204**	0.666	0.985	1.166**	1.397**	0.948
	[0.584]	[0.605]	[0.621]	[0.564]	[0.593]	[0.599]
Financial openness (lagged)	−0.249***	−0.264***	−0.253***	−0.232***	−0.218***	−0.231***
	[0.0479]	[0.0525]	[0.0501]	[0.0512]	[0.0498]	[0.0537]
Rest of the world output growth × Trade openness		0.272***	0.210***			0.208***
		[0.0837]	[0.0670]			[0.0667]
Rest of the world output growth × Global recession dummy			0.875***		1.103***	0.925***
			[0.302]		[0.319]	[0.305]
Real LIBOR rate × Global recession dummy			0.157**		0.196***	0.182**
			[0.0725]		[0.0739]	[0.0739]
Real LIBOR rate × Financial openness				0.0292*	0.0380**	0.0377**
				[0.0169]	[0.0177]	[0.0174]
Global recession dummy			−0.145		−0.127	−0.192
			[0.386]		[0.389]	[0.386]
Constant	−0.344	0.0881	0.120	−0.330	−0.179	0.154
	[0.419]	[0.428]	[0.441]	[0.404]	[0.418]	[0.421]
Number of observations	3,465	3,465	3,465	3,465	3,465	3,465
Number of economies	97	97	97	97	97	97
R^2 adjusted	0.603	0.597	0.570	0.610	0.555	0.564

Note: The dependent variable is the growth rate of per capita real GDP in each country. LIBOR = London interbank offered rate. Robust and clustered standard errors in brackets. All regressions include fixed effects. ***,**,* denote significance at the 1 percent, 5 percent, and 10 percent levels, respectively.

Bibliography

Abberger, K., and W. Nierhaus. 2008. "How to Define a Recession?" *CESifo Forum* 4: 74–76.

Abiad, A., R. Balakrishnan, P. Koeva Brooks, D. Leigh, and I. Tytell. 2009. "What's the Damage? Medium-term Output Dynamics after Banking Crises." IMF Working Paper 09/245. International Monetary Fund, Washington.

Abiad, A., D. Furceri, and P. Topalova. 2015. "The Macroeconomic Effects of Public Investment: Evidence from Advanced Economies." IMF Working Paper 15/95. International Monetary Fund.

Acosta, P. A., E. K. K. Lartey, and F. S. Mandelman. 2009. "Remittances and the Dutch Disease." *Journal of International Economics* 79 (1): 102–16.

Adrian, T., and H. S. Shin. 2008. "Liquidity, Monetary Policy, and Financial Cycles." Federal Reserve Bank of New York *Current Issues in Economics and Finance* 14 (1): 1–7.

Ahmed, S., A. Levin, and B. A. Wilson. 2004. "Recent U.S. Macroeconomic Stability: Good Policies, Good Practices, or Good Luck?" *Review of Economics and Statistics* 86 (3): 824–32.

Aiolfi, M., L. A. V. Catão, and A. Timmermann. 2011. "Common Factors in Latin America's Business Cycles." *Journal of Development Economics* 95 (2): 212–28.

Akin, C., and M. A. Kose. 2008. "Changing Nature of North-South Linkages: Stylized Facts and Explanations." *Journal of Asian Economics* 19: 1–28.

Alesina, A. 2012. "Fiscal Policy after the Great Recession." *Atlantic Economic Journal* 40 (4): 429–35.

Alesina A., and S. Ardagna. 2010. "Large Changes in Fiscal Policy: Taxes versus Spending." *Tax Policy and the Economy* 24: 35–68.

Alesina, A., and F. Giavazzi. 2013. *Fiscal Policy after the Financial Crisis.* Chicago: University of Chicago Press and National Bureau of Economic Research.

Alessandria, G., J. P. Kaboski, and V. Midrigan. 2010. "The Great Trade Collapse of 2008–09: An Inventory Adjustment." *IMF Economic Review* 58 (2): 254–94.

Allen, R. E., 2010. *Financial Crises and Recession in the Global Economy.* Cheltenham, United Kingdom: Edward Elgar, 3rd ed.

Almunia, M., A. Benetrix, B. Eichengreen, K. O'Rourke, and G. Rua. 2010. "From Great Depression to Great Credit Crisis: Similarities, Differences, and Lessons." *Economic Policy* 25 (62): 219–65.

Altig, D., S. M. Byrne, and K. A. Samolyk. 1992. "Is Household Debt Inhibiting the Recovery?" *Economic Commentary.* Federal Reserve Bank of Cleveland.

Ambler, S., E. Cardia, and C. Zimmermann. 2004. "International Business Cycles: What Are the Facts?" *Journal of Monetary Economics* 51 (2): 257–76.

Amiti, M., and D. E. Weinstein. 2011. "Exports and Financial Shocks." *Quarterly Journal of Economics* 126 (4): 1841–77.

Angeloni, I., and J. Pisani-Ferry. 2012. "The G20: Characters in Search of an Author," Bruegel Working Paper 2012/04.

Aoki, K., J. Proudman, and G. Vlieghe. 2004. "House Prices, Consumption, and Monetary Policy: A Financial Accelerator Approach." *Journal of Financial Intermediation* 13 (4): 414–35.

Arellano, C., Y. Bai, and P. Kehoe. 2012. "Financial Markets and Fluctuations in Uncertainty." Federal Reserve Bank of Minneapolis Research Department Staff Report.

Arora, V., and A. Vamvakidis. 2004. "How Much Do Trading Partners Matter for Economic Growth?" IMF Working Paper 04/26, International Monetary Fund, Washington.

Artis, M. J., Z. G. Kontolemis, and D. R. Osborn. 1997. "Business Cycles for G-7 and European Countries." *Journal of Business* 70: 249–79.

Artis, M. J., M. Marcellino, and T. Proietti. 2003. "Dating the Euro Area Business Cycle." CEPR Discussion Paper 3696, Centre for Economic Policy Research, London.

Aslam, A., S. Beidas-Strom, M. E. Terrones, and J. Yepez. 2014. "Are Global Imbalances at a Turning Point?." *World Economic Outlook*. October. International Monetary Fund, Washington.

Atkinson, T., D. Luttrell, and H. Rosenblum. 2013. "How Bad Was It? The Costs and Consequences of the 2007–09 Financial Crisis." Federal Reserve Bank of Dallas Staff Paper No. 20.

Auerbach, A., and Y. Gorodnichenko. 2012. "Measuring the Output Responses to Fiscal Policy." *American Economic Journal—Economic Policy* 4: 1–27.

Bacchetta, P., and E. van Wincoop. 2013. "The Great Recession: A Self-Fulfilling Global Panic." NBER Working Paper 19062, National Bureau of Economic Research, Cambridge, Massachusetts.

Bachmann, R., and C. Bayer. 2011. "Uncertainty Business Cycles—Really?" NBER Working Paper 16862. National Bureau of Economic Research, Cambridge, Massachusetts.

———. 2013. "'Wait-and-See' Business Cycles?" *Journal of Monetary Economics* 60 (6): 704–19.

———. 2014. "Investment Dispersion and the Business Cycle." *American Economic Review*, 104 (4): 1392–416.

Bachmann, R., and G. Moscarini. 2011. "Business Cycles and Endogenous Uncertainty." 2011 Meeting Papers 36, Society for Economic Dynamics.

Baffes, J., M. A. Kose, F. Ohnsorge, and M. Stocker. 2015. "The Great Plunge in Oil Prices: Causes, Consequences, and Policy Responses," Policy Research Note: 1, World Bank.

Baily, M. N., and B. Bosworth. 2013. "The United States Economy: Why Such a Weak Recovery?" paper presented at the Nomura Foundation's Macro Economy Research Conference, Prospects for Growth in the World's Four Major Economies, September 11, Brookings Institution.

Baker, S., and N. Bloom. 2013. "Does Uncertainty Reduce Growth? Using Disasters as Natural Experiments." NBER Working Paper 19475, National Bureau of Economic Research, Cambridge, Massachusetts.

Baker, S., N. Bloom, B. Canes-Wrone, S. J. Davis, and J. A. Rodden. 2014. "Why Has U.S. Policy Uncertainty Risen Since 1960?" NBER Working Paper, No. 19826.

Baker, S., N. Bloom, and S. J. Davis. 2012. "The Rocky Balboa Recovery" *VoxEU,* June 20.

———. 2013. "Measuring Economic Policy Uncertainty." Stanford University Working Paper, Stanford University, Palo Alto, California.

Baldwin, R., and S. Evenett, eds. 2009. *The Collapse of Global Trade, Murky Protectionism, and the Crisis: Recommendations for the G20, VoxEU.*

Balke, N. S., and M. A. Wynne. 1995. "Recessions and Recoveries in Real Business Cycle Models," *Economic Inquiry* 33: 640–63.

Ball, L. 2014. "Long-term Damage from the Great Recession in OECD Countries," NBER Working Paper, No. 20185.

Ball, L., D. Leigh, and P. Loungani. 2013. "Okun's Law: Fit at 50?" IMF Working Paper 13/10, International Monetary Fund, Washington.

Barro, R. J. 1981. *Money, Expectations, and Business Cycles*. New York.

Barsky, R. B., and L. Kilian. 2004. "Oil and the Macroeconomy since the 1970s." *Journal of Economic Perspectives* 18 (4): 115–34.

Barth, J. R., S. Trimbath, and G. Yago. 2004. *The Savings and Loan Crisis: Lessons from a Regulatory Failure*. Milken Institute Series on Financial Innovation and Economic Growth.

Basu, S., and J. Fernald. 2000. "Why Is Productivity Procyclical? Why Do We Care?" NBER Working Paper 7940, National Bureau of Economic Research, Cambridge, Massachusetts.

Bauer, M. D., and G. D. Rudebusch. 2012. "The Signaling Channel for Federal Reserve Bond Purchases." Federal Reserve Bank of San Francisco Working Paper 2011–21.

Baumeister, C., and L. Benati. 2010. "Unconventional Monetary Policy and the Great Recession." ECB Working Paper 1258, European Central Bank, Frankfurt.

Baxter, M., and M. A. Kouparitsas. 2005. "Determinants of Business Cycle Comovement: A Robust Analysis." *Journal of Monetary Economics* 52 (1): 113–57.

Bayer, A., V. Gaspar, C. Gerberding, and M. Issing. 2009. "Opting Out of the Great Inflation: German Monetary Policy after the Break Down of Bretton Woods." ECB Working Paper 1020, European Central Bank, Frankfurt.

BBC News. 1973. "Arab States Attack Israeli Forces," October 6.

———. 1989. "Berliners Celebrate the Fall of the Wall," November 9.

———. 1990. "Iraq Invades Kuwait," August 2.

———. 1992. "UK Crashes out of ERM," September 16.

———. 2010a. "Eurozone Approves Massive Greece Bail-out," May 2.

———. 2010b. "Irish Republic 85bn Euro Bail-out Agreed," November 28.

———. 2011. "Eurozone Agrees New 109bn Euros Greek Bailout," July 21.

Beauchemin, K. R. 2011. "Not Your Father's Recovery?" FRB Cleveland *Economic Commentary* (September).

Bems, R., R. C. Johnson, and K. Yi. 2010. "Demand Spillovers and the Collapse of Trade in the Global Recession." *IMF Economic Review* 58 (2): 295–326.

———. 2012. "The Great Trade Collapse." NBER Working Paper 18632, National Bureau of Economic Research, Cambridge, Massachusetts.

Bergman, U. M., M. D. Bordo, and L. Jonung. 1998. "Historical Evidence on Business Cycles: The International Experience," in *Beyond Shocks: What Causes Business Cycles?* edited by J. C. Fuhrer and S. Schuh. Federal Reserve Bank of Boston Conference Series 42: 65–113.

Berkmen, P., G. Gelos, R. Rennhack, and J. P. Walsh. 2009. "The Global Financial Crisis: Explaining Cross-Country Differences in the Output Impact." IMF Working Paper 09/280, International Monetary Fund, Washington.

Berle, A. A., Jr. 1953. "Wesley Clair Mitchell: The Economic Scientist." *Journal of the American Statistical Association* 48 (262): 169–75.

Bernanke, B. S. 1983. "Irreversibility, Uncertainty, and Cyclical Investment." *Quarterly Journal of Economics* 98 (1): 85–106.

———. 1993. "Credit in the Macroeconomy," Federal Reserve Bank of New York *Quarterly Review* (Spring): 50–70.

———. 2004. "The Great Moderation," remarks at the meetings of the Eastern Economic Association, Washington, February 20.

———. 2012a. "Monetary Policy since the Onset of the Crisis," Federal Reserve Bank of Kansas City Economic Symposium, Jackson Hole, Wyoming.

———. 2012b. "The Economic Recovery and Economic Policy," remarks at the Economic Club of New York.

———. 2013. *The Federal Reserve and the Financial Crisis.* Princeton, New Jersey: Princeton University Press.

———. 2014. "The Federal Reserve: Looking Back, Looking Forward," speech at the Annual Meeting of the American Economic Association, Philadelphia, Pennsylvania, January 3.

———. 2015a. "Why Are Interest Rates So Low?" Ben Bernanke's Blog, Brookings Institute.

———. 2015b. "Why Are Interest Rates So Low, Part 2: Secular Stagnation" Ben Bernanke's Blog, Brookings Institute.

————. 2015c. "Why Are Interest Rates So Low, Part 3: The Global Savings Glut" Ben Bernanke's Blog, Brookings Institute.

————. 2015d. "Why Are Interest Rates So Low, Part 4: Term Premiums" Ben Bernanke's Blog, Brookings Institute.

————. 2015e. "WSJ Editorial Page Watch: The Slow-Growth Fed?" Ben Bernanke's Blog, Brookings Institute.

Bernanke, B. S., and M. Gertler. 1989. "Agency Costs, Net Worth, and Business Fluctuations," *American Economic Review* 79: 14–31.

Bernanke, B. S., and C. S. Lown. 1991. "The Credit Crunch." *Brookings Papers on Economic Activity* 2: 205–47.

Bernanke, B. S., M. Gertler, and S. Gilchrist. 1999. "The Financial Accelerator in a Quantitative Business Cycle Framework," in *Handbook of Macroeconomics* Vol. 1, edited by J. B. Taylor and M. Woodford, 1341–393.

Blanchard, O. J. 1993. "Consumption and the Recession of 1990–1991," *American Economic Review* 83 (2): 270–74.

————. 2001. "Close Encounters with Recessions of the Third Kind." *Project Syndicate*, March 12.

————. 2008. "Press Conference on the *World Economic Outlook*," October 9. http://www.imf.org/external/index.htm.

————. 2009a. "The State of Macro." *Annual Review of Economics* 1 (1): 209–28.

————. 2009b. "The Crisis: Basic Mechanism and Appropriate Policies," *CESifo Forum* 10 (1): 3–14.

————. 2009c. "(Nearly) Nothing to Fear but Fear Itself." Guest Article, *Economist*, January 29.

————. 2010. "Sustaining a Global Recovery." *Journal of Policy Modeling* 32 (5): 604–9.

————. 2013. "Rethinking Macroeconomic Policy." *VoxEU,* May 9.

Blanchard, O. J., and S. Fischer. 1989. *Lectures on Macroeconomics.* Cambridge, Massachusetts: MIT Press.

Blanchard, O. J., and D. Leigh. 2013a. "Fiscal Consolidation: At What Speed?" *VoxEU*, May 3.

————. 2013b. "Growth Forecast Errors and Fiscal Multipliers." IMF Working Paper 13/1, International Monetary Fund, Washington.

Blanchard, O. J., and G. M. Milesi-Ferretti. 2012. "(Why) Should Current Account Balances Be Reduced?" *IMF Economic Review* 60 (1): 139–50.

————. 2009. "Global Imbalances: In Midstream?" IMF Staff Position Note 09/29, International Monetary Fund, Washington.

Blanchard, O. J., and R. Perotti. 2002. "An Empirical Characterization of the Dynamic Effects of Changes in Government Spending and Taxes on Output." *Quarterly Journal of Economics* 117 (4): 1329–68.

Blanchard, O. J., and J. Simon. 2001. "The Long and Large Decline in U.S. Output Volatility." *Brookings Papers on Economic Activity* 1: 135–64.

Blanchard, O. J., and J. Viñals. 2009. "Joint Foreword to *World Economic Outlook* and *Global Financial Stability Report*." *World Economic Outlook*, April: xii–xiv. Washington: International Monetary Fund.

Blanchard, O. J., G. Dell'Ariccia, and P. Mauro. 2010. "Rethinking Macroeconomic Policy." *Journal of Money, Credit and Banking* 42 (1): 199–215.

————. 2013. "Rethinking Macroeconomic Policy II: Getting Granular." IMF Staff Discussion Note13/03, International Monetary Fund, Washington.

Blanchard, O. J., H. Faruqee, and M. Das. 2010. "The Initial Impact of the Crisis on Emerging Market Countries." *Brookings Papers on Economic Activity* (Spring): 264–323.

Blanchard, O. J., F. Jaumotte, and P. Loungani. 2013. "Labor Market Policies and IMF Advice in Advanced Economies during the Great Recession." IMF Staff Discussion Note 13/02, International Monetary Fund, Washington.

Blanchard, O. J., D. Romer, J. Stiglitz, and M. Spence. 2012. *In the Wake of the Crisis: Leading Economists Reassess Economic Policy.* Cambridge, Massachusetts: MIT Press.

Blinder, A. S. 2013. *After the Music Stopped: The Financial Crisis, the Response, and the Work Ahead.* New York: Penguin Press.

Blinder, A. S., and J. B. Rudd. 2012. "The Supply-Shock Explanation of the Great Stagflation Revisited," in *The Great Inflation: The Rebirth of Modern Central Banking.* Cambridge, Massachusetts: National Bureau of Economic Research.

Bloom, N. 2009. "The Impact of Uncertainty Shocks." *Econometrica* 77 (3): 623–85.

———. 2013. "Fluctuations in Uncertainty." NBER Working Paper 19714, National Bureau of Economic Research, Cambridge, Massachusetts.

Bloom, N., M. A. Kose, and M. E. Terrones. 2013. "Held Back by Uncertainty." *Finance & Development* 50 (1): 38–41.

Bloom, N., M. Floetotto, N. Jaimovich, I. Saporta-Eksten, and S. Terry. 2012. "Really Uncertain Business Cycles." NBER Working Paper, National Bureau of Economic Research, Cambridge, Massachusetts.

Bloomberg News. 2012. "Draghi Says ECB Will Do What's Needed to Preserve Euro," July 26.

Bluedorn, J. C., J. Decressin, and M. E. Terrones. 2013. "Do Asset Price Drops Foreshadow Recessions?" IMF Working Paper 13/203, International Monetary Fund, Washington.

Board of Governors of the Federal Reserve System. 2008. Press Release, December 16.

———. 2013. Press Release, December 18.

———. 2014. "Monetary Policy Report," February 11.

Bordo, M. D. 2012a. "Financial Recessions Don't Lead to Weak Recoveries." *Wall Street Journal*, September 27.

Bordo, M. D. 2012b. "The Great Depression and the Great Recession: What Have We Learnt?" Fourth P.R. Brahmananda Memorial Lecture in Mumbai. Reserve Bank of India.

Bordo, M. D., and J. G. Haubrich. 2012. "Deep Recessions, Fast Recoveries, and Financial Crises: Evidence from the American Record." Federal Reserve Bank of Cleveland Working Paper 12/14.

Bordo, M., and T. Helbling. 2004. "Have National Business Cycles Become More Synchronized?" in *Macroeconomic Policies in the World Economy*, edited by H. Siebert. Berlin: Springer.

Boskin, M. J. 2009. "Global Disaster Recovery." *Project Syndicate,* March 23.

Bosworth, B., and S. Collins, 2010. "Rebalancing the U.S. Economy in a Post-Crisis World." Paper presented at the Trans-Pacific Rebalancing Conference organized by the Asian Development Bank Institute and the Brookings Institution, March 3–4, Tokyo.

Bosworth, B., and A. Flaaen. 2009. "America's Financial Crisis: The End of an Era." Paper presented at Global Financial and Economic Crisis: Impacts, Lessons, and Growth Rebalancing Conference, April 22–23, Tokyo.

Bown, C. P., ed. 2011, *The Great Recession and Import Protection: The Role of Temporary Trade Barriers.* London: Centre for Economic Policy Research and World Bank.

Broda, C., and C. Tille. 2003. "Coping with Terms-of-Trade Shocks in Developing Countries." *Current Issues in Economics and Finance*, Federal Reserve Bank of New York (November).

Bronfenbrenner, M. 1969. *Is the Business Cycle Obsolete?* New York: Wiley.

Brunnermeier, M. K. 2009. "Deciphering the 2007–08 Liquidity and Credit Crunch." *Journal of Economic Perspectives* 23 (1): 77–100.

———, and Y. Sannikov. 2012. "A Macroeconomic Model with a Financial Sector." *2012 Meeting Papers* 507, Society for Economic Dynamics.

Bry, G., and C. Boschan. 1971. *Cyclical Analysis of Time Series: Selected Procedures and Computer Programs*. Cambridge, Massachusetts: National Bureau of Economic Research.

Buiter, W. H., G. M. Corsetti, and P. A. Pesenti. 1998. "Interpreting the ERM Crisis: Country-Specific and Systemic Issues." *Princeton Studies in International Finance* 84.

Buiter, W. H., E. Rahbari, and J. Seydl. 2014. "Secular Stagnation: Only If We Really Ask for It." *Global Economic View*, Citi Research, January 13.

Buiter, W. 2015. "Is China Leading the World into Recession?" *Global Economic View*, Citi Research, September 8.

Burns, A. F., ed. 1952. *Wesley Clair Mitchell: The Economic Scientist*. New York: National Bureau of Economic Research.

Burns, A. F., and W. C. Mitchell. 1947. *Measuring Business Cycles*. Cambridge, Massachusetts: National Bureau of Economic Research.

Burstein, A., C. Kurz, and L. Tesar. 2008. "Trade, Production Sharing, and the International Transmission of Business Cycles." *Journal of Monetary Economics* 55 (4): 775–95.

Businessweek. 2000. "The New Economy," January 30.

Bussière, M., E. Perez-Barreiro, R. Straub, and D. Taglioni. 2010. "Protectionist Responses to the Crisis: Global Trends and Implications." ECB Working Paper 110, European Central Bank, Frankfurt.

Bussière, M., G. Callegari, F. Ghironi, G. Sestieri, and N. Yamano. 2013. "Estimating Trade Elasticities: Demand Composition and the Trade Collapse of 2008–09." *American Economic Journal: Macroeconomics* 5 (3): 118–51.

Byrne, D. M., S. D. Oliner, and D. E. Sichel. 2013. "Is the Information Technology Revolution Over?" Federal Reserve Board Finance and Economics Discussion Series.

Caballero, R. J. 2010. "Macroeconomics after the Crisis: Time to Deal with the Pretense-of-Knowledge Syndrome." *Journal of Economic Perspectives* 24 (4): 85–102.

Callen, T. 2007. "PPP versus the Market: Which Weight Matters?" *Finance and Development* 44: 50–51.

———. 2008. "Gross Domestic Product: An Economy's All." *Finance and Development* 45 (March): 48–49.

Calomiris, C. W. 2009. "The Subprime Turmoil: What's Old, What's New, and What's Next." *Journal of Structured Finance* 15 (1): 6–52.

Calomiris, C. W., and S. H. Haber. 2014. *Fragile by Design: The Political Origins of Banking Crises and Scarce Credit*. Princeton, New Jersey: Princeton University Press.

Calvo, G., and R. Loo-Kung. 2010. "US Recovery: A New 'Phoenix Miracle'?" *VoxEu*.

Calvo, G. A., C. Reinhart, E. Fernández-Arias, and E. Talvi. 2001. "Growth and External Financing in Latin America," Working Paper 4277, Inter-American Development Bank, Washington.

Canova, F. 1998. "Detrending and Business Cycle Facts." *Journal of Monetary Economics* 41 (3): 475–512.

———. 2005. "The Transmission of US Shocks to Latin America." *Journal of Applied Econometrics* 20 (2): 229–51.

———, M. Ciccarelli, and E. Ortega. 2007. "Similarities and Convergence in G-7 Cycles." *Journal of Monetary Economics* 54 (3): 850–78.

Cardarelli, R., S. Elekdag, and M. A. Kose. 2010. "Capital Inflows: Macroeconomic Implications and Policy Responses." *Economic Systems* 34: 333–56.

Carlson, M. 2006. "A Brief History of the 1987 Stock Market Crash." Board of Governors of the Federal Reserve Working Paper.

Carrell, P. 2011. "ECB Says Will 'Actively Implement' Bond-buying," August 7, *Reuters*.

Carrière-Swallow, Y., and L. F. Céspedes. 2013. "The Impact of Uncertainty Shocks in Emerging Economies." *Journal of International Economics* 90 (2): 316–25.

Carroll, C. D., M. Otsuka, and J. Slacalek. 2006. "How Large Is the Housing Wealth Effect? A New Approach." Economics Working Paper Archive Vol. 535, Johns Hopkins University Department of Economics, Baltimore, Maryland.

Caruana, J. 2013. "Hitting the Limits of 'Outside the Box' Thinking? Monetary Policy" in *The Crisis and Beyond*, Official Monetary and Financial Institutions Forum lecture. London.

Carvalho C., S. Eusipe, and C. Grisse. 2012. "Policy Initiatives in the Global Recession: What Did Forecasters Expect?" *Current Issues in Economics and Finance.* New York: Federal Reserve Bank.

Case, K., J. Quigley, and R. Shiller. 2013. "Wealth Effects Revisited: 1975–2012," NBER Working Paper 18667, National Bureau of Economic Research, Cambridge, Massachusetts.

Cassidy, K. 2014. "Is Larry Summers Right about 'Secular Stagnation'?" *New Yorker*, January 8.

Castle, S. 2012. "O.E.C.D., Slashing Growth Outlook, Warns of Global Recession," *New York Times,* November 27.

Cecchetti, S. G. 2006. "Measuring the Macroeconomic Risks Posed by Asset Price Booms." NBER Working Paper 12542, National Bureau of Economic Research, Cambridge, Massachusetts.

———. 2009. "Crisis and Responses: The Federal Reserve in the Early Stages of the Financial Crisis." *Journal of Economic Perspectives* 23 (1): 51–75.

Cecchetti, S. G., M. Kohler, and C. Upper. 2009. "Financial Crises and Economic Activity." *Proceedings—Economic Policy Symposium—Jackson Hole, Federal Reserve Bank of Kansas City,* 89–135.

Centre for Economic Policy Research (CEPR). 2003. "Business-Cycle Dating Committee Report," London.

———. 2009. "Euro Area Business Cycle Dating Committee: Determination of the 2008 Q1 Peak in Economic Activity," London.

———. 2010. Euro Area Business Cycle Dating Committee: Determination of the 2009 Q2 Trough in Economic Activity," London.

———. 2012. Euro Area Business Cycle Dating Committee: Euro Area Business Cycle Peaked in Third Quarter of 2011, Has Been in Recession Since," London.

———. 2014. Euro Area Business Cycle Dating Committee: Euro Area Mired in Recession Pause," London.

Cesa-Bianchi, A., M. H. Pesaran, and A. Rebucci. 2014. "Uncertainty and Economic Activity: A Global Perspective" Unpublished Working Paper.

Chandra, S. 2009. "U.S. Factories Contracted at Fastest Pace since 1980 (Update2)," Bloomberg, January 2.

Chari, A., and P. B. Henry. 2013. "Two Tales of Adjustment: East Asian Lessons for European Growth." Paper Presented at the 14th Jacques Polak Annual Research Conference, November 7–8, Washington.

Chen, H., V. Cúrdia, and A. Ferrero. 2012. "The Macroeconomic Effects of Large-Scale Asset Purchase Programs." *The Economic Journal* 122 (564): 289–315.

Chinn, M. D. 2011. "Regulatory Uncertainty, Macro Policy Uncertainty, and Demand." Econbrowser. com, December 22.

———. 2013. "Global Supply Chains and Macroeconomic Relationships in Asia." Unpublished, University of Wisconsin.

———. 2014. "Fiscal Multipliers." *The New Palgrave Dictionary of Economics*, forthcoming.

Chor, D., and K. Manova. 2012. "Off the Cliff and Back? Credit Conditions and International Trade during the Global Financial Crisis." *Journal of International Economics* 87: 117–33.

Christiano, L., M. Eichenbaum, and S. Rebelo. 2011. "When Is the Government Spending Multiplier Large?" *Journal of Political Economy* 119: 78–121.

Christiano, L., M. Eichenbaum, and M. Trabandt. 2014. "Understanding the Great Recession," NBER Working Paper, No. 20040.

Chui, M., P. Levine, S. M. Murshed, and J. Pearlman. 2002. "North-South Models of Growth and Trade." *Journal of Economic Surveys* 16: 123–43.

Cimilluca, D., A. Macdonald, and S. S. Munoz. 2008. "Lloyds TSB to Acquire HBOS as U.K. Seeks Bank Stability." *Wall Street Journal*, September 18.

Claessens, S., and K. Forbes. 2001. "International Financial Contagion: An Overview of the Issues and the Book," in *International Financial Contagion*, edited by S. Claessens and K. Forbes. Boston: Kluwer Academic Press.

Claessens, S., and M. A. Kose. 2009. "What Is a Recession?" *Finance and Development* 46 (1): 52–53.

———. 2014a. "Asset Prices and Macroeconomic Outcomes." Forthcoming IMF Working Paper, International Monetary Fund, Washington.

———. 2014b. "Macroeconomic Implications of Financial Imperfections." Forthcoming IMF Working Paper, International Monetary Fund Washington.

———. 2014c. "Financial Crises: Explanations, Types and Implications," in *Financial Crises: Causes, Consequences, and Policy Responses,* edited by S. Claessens, M. A. Kose, L. Laeven, and F. Valencia. Washington: International Monetary Fund.

Claessens, S., M. A. Kose, and M. E. Terrones. 2008a. "When Crises Collide." *Finance and Development* 45 (4).

———. 2008b. "Global Financial Crisis: How Long? How Deep?" *VoxEU*, October 7.

———. 2009. "What Happens during Recessions, Crunches, and Busts?" *Economic Policy* 60: 653–700.

———. 2010. "The Global Financial Crisis: How Similar? How Different? How Costly?" *Journal of Asian Economics* 21 (3): 247–64.

———. 2011a. "Financial Cycles: What? How? When?" in *NBER International Seminar on Macroeconomics (ISOM) 2010,* edited by R. Clarida and F. Giavazzi. Chicago: University of Chicago Press, 303–43.

———. 2011b. "Gyrations in Financial Markets." *Finance and Development* 48 (1).

———. 2012. "How Do Business and Financial Cycles Interact?" *Journal of International Economics* 87 (1): 178–90.

Claessens, S., M. A. Kose, L. Laeven, and F. Valencia, eds. 2014. *Financial Crises: Causes, Consequences, and Policy Responses.* Washington: International Monetary Fund.

Cleveland, H., and B. Brittain. 1975. "A World Depression?" *Foreign Affairs* 53 (2): 223–41.

CNN. 2009. "G-20 Pumps $1 Trillion into Beating Recession," April 2.

Cochrane, J. H., ed. 2006. "Financial Markets and the Real Economy," in *International Library of Critical Writings in Financial Economics* (18): 11–19.

———. 2009a. "How Did Paul Krugman Get It So Wrong?" Unpublished.

———. 2009b. "Fiscal Stimulus, Fiscal Inflation, or Fiscal Fallacies?" University of Chicago, Booth School of Business.

———. 2012. "Austerity, Stimulus, or Growth Now?" The Grumpy Economist, March 21.

———. 2014. "An Autopsy for the Keynesians," *Wall Street Journal*, December 26.

Coenen, G., C. J. Erceg, C. Freedman, D. Furceri, M. Kumhof, R. Lalonde, D. Laxton, J. Lindé, A. Mourougane, D. Muir, S. Mursula, C. de Resende, J. Roberts, W. Roeger, S. Snudden, M. Trabandt, and J. Veld. 2012. "Effects of Fiscal Stimulus in Structural Models." *American Economic Journal: Macroeconomics* 4: 1–47.

Cogan, J. F., and J. B. Taylor. 2012. "What the Government Purchases Multiplier Actually Multiplied in the 2009 Stimulus Package," in *Government Policies and the Delayed Economic Recovery*, edited by L. E. Ohanian, J. B. Taylor, and I. J. Wright. Stanford, California: Stanford University.

Cotis, J., and J. Coppel. 2005. "Business Cycle Dynamics in OECD Countries: Evidence, Causes and Policy Implications." RBA Annual Conference Volume, in *The Changing Nature of the Business Cycle*, edited by C. C. Kent and D. D. Norman. Sydney: Reserve Bank of Australia.

Council of Economic Advisers. 2009. "Housing and Financial Markets." Chapter 2, *Economic Report to the President*.

———. 2010. "Crisis and Recovery in the World Economy." Chapter 3, *Economic Report to the President*.

———. 2012. "To Recover, Rebalance, and Rebuild." Chapter 1, *Economic Report to the President*.

———. 2014a. "The Economic Impact of the American Recovery and Reinvestment Act Five Years Later." *Final Report to Congress*.

———. 2014b. "The Fifth Anniversary of the American Recovery and Reinvestment Act."

Coyle, D. 2014. *GDP: A Brief but Affectionate History*. Princeton, New Jersey: Princeton University Press.

Currie, D., and D. Vines. 1988. *Macroeconomic Interactions between North and South*. New York: Cambridge University Press.

Curry, T., and L. Shibut. 2000. "The Cost of the Savings and Loan Crisis: Truth and Consequences." *FDIC Banking Review* 13 (2): 26–35.

Daly, M. C., J. Fernald, O. Jorda, and F. Nechid. 2013. "Labor Markets in the Global Financial Crisis." *FRBSF Economic Letter* 38.

D'Amico, S., W. English, D. Lopez-Salido, and E. Nelson. 2012. "The Federal Reserve's Large-Scale Asset Purchase Programs: Rationale and Effects." Finance and Discussion Series Paper 2012-85, Federal Reserve Board, Washington.

Dao, M., and P. Loungani. 2010. "The Human Cost of Recessions: Assessing It, Reducing It." IMF Staff Position Note 10/17, International Monetary Fund, Washington.

Davies, G. 2011. "Monitoring the Risk of Global Recession." *Financial Times*, September 5.

———. 2014. "Global Policy Mix Turns More Growth Friendly," *Financial Times*, November 24.

Davies, P. 2012. "Asian Crisis: 10 Lessons for Europe." *Financial Times*, June 8.

Davis, S. J. 2013. "Straw Man Bites the Dust: A Response to Paul Krugman on Policy Uncertainty." Capital Ideas (website), University of Chicago, Booth School of Business.

Davis, S. J., and J. A. Kahn. 2008. "Interpreting the Great Moderation: Changes in the Volatility of Economic Activity at the Macro and Micro Levels." *Journal of Economic Perspectives* 22 (4): 155–80.

De Gregorio, J. 2014. *How Latin America Weathered the Global Financial Crisis*. Washington: Peterson Institute for International Economics.

de Haan, J., R. Inklaar, and R. Jong-A-Pin. 2008. "Will Business Cycles in the Euro Area Converge? A Critical Survey of Empirical Research." *Journal of Economic Surveys* 22 (2): 234–73.

DeLong, J. B. 2011a. "The Little Depression." Blog, June 10.

———, J. B. 2011b. "The Anatomy of Slow Recovery." *Project Syndicate*, March 31.

DeLong, and L. H. Summers. 2012. "Fiscal Policy in a Depressed Economy." *Brookings Papers on Economic Activity* (March).

Dées, S., and N. Zorell. 2012. "Business Cycle Synchronization: Disentangling Trade and Financial Linkages." *Open Economies Review* 23 (4): 623–43.

Department of the Treasury. 1992. "International Economic and Exchange Rate Policy." Report to the U.S. Congress, May 12.

Dervis, K. 2012. "Convergence, Interdependence, and Divergence." *Finance and Development* 49 (3).

———. 2013. "Catching up at Different Speeds." Brookings Institution, December 17.

———. 2014. "Tailspin or Turbulence?" Brookings Institution, February 18.

Desai, S., and M. Jones. 2008. "Northern Rock Nationalised." *Reuters*, February 17.

di Giovanni, J., and A. A. Levchenko. 2010. "Putting the Parts Together: Trade, Vertical Linkages, and Business Cycle Comovement." *American Economic Journal: Macroeconomics* Vol. 2: 95–124.

Diebold, F. X., and K. Yilmaz. 2009. "Measuring Financial Asset Return and Volatility Spillovers with Application to Global Equity Markets." *The Economic Journal* 119 (534): 158–71.

———. 2014. "Measuring the Dynamics of Global Business Cycle Connectedness," in Unobserved Components and Time Series Econometrics: Essays in Honor of Andrew C. Harvey, edited by S. J. Koopman and N. Shephard. Oxford: Oxford University Press, forthcoming.

Dixit, A. K., and R. S. Pindyck. 1994. *Investment under Uncertainty*. Princeton, New Jersey: Princeton University Press.

Dornbusch, R. 1985. "Policy and Performance Links between LDC Debtors and Industrial Nations." *Brookings Papers on Economic Activity* 2: 303–56.

Dornbusch, R., T. Johnson, and A. Krueger. 1988. "Our LDC Debts," in *The United States in the World Economy*, edited by Martin Feldstein. Chicago: University of Chicago Press.

Draghi, M. 2012 Speech at the Global Investment Conference in London, July 26.

Dua, P., and A. Banerji. 2010. "Synchronization of Recessions in Major Developed and Emerging Economies." *Journal of Applied Economic Research* 4 (2): 197–223.

Dudley, W. C. 2014 "U.S. Monetary Policy and Emerging Market Economies." Speech, March 27.

Du Plesis, S., and B. Smit. 2004. "Reconsidering the Business Cycle and Stabilization Policies in South Africa." Paper presented at the Ninth Annual Conference on Econometric Modelling for Africa, June 30–July 2.

Durdu, C. B., and S. Sayan. 2010. "Emerging Market Business Cycles with Remittance Fluctuations." *IMF Staff Papers* 57 (2): 303–25.

Durdu, C. B., E. G. Mendoza, and M. E. Terrones. 2009. "Precautionary Demand for Foreign Assets in Sudden Stop Economies: An Assessment of the New Mercantilism." *Journal of Development Economics* 89 (2): 194–209.

Eckstein, O., and A. Sinai. 1986. "The Mechanisms of the Business Cycle in the Postwar Era," in *The American Business Cycle: Continuity and Change*, edited by R. Gordon. Chicago: University of Chicago Press for National Bureau of Economic Research.

The Economist. 1971. "When the Dollar Was Devalued." August 21.

———. 1973. "What's the German for Stagflation?" November 10.

———. 1974a. "When the Balloon Goes Up." December 21.

———. 1974b. "Who Will Survive the slump?" December 28.

———. 1974c. "A Cold, Dark, Three-Day Week." January 5.

———. 1974d. "Oil Unblocked." March 23, 50.

———. 1975a. "Beware the Coming Boom." April 12.

———. 1975b. "A World of Slow Growth." July 26.

———. 1975c. "Summit in a Slump." November 15.

———. 1978a. "Iran's Oil Strike: Time for a Little Studied Western Calm." November 4.

———. 1978b. "Where Is the Oil to Replace Iran's?" November 11.

———. 1979a. "Hello Freedom, If That's What You Are." January 20.

———. 1979b. "What to Do about Oil Prices?" May 26.

———. 1979c. "Dollar Surgery." October 13.

———. 1980a. "The Price of War." November 15.

———. 1980b. "Face the Worst." July 12.

———. 1981a. "1931 and 1981." September 5.

———. 1981b. "Summer Slump and Less Inflation Won't Bring Easier Money." July 11.

———. 1982a. "Recyclers' Recession." August 7.

———. 1982b. "Recession as Usual." August 21.

———. 1983. "Helmut Schmidt's Prescription: The World Economy at Stake," February 26.

———. 1989. "The Business Cycle Gets a Puncture." August 5.

———. 1990. "All Fall Down." September 22.

———. 1991. "Economics Focus—After the Recession." March 16.

———. 1992a. "What Recession?" June 20.

———. 1992b. "Recession or Doom?" October 24.

———. 1998. "Puncture Ahead." December 3.

———. 1999. "Depressing Jargon." January 21.

———. 2001a. "A Global Game of Dominoes." August 23.

———. 2001b. "Going Downhill." September 27.

———. 2002. "After the Bubbles: Brace Yourself for a Bumpier Time Ahead." September 26.

———. 2008a. "The Global Slumpometer." November 6.

———. 2008b. "Diagnosing Depression." December 30.

———. 2010. "The Volcker Recession: Who Beat Inflation?" March 31.

———. 2014. "Why Is Stagnation Bubbly?" January 6.

———. 2015. "Watch Out" June 13.

Edwards, S. 1995. *Crisis and Reform in Latin America: From Despair to Hope.* New York: Oxford University Press for World Bank.

Eggertsson, G., and N. Mehrotra. 2014. "A Model of Secular Stagnation." Brown University Working Paper.

Eggertsson, G., and M. Woodford. 2003. "The Zero Bound on Interest Rates and Optimal Monetary Policy." *Brookings Papers on Economic Activity* (Spring): 139–211.

Eichengreen, B. 1996. *Golden Fetters.* Oxford: Oxford University Press.

———. 2015. *Hall of Mirrors: The Great Depression, The Great Recession, and the Uses-and Misuses-of History,* Oxford University Press.

Eichengreen, B., and K. H. O'Rourke. 2009. "A Tale of Two Depressions." *VoxEU,* September 1.

Eicher, T. S., S. F. Schubert, and S. J. Turnovsky. 2008. "Dynamic Effects of Terms of Trade Shocks: The Impact on Debt and Growth." *Journal of International Money and Finance* 27 (6): 876–96.

El-Erian, M. A. 2009. "A New Normal." *Economic Outlook* (May), pimco.com.

———. 2011. "Secular Outlook: Navigating the Multi-Speed World." *Economic Outlook* (May), pimco.com.

———. 2015. "The Messy Politics of Economic Divergence," Project Syndicate, March.

Elsby, M. W. L., B. Hobijn, and A. Sahin. 2010. "The Labor Market in the Great Recession." *Brookings Papers on Economic Activity* 41: 1–69.

———, and R. G. Valletta. 2011. "The Labor Market in the Great Recession—An Update to September 2011." *Brookings Papers on Economic Activity* (Fall): 353–84.

English, W. B., J. D. Lopez-Salido, and R. J. Tetlow. 2013. "The Federal Reserve's Framework for Monetary Policy—Recent Changes and New Questions." Paper Presented at the 14th Jacques Polak Annual Research Conference, November 7–8, Washington.

European Central Bank. 1998. "Euro Central Rates and Intervention Rates in ERM II." Press release, December 31.

Faber, M. 2012. "Marc Faber: 100% Chance of Global Recession." CNBC Interview by Lee Brodie, May 25.

Faruqee, H., and K. Srinivasan. 2012. "The G-20 Mutual Assessment Process—A Perspective from IMF Staff." *Oxford Review of Economic Policy* 28 (3): 493–511.

Fatas, A., and I. Mihov. 2013. "Recoveries." INSEAD Working Paper.

Federal Deposit Insurance Corporation (FDIC). 1997. "The LDC Debt Crisis," Chapter 5 in *History of Eighties—Lessons for the Future, Vol. 1: An Examination of the Banking Crises of the 1980s and Early 1990s.*

Federal Reserve Bank of Kansas City. 2002. *Rethinking Stabilization Policy.* Symposium Publication, Jackson Hole, Wyoming.

Federal Open Market Committee (FOMC). 2008. "Minutes of the Federal Open Market Committee." Board of Governors of the Federal Reserve System, April 29–30.

———. 2009. "Minutes of the Federal Open Market Committee," Board of Governors of the Federal Reserve System, June 23–24.

———. 2010. "Minutes of the Federal Open Market Committee," Board of Governors of the Federal Reserve System, September 21.

———. 2013. "Minutes of the Federal Open Market Committee," Board of Governors of the Federal Reserve System, December 17-18.

Feldstein, M. 2010 "Why Has America's Economic Recovery Stalled?" *Project Syndicate*, October 25.

———. 2013. "The Taper Chase." *Project Syndicate*, September 30.

Ferguson, R. W. 2005 "Recessions and Recoveries Associated with Asset-Price Movements: What Do We Know?" Speech given at the Stanford Institute for Economic Policy Research, Stanford, California.

Fernald, J. 2014. "Productivity and Potential Output Before, During, and After the Great Recession," NBER Working Paper, No. 20248.

Fidrmuc, J., and I. Korhonen. 2010. "The Impact of the Global Financial Crisis on Business Cycles in Asian Emerging Economies." *Journal of Asian Economics* 21 (3): 293–303.

Fisher, I. 1933. "The Debt-Deflation Theory of Great Depressions." *Econometrica* 1: 337–57.

Fischer, S. 1998. "Lessons from a Crisis." *Economist*, October 3.

———. 2014. "The Great Recession: Moving Ahead," August 11, speech at a conference sponsored by the Swedish Ministry of Finance, Stockholm, Sweden.

———. 2015. "Conducting Monetary Policy with a Large Balance Sheet," speech given on February 27.

———, R. Sahay, and C. Végh. 1996. "Stabilization and Growth in Transition Economies: The Early Experience." *Journal of Economic Perspectives* 10 (2): 45–66.

Forbes, K. 2013. "The 'Big C': Identifying and Mitigating Contagion." *The Changing Policy Landscape 2012.* Jackson Hole Symposium hosted by the Federal Reserve Bank of Kansas City, 23–87.

———, and R. Rigobon. 2002. "No Contagion, Only Interdependence: Measuring Stock Market Comovements." *Journal of Finance* 152: 2223–61.

Forbes, K. J., and F. E. Warnock. 2012. "Capital Flows Waves: Surges, Stops, Flight, and Retrenchment." *Journal of International Economics* 88 (2): 235–51.

Foster, L., C. Grim, and J. Haltiwanger,. 2014. "Reallocation in the Great Recession: Cleansing or Not?" NBER Working Paper, No. 20427.

Frankel, J. 2011. "Are Bilateral Remittances Countercyclical?" *Open Economies Review* 22 (1): 1–16.

———. 2013. "Monetary Alchemy, Fiscal Science." *Project Syndicate*, January 26.

———, and A. Rose. 1998. "The Endogeneity of the Optimum Currency Area Criteria." *Economic Journal* 108 (149): 1009–25.

Frankel, J. A., and N. Roubini. 2001. "The Role of Industrial Country Policies in Emerging Market Crises." NBER Working Paper 8634, National Bureau of Economic Research, Cambridge, Massachusetts.

Freedman, C., M. Kumhof, D. Laxton, and J. Lee. 2009. "The Case for Global Fiscal Stimulus." IMF Staff Position Paper 09/04, International Monetary Fund, Washington.

Freund, C. 2009. "The Trade Response to Global Downturns: Historical Evidence." World Bank Policy Research Working Paper 5015, World Bank, Washington.

Friedman, M. 1964. "The Monetary Studies of the National Bureau." *The National Bureau Enters Its 45th Year*, 44th Annual Report, 7–25.

———. 1993. "The 'Plucking Model' of Business Fluctuations Revisited." *Economic Inquiry* 31 (2): 171–78.

Fuerbringer, J. 1991. "Why a U.S. Recession Still Matters." *New York Times*, January 6.

Furceri, D., and A. Zdzienicka. 2012. "How Costly Are Debt Crises?" *Journal of International Money and Finance* 31 (4): 726–42.

Furman, J. 2014. "The Fifth Anniversary of the American Recovery and Reinvestment Act." Council of Economic Advisers, February 17.

Gagnon, J., M. Raskin, J. Remache, and B. Sack. 2011. "Large-Scale Asset Purchases by the Federal Reserve: Did They Work?" *FRBNY Economic Policy Review* (May): 41–59.

Gagnon, J., and B. Sack. 2014. "Monetary Policy with Abundant Liquidity: A New Operating Framework for the Federal Reserve." Policy Brief, Peterson Institute for International Economics, Washington.

Garcia, R., and H. Schaller. 2002. "Are the Effects of Monetary Policy Asymmetric?" *Economic Inquiry* 40 (1): 102–19.

Geithner, T. F. 2014. *Stress Test: Reflections on Financial Crises*. New York: Crown.

Gerlach, H. M. S. 1988. "World Business Cycles under Fixed and Flexible Exchange Rates" *Journal of Money, Credit and Banking* 20 (4): 621–32.

Gertler, M. 1988. "Financial Structure and Aggregate Economic Activity: An Overview." *Journal of Money, Credit and Banking* 20 (3): 559–88.

———, and N. Kiyotaki. 2010. "Financial Intermediation and Credit Policy in Business Cycle Analysis," in *Handbook of Monetary Economics*, edited by B. Friedman and M. Woodford. Amsterdam: Elsevier.

Giannone, D., M. Lenza, and L. Reichlin. 2011. "Market Freedom and the Global Recession." *IMF Economic Review* 59: 111–35.

Gilchrist, S., J. Sim, and E. Zakrajsek. 2010. "Uncertainty, Financial Frictions, and Investment Dynamics." *2010 Meeting Papers* 1285, Society for Economic Dynamics.

Giuliano, P., and A. Spilimbergo. 2009. "Growing Up in a Recession: Beliefs and the Macroeconomy." NBER Working Paper 15321, National Bureau of Economic Research, Cambridge, Massachusetts.

Golden, S. 1975. "Is It a Depression—Or Just a Bad Recession." *New York Times*, March 9.

Goldstein, M. 2008. "Bear Stearns' Big Bailout." *Bloomberg Businessweek*, March 14.

Goldstein, M., and M. S. Khan. 1982. *Effects of Slowdown in Industrial Countries on Growth in Non-oil Developing Countries*. Washington: International Monetary Fund.

Gomes, S., P. Jacquinot, R. Mestre, and J. Sousa, 2015. "Global Policy at the Zero Lower Bound In a Large-scale DSGE Model," *Journal of International Money and Finance* 50: 134–53.

Goodfriend, M., and R. G. King. 2005. "The Incredible Volcker Disinflation." *Journal of Monetary Economics* 52 (5): 981–1015.

Goodley, S. 2012. "How Black Monday Sowed the Seeds for the Current Financial Crisis." *Guardian*, October 13.

Goodman, P. S. 2008. "U.S. and Global Economies Slipping in Unison." *New York Times*, August 23.

Gordon, R. A. 1970. "How Obsolete Is the Business Cycle?" *National Affairs* 21: 127–39.

Gordon, R. J. 2009. "Is Modern Macro or 1978-era Macro More Relevant to the Understanding of the Current Economic Crisis?" Working Paper, Northwestern University.

———. 2012. "Is U.S. Economic Growth Over? Faltering Innovation Confronts the Six Headwinds." NBER Working Paper 18315, National Bureau of Economic Research, Cambridge, Massachusetts.

———. 2014. "The Demise of U.S. Economic Growth: Restatement, Rebuttal, and Reflections." NBER Working Paper 19895, National Bureau of Economic Research, Cambridge, Massachusetts.

Gorton, G. 2012. *Misunderstanding Financial Crises: Why We Don't See Them Coming.* Oxford: Oxford University Press.

Gourinchas, P. 2012. "Global Imbalances and Global Liquidity," in *Asia's Role in the Post Crisis Global Economy*, edited by M. Spiegel and R. Glick, 305–40.

———, and M. A. Kose. 2010. "Economic Linkages, Spillovers, and the Financial Crisis-1." *IMF Economic Review* 58: 209–13.

———. 2011. "Economic Linkages, Spillovers, and the Financial Crisis-2." *IMF Economic Review* 59: 1–5.

———. 2013a. "Labor Markets through the Lens of the Great Recession—1." *IMF Economic Review* 61 (3): 405–9.

———. 2013b. "Labor Markets through the Lens of the Great Recession—2." *IMF Economic Review* 61 (4): 561–65.

Gourinchas P., and M. A. Kose, 2014. "Crises: Yesterday and Today—1," *IMF Economic Review* 62(4): 465-469.

———. 2015. "Crises: Yesterday and Today—2," *IMF Economic Review* 63(1):1–5.

Gourinchas, P., and M. Obstfeld. 2012. "Stories of the Twentieth Century for the Twenty-First." *American Economic Journal: Macroeconomics* 4 (1): 226–65.

Gourinchas, P., and H. Rey. 2014. "External Adjustment, Global Imbalances, Valuation Effects." forthcoming in *Handbook of International Economics.*

Greenspan, A. 2013. "Uncertainty Unbundled: The Metrics of Activism," in *Government Policies and the Delayed Economic Recovery*, edited by L. E. Ohanian, J. B. Taylor, and I. J. Wright. Stanford, California: Hoover Institution Press.

Gregory, A. W., and A. C. Head. 1999. "Common and Country-Specific Fluctuations in Productivity, Investment, and the Current Account." *Journal of Monetary Economics* 44 (3): 423–51.

Gregory, A. W., and J. Raynauld. 1997. "Measuring World Business Cycles." *International Economic Review* 38 (3): 677–701.

Gross, W. H. 2009 "On the 'Course' to a New Normal." *Investment Outlook* (September), pimco.com.

Guajardo, J., D. Leigh, and A. Pescatori. 2011. "Expansionary Austerity: New International Evidence." IMF Working Paper 11/158, International Monetary Fund, Washington.

Guardian. 1973. "OPEC Oil Embargo Leads to Global Fuel Crisis," November 13.

Hall, R. E. 1993. "Macro Theory and the Recession of 1990–1991." *American Economic Review* 83 (2): 275–79.

Hall, V., and J. McDermott. 2007. "Regional Business Cycles in New Zealand: Do They Exist? What Might Drive Them?" *Papers in Regional Science* 86 (2): 167–91.

Haltmaier, J. 2012 "Do Recessions Affect Potential Output?" International Finance Discussion Papers 1066, Federal Reserve Board.

Hamilton, J. D. 1989. "A New Approach to the Economic Analysis of Nonstationary Time Series and the Business Cycle." *Econometrica* 57 (2): 357–84.

———. 2003. "Comment on 'A Comparison of Two Business Cycle Dating Methods.'" *Journal of Economic Dynamics and Control* 27 (9): 1691–93.

———. 2009a. "Oil Prices and the Economic Recession of 2007–08." *VoxEU*, June 16.

———. 2009b. "Causes and Consequences of the Oil Shock of 2007–08," *Brookings Papers on Economic Activity* 40: 215–83.

———. 2011. "Historical Oil Shocks." Unpublished, University of California, San Diego.

———, E. S. Harris, J. Hatzius, and K. D. West. 2015. "The Equilibrium Real Funds Rate: Past, Present and Future," University of Chicago, Working Paper.

Hansen, A. 1939. "Economic Progress and Declining Population Growth."*American Economic Review* 29 (1): 1–15.

Hansen, G. D., and E. C. Prescott. 1993. "Did Technology Shocks Cause the 1990–1991 Recession?" *American Economic Review* 83 (2): 280–86.

Harding, D., and A. Pagan. 2002. "Dissecting the Cycle: A Methodological Investigation." *Journal of Monetary Economics* 49: 365–81.

Harding, R. 2014. "Yellen Says Emerging Market Turmoil Will Not Sway the Fed." *Financial Times*, February 11.

Hassett, K., and G. Hubbard. 2012. "Obama Inconsistent on Pace of Economic Recovery." *Washington Post*, August, 15.

He, D., and W. Liao. 2012. "Asian Business Cycle Synchronization." *Pacific Economic Review* 17 (1): 105–35.

Helbling, T. 2009. "How Similar Is the Current Crisis to the Great Depression?" *VoxEU*, April 29.

Helbling, T., P. Berezin, M. A. Kose, M. Kumhof, D. Laxton, and N. Spatafora. 2007. "Decoupling the Train? Spillovers and Cycles in the Global Economy," in *World Economic Outlook*. Washington: International Monetary Fund, April: 121–60.

Helbling, T., and M. E. Terrones. 2004. "Asset Price Booms and Busts—Stylized Facts from the Last Three Decades of the 20th Century." Unpublished, International Monetary Fund, Washington.

Helbling, T., R. Huidrom, M. A. Kose, and C. Otrok. 2011. "Do Credit Shocks Matter? A Global Perspective." *European Economic Review* 55: 340–53.

Henn, C., and B. McDonald. 2011. "Protectionist Responses to the Crisis: Damage Observed in Product-Level Trade." IMF Working Paper 11/139, International Monetary Fund, Washington.

Herndon, T., M. Ash, and R. Pollin. 2013. "Does High Public Debt Consistently Stifle Economic Growth? A Critique of Reinhart and Rogoff." Working Paper, University of Massachusetts, Amherst.

Higgins, B. 1993. "Was the ERM Crisis Inevitable?" Federal Reserve Bank of Kansas City *Economic Review* 78 (4): 27–40.

Hirata, H., M. A. Kose, and C. Otrok. 2013. "Globalization vs. Regionalization," IMF Working Paper 13/19, International Monetary Fund, Washington.

———, and M. E. Terrones. 2012. "Global House Price Fluctuations: Synchronization and Determinants," in *NBER International Seminar on Macroeconomics 2012*.

Hoffmaister, A., M. Pradhan, and H. Samiei. 1998. "Have North-South Growth Linkages Changed?" *World Development* 26 (5): 791–808.

Hoshi, T., and A. K. Kashyap. 2013. "Will the US and Europe Avoid a Lost Decade? Lessons from Japan's Post Crisis Experience." Paper presented at the 14th Jacques Polak Annual Research Conference, November 7–8, Washington.

Howard, G., R. Martin, and B. A. Wilson. 2011. "Are Recoveries from Banking and Financial Crises Really So Different?" International Finance Discussion Paper 1037, Federal Reserve Board, Washington.

Hutchens, G., and P. Martin. 2014. "OECD Warns of New Era of Low Economic Growth Globally." *Sydney Morning Herald*, February 22.

Iacoviello, M. 2005. "House Prices, Borrowing Constraints, and Monetary Policy in the Business Cycle." *American Economic Review* 95 (3): 739–64.

Imbs, J. 2004. "Trade, Finance, Specialization, and Synchronization." *Review of Economics and Statistics* 86 (3): 723–34.

———. 2006. "The Real Effects of Financial Integration." *Journal of International Economics* 68 (2): 296–324.

———. 2010. "The First Global Recession in Decades." *IMF Economic Review* 58 (2): 327–54.

Independent Evaluation Office of the International Monetary Fund. 2012. "International Reserves: IMF Concerns and Country Perspectives." Evaluation Report, Washington.

International Labour Organization (ILO). 2013. *Global Employment Trends 2013.* Geneva.

———. 2014. *Global Employment Trends 2014.* Geneva.

International Monetary Fund (IMF). 1998a. "Financial Crises: Causes and Indicators." *World Economic Outlook.* Washington, May.

———. 1998b. "Financial Turbulence and the World Economy." *World Economic Outlook.* Washington, October.

———. 2000. "Transition Economies: An IMF Perspective on Progress and Prospects." Brief Note 00/08, Washington.

———. 2001a. "Fiscal Policy and Macroeconomic Stability." *World Economic Outlook.* Washington, May.

———. 2001b. "The Information Technology Revolution." *World Economic Outlook.* Washington, October.

———. 2001c. "The Global Economy after September 11," *World Economic Outlook Update* Washington, December.

———. 2001d. "How Do Fluctuations in the G-7 Countries Affect Developing Countries?" *World Economic Outlook.* Washington, October.

———. 2008. "Housing and Business Cycle." *World Economic Outlook.* Washington, April.

———. 2009a. "What's the Damage? Medium-Term Output Dynamics after Financial Crises." *World Economic Outlook.* Washington, October.

———. 2009b. "Executive Summary." *Regional Economic Outlook: Middle East and Central Asia.* Washington, May.

———. 2010a. "A Policy-Driven, Multispeed Recovery." *World Economic Outlook Update.* Washington, January.

———. 2010b. "Executive Summary." *Regional Economic Outlook: Asia and Pacific.* Washington, October.

———. 2010c. "Executive Summary." *Regional Economic Outlook: Western Hemisphere.* Washington, May.

———. 2011a. "Global Recovery Advances but Remains Uneven." *World Economic Outlook Update.* Washington, January.

———. 2011b. "IMF Welcomes Agreement to Tackle Eurozone Crisis." *IMF Survey* online, July 22.

———. 2012a. "Global Recovery Stalls, Downside Risks Intensify." *World Economic Outlook Update.* Washington, January.

———. 2012b. "Coping with High Debt and Sluggish Growth." *World Economic Outlook.* Washington, October.

———. 2013a. "Gradual Upturn in Global Growth during 2013." *World Economic Outlook Update.* Washington, January.

———. 2013b. "Fiscal Monitor: Fiscal Adjustment in an Uncertain World." *World Economic and Financial Surveys.* Washington, April.

———. 2013c. "Unconventional Monetary Policies—Recent Experience and Prospects." Policy Paper, Washington, April.

———. 2013. "Transitions and Tensions," *World Economic Outlook.* Washington, October.

———. 2014a. "Is the Tide Rising?" *World Economic Outlook Update.* Washington, January.

———. 2014b. "Recovery Strengthens, Remains Uneven." *World Economic Outlook.* Washington, April.

———. 2014c. "Public Expenditures Reform: Making Difficult Choices." *Fiscal Monitor.* Washington, April.

———. 2015a. "Uneven Growth: Short- and Long-Term Factors," *World Economic Outlook*, April, Chapter 1, 1–42.

———. 2015b. "Slower Growth in Emerging Markets, a Gradual Pickup in Advanced Economies" *World Economic Outlook Update*, July 2015.

———. 2015c. "Where Are We Headed? Perspectives on Potential Output," *World Economic Outlook*, April, Chapter 3, 69–110.

Jansen, W. J., and A. C. J. Stokman. 2004. "Foreign Direct Investment and International Business Cycle Comovement." ECB Working Paper 401, European Central Bank, Frankfurt.

Jeanne, O. 2007. "International Reserves in Emerging Market Countries: Too Much of a Good Thing?" *Brookings Papers on Economic Activity* 38: 1–80.

———. 2014. "Macroprudential Policies in a Global Perspective." IMES Discussion Paper 2014-E-1.

Journal of Commerce. 1998. "Global Recession?" (September 2): 6A.

Joyce M., A. Lasaosa, I. Stevens, and M. Tong. 2010. "The Financial Market Impact of Quantitative Easing." Bank of England Working Paper, London.

Kalemli-Ozcan, S., E. Papaioannou, and J. L. Peydró. 2013. "Financial Regulation, Financial Globalization and the Synchronization of Economic Activity." *Journal of Finance* 68: 1179–228.

Kamin, S. B., and L. P. DeMarco. 2012. "How Did a Domestic Slump Turn into a Global Financial Crisis?" *Journal of International Money and Finance* 31: 10–41.

Kaminsky, G. L., C. M. Reinhart, and C. A. Végh. 2005. "When It Rains, It Pours: Procyclical Capital Flows and Macroeconomic Policies," in *NBER Macroeconomics Annual 2004* Vol. 19. Cambridge, Massachusetts: National Bureau of Economic Research, 11–82.

Kanaya, A., and D. Woo. 2000. "The Japanese Banking Crisis of the 1990s: Sources and Lessons." IMF Working Paper 00/7, International Monetary Fund, Washington.

Kannan, P. 2012. "Credit Conditions and Recoveries from Financial Crises." *Journal of International Money and Finance* 31 (5): 930–47.

Karnitschnig, M., D. Solomon, L. Pleven, and J. E. Hilsenrath. 2008. "U.S. to Take over AIG in $85 Billion Bailout; Central Banks Inject Cash as Credit Dries Up." *Wall Street Journal*, September 16.

Karras, G. 1996. "Why Are the Effects of Money-Supply Shocks Asymmetric? Convex Aggregate Supply or 'Pushing on a String'?" *Journal of Macroeconomics* 18 (4): 605–19.

Katz, L. F., K. Kroft, F. Lange, and M. Notowidigdo. 2014. "Addressing Long-Term Unemployment in the Aftermath of the Great Recession," VoxEU, December 3.

Kenen, P. B. 1983. "The Costly Blunders of Central Bankers." *New York Times.*

Keynes, J. M. [1936] 1973. "The General Theory of Employment, Interest, and Money." *The Collected Writings of John Maynard Keynes*, Vol. VII, edited by D. E. Moggridge. London: Macmillan.

Kiley, M. T. 2013. "The Response of Equity Prices to Movements in Long-Term Interest Rates Associated with Monetary Policy Statements: Before and after the Zero Lower Bound." Finance and Economics Discussion Series 2013–15, Federal Reserve Board, Washington.

Kim, S. 2001. "International Transmission of U.S. Monetary Policy Shocks: Evidence from VAR's." *Journal of Monetary Economics* 48 (2): 339–72.

King, S. D. 2010. *Losing Control: The Emerging Threats to Western Prosperity.* New Haven, Connecticut: Yale University Press.

Kishor, N. K. 2007. "Does Consumption Respond More to Housing Wealth Than to Financial Market Wealth? If So, Why?" *The Journal of Real Estate Finance and Economics* 35 (4): 427–48.

Kiyotaki, N., and J. Moore. 1997. "Credit Cycles." *Journal of Political Economy* 105: 211–48.

Knoop, T. A. 2004. *Recessions and Depressions: Understanding Business Cycles.* Westport, Connecticut: Praeger.

Kocherlakota, N. 2010. "Modern Macroeconomic Models as Tools for Economic Policy." *The Region, Banking and Policy Issues Magazine of the Federal Reserve Bank of Minneapolis* (May 4): 5–21.

Kollmann, R., W. Roeger, and J. Veld. 2012. "Fiscal Policy in a Financial Crisis: Standard Policy versus Bank Rescue Measures." *American Economic Review* 102 (3): 77–81.

Kose, M. A. 2002. "Explaining Business Cycles in Small Open Economies: How Much Do World Prices Matter?" *Journal of International Economics* 56 (2): 299–327.

Kose, M. A., and E. Prasad. 2010. *Emerging Markets: Resilience and Growth Amid Global Turmoil.* Washington: Brookings Institution Press.

Kose, M. A. and E. O. Ozturk, 2014. "A World of Change: Taking Stock of the Past Half Century," *Finance and Development*, September, 6–11.

———. 2015. "How Has the Global Economy Changed? A Summary of the Past Fifty Years," Working Paper, World Bank.

Kose, M. A., and A. Rebucci. 2005. "How Might CAFTA Change Macroeconomic Fluctuations in Central America?: Lessons from NAFTA." *Journal of Asian Economics* 16 (1): 77–104.

Kose, M. A., and R. Riezman. 2001. "Trade Shocks and Macroeconomic Fluctuations in Africa." *Journal of Development Economics* 65 (1): 55–80.

Kose, M. A., and M. E. Terrones. 2012. "How Does Uncertainty Affect Economic Performance?" *World Economic Outlook.* Washington: International Monetary Fund, October.

———. 2015. "Global Recessions." Forthcoming IMF Working Paper, International Monetary Fund, Washington.

Kose, M. A., and K. Yi. 2001. "International Trade and Business Cycles: Is Vertical Specialization the Missing Link?" *American Economic Review* 91 (2): 371–75.

———. 2006. "Can the Standard International Business Cycle Model Explain the Relation between Trade and Comovement?" *Journal of International Economics* 68 (2): 267–95.

Kose, M. A., P. Loungani, and M. E. Terrones. 2009. "Out of the Ballpark." *Finance & Development* 46: 25–28.

———. 2012. "Tracking the Global Recovery." *Finance & Development* 49 (2): 10–13.

———. 2013a. "The Great Divergence of Policies." *World Economic Outlook.* Washington: International Monetary Fund, April.

———. 2013b. "From the Global to the National Cycle: An Intricate Liaison." *Pacific Economic Review* 18 (3): 270–402.

Kose, M. A., G. M. Meredith, and C. M. Towe. 2005. "How Has NAFTA Affected the Mexican Economy? Review and Evidence." *Monetary Policy and Macroeconomic Stabilization in Latin America.* Berlin: Springer), 35–81.

Kose, M. A., C. Otrok, and E. Prasad. 2012. "Global Business Cycles: Convergence or Decoupling?" *International Economic Review* 53: 511–38.

Kose, M. A, C. Otrok, and C. H. Whiteman. 2003. "International Business Cycles: World, Region, and Country Specific Factors." *American Economic Review* 93: 1216–39.

———. 2008. "Understanding the Evolution of World Business Cycles." *Journal of International Economics* 75 (1): 110–30.

Kose, M. A., E. Prasad, K. Rogoff, and S. Wei. 2010. "Financial Globalization and Economic Policies." *Handbook of Development Economics* 5 (6): 4283–359.

Kose, M. A., E. S. Prasad, and M. E. Terrones. 2003a. "How Does Globalization Affect the Synchronization of Business Cycles?" *American Economic Review* 93 (2): 57–62.

———. 2003b. "Financial Integration and Macroeconomic Volatility." *IMF Staff Papers* 50 (Special Issue): 119–43.

———. 2005. "Growth and Volatility in an Era of Globalization." *IMF Staff Papers* 52: 31–63.

———. 2006. "How Do Trade and Financial Integration Affect the Relationship between Growth and Volatility?" *Journal of International Economics* 69: 176–202.

———. 2009a. "Does Financial Globalization Promote Risk Sharing?" *Journal of Development Economics* 89 (2): 258–70.

———. 2009b. "Does Openness to International Financial Flows Contribute to Productivity Growth?" *Journal of International Money and Finance* 28(4): 549–738.

Kowsmann, P. 2011. "Portugal Bailout Plan Detailed" *Wall Street Journal*, May 5.

Krishnamurthy, A., and A. Vissing-Jorgensen. 2011. "The Effects of Quantitative Easing on Interest Rates: Channels and Implications for Policy." *Brookings Papers on Economic Activity* (Fall): 215–65.

———. 2013. "The Ins and Outs of LSAPs." *Proceedings–Economic Policy Symposium*, Jackson Hole, Federal Reserve Bank of Kansas City.

Krugman, P. 1993. "Lessons from Massachusetts for EMU," in *Adjustment and Growth in the European Monetary Union*, edited by F. Torres and F. Giavazzi. London: Centre for Economic Policy Research and Cambridge University Press.

———. 2008a. "Stimulus Math (Wonkish)." *New York Times*, November 10.

———. 2008b. "Synchronized Sinking," *New York Times*, August 23.

———. 2009a. *The Return of Depression Economics and the Crisis of 2008*. New York: W.W. Norton.

———. 2009b. "How Did Economists Get It So Wrong?" *New York Times*, September 2.

———. 2011a. "The Lesser Depression," *New York Times*, July 21.

———. 2011b. "This Week Transcript: Gen. Jim Jones (Ret.)." ABC News interview, March 27.

———. 2012a. "Financial Crisis Denialism." *New York Times*, October 17.

———. 2012b. "The 'Uncertainty' Scam." *New York Times*, October 22.

———. 2013a. "How the Case for Austerity Has Crumbled." *New York Review of Books*.

———. 2013b. "Phony Fear Factor." *New York Times*, August 8.

———. 2013c. "Secular Stagnation, Coalmines, Bubbles, and Larry Summers." *New York Times*, November 16.

———. 2014a. "The Stimulus Tragedy." *New York Times*, February 21.

———. 2014b. "The Inflation Obsession." *New York Times*, March 2.

———. 2014c. "Euphemistic at the IMF." *New York Times*, April 4.

———. 2014d. "Inflation Targets Reconsidered." Draft paper for European Central Bank Sintra conference, May.

Kuczynski, P. 1982. "Latin American Debt." *Foreign Affairs* 61 (2): 344.

Laeven, L., and F. Valencia. 2008. "Systemic Banking Crises: A New Database." IMF Working Paper 08/224, International Monetary Fund, Washington.

———. 2011. "The Real Effects of Financial Sector Interventions during Crises." IMF Working Paper 11/45, International Monetary Fund, Washington.

———. 2012. "Systemic Banking Crises Database: An Update." IMF Working Paper 12/163, International Monetary Fund, Washington.

———. 2013. "Systemic Banking Crises Database." *IMF Economic Review* 61 (2): 225–70.

Lagarde, C. 2011. "Global Action for Global Recovery." *Project Syndicate*, September 25.

————. 2014. "The Global Economy in 2014." Speech at the National Press Club, January 15.

Lane, P. R. 2012. "Financial Globalization and the Crisis." BIS Working Paper 397, Bank for International Settlements, Basel.

Lane, P. R., and G. M. Milesi-Ferretti. 2007. "The External Wealth of Nations Mark II: Revised and Extended Estimates of Foreign Assets and Liabilities, 1970–2004." *Journal of International Economics* 73: 223–50.

————. 2011. "The Cross-Country Incidence of the Global Crisis." *IMF Economic Review* 59: 77–110.

————. 2012. "External Adjustment and the Global Crisis." *Journal of International Economics* 88 (2): 252–65.

Lang, S. 2010. "Economist Alfred Kahn, 'Father of Airline Regulation' and Former Presidential Adviser, Dies at 93." *Cornell Chronicle*, December 27.

Leamer, E. E. 2007. "Housing Is the Business Cycle." *Proceedings*, Federal Reserve Bank of Kansas City, 149–233.

————. 2008. "What's a Recession, Anyway?" NBER Working Paper 14221, National Bureau of Economic Research, Cambridge, Massachusetts.

————. 2009. *Macroeconomic Patterns and Stories*. Springer.

Lee, W. 2014. "Policy Uncertainty Stalls Global Investment." *Citi GPS: Global Perspectives & Solutions* opinion article.

Levchenko, A., L. T. Lewis, and L. L. Tesar. 2010. "The Collapse of International Trade during the 2008–09 Crisis: In Search of the Smoking Gun." *IMF Economic Review* 58 (2): 214–53.

Lewis, A. 1980. "The Slowing Down of the Engine of Growth." *American Economic Review* 70 (4): 555–64.

Lewis, M. 2010. *The Big Short: Inside the Doomsday Machine*. New York: W.W. Norton.

Lo, A. W. 2012. "Reading about the Financial Crisis: A Twenty-One-Book Review." *Journal of Economic Literature* 50: 151–78.

Loungani, P. 2012. "Seven Questions: Unemployment through the Prism of the Great Recession." *IMF Research Bulletin* 13 (1).

Lucas, R. E. 1975. "An Equilibrium Model of the Business Cycle." *Journal of Political Economy* 83: 1113–44.

————. 1977. "Understanding Business Cycles," in *Stabilization of the Domestic and International Economy*, edited by K. Brunner and A. H. Meltzer. Carnegie-Rochester Conference Series on Public Policy 5. Amsterdam.

————. 1995. "Monetary Neutrality." Economic Science Prize Lecture.

————. 2012. "Interview on Modern Macroeconomics." *Economic Dynamics* 14 (1).

————, and T. Sargent. 1978. "After Keynesian Economics, After the Phillips Curve: Persistence of High Inflation and High Unemployment." Federal Reserve Bank of Boston Conference volume.

Luce, E. 2014. "RIP Obama's Stimulus: Funeral for a Policy Success." *Financial Times*, February 23.

Lumsdaine, R., and E. S. Prasad. 2003. "Identifying the Common Component of International Economic Fluctuations: A New Approach." *Economic Journal* 113: 101–27.

Magnus, G. 2011. *Uprising: Will Emerging Markets Shape or Shake the World Economy?* Hoboken, New Jersey: John Wiley and Sons.

Mandelman, F. S., and A. Zlate. 2012. "Immigration, Remittances and Business Cycles." *Journal of Monetary Economics* 59 (2): 196–213.

Mankiw, N. G. 2007. "How to Avoid Recession? Let the Fed Work." *New York Times*, December 23.

————. 2009. "Are Fiscal Multipliers Now Big or Small?" Blog, March 5.

————. 2012. *Macroeconomics*. Worth Publishers.

Matthews, D. 2011. "Did the Stimulus Work? A Review of the Nine Best Studies on the Subject." Wonkblog, *Washington Post*, August 24.

McKinsey Global Institute. 2013. *Financial Globalization: Retreat or Reset?* Seoul.

Meltzer, A. 2010. *A History of the Federal Reserve*, Vol. 2, Book 2. Chicago: University of Chicago Press.

———. 2012. "Federal Reserve Policy in the Great Recession." *Cato Journal* 32 (2): 255–63.

Mendoza, E. G. 2001. "Credit, Prices, and Crashes: Business Cycles with a Sudden Stop." NBER Working Paper 8338, National Bureau of Economic Research, Cambridge, Massachusetts.

———. 2010. "Sudden Stops, Financial Crises and Leverage." *American Economic Review* 100: 1941–66.

Mendoza, E. G., and M. E. Terrones. 2008. "An Anatomy of Credit Booms: Evidence from Macro Aggregates and Micro Data." IMF Working Paper 08/226, International Monetary Fund, Washington.

———. 2012. "An Anatomy of Credit Booms and Their Demise." NBER Working Paper 18379, National Bureau of Economic Research, Cambridge, Massachusetts.

Mian, A., and A. Sufi. 2012. "What Explains High Unemployment: The Aggregate Demand Channel." Unpublished, Princeton, New Jersey: Princeton University.

———. 2014. *House of Debt*. Chicago: University of Chicago Press.

Milesi-Ferretti, G. M., and C. Tille. 2011. "The Great Retrenchment: International Capital Flows During the Global Financial Crisis." *Economic Policy* 26: 285–342.

Miller, P. J. 1994. *The Rational Expectations Revolution*. Cambridge, Massachusetts: MIT Press.

Mishkin, F. 2009. "Is Monetary Policy Effective During Financial Crises?" *American Economic Review* 99 (2): 573–77.

Mitchell, W. C. 1927. "The Processes Involved in Business Cycles." *Business Cycles: The Problem and Its Setting*, Chapter 1, 1–60.

Mitchener, B. 1992. "EC Devalues the Lira by 7%; Bundesbank to Lower Rates." *New York Times*, September 14.

Mokyr, J. 2014. "Secular Stagnation? Not In Your Life," in *Secular Stagnation: Facts, Causes and Cures*, edited by Coen Teulings and Richard Baldwin, pp. 83–90, CEPR Press.

Mollenkamp, C., S. Craig, S. Ng, and A. Lucchetti. 2008. "Lehman Files for Bankruptcy; Merrill Is Sold, AIG Seeks Cash." *Wall Street Journal*, September 16.

Moneta, F., and R. Rüffer. 2009. "Business Cycle Synchronisation in East Asia." *Journal of Asian Economics* 20: 1–12.

Mullaney, T. E. 1977. "A Slow World Recovery." *New York Times*, June 19.

Mulligan, C. 2012. *The Redistribution Recession: How Labor Market Distortions Contracted the Economy*. Oxford: Oxford University Press.

Mumtaz, H., S. Simonelli, and S. Surico. 2011. "International Comovements, Business Cycle and Inflation: A Historical Perspective." *Review of Economic Dynamics* 14 (1): 176–98.

Mussa, M. 2009. "World Recession and Recovery: A V or an L?" Peterson Institute for International Economics Working Paper, Washington.

National Association for Business Economics. 2014. "Economists Align on Monetary Policy but not on Fiscal Issues."

NBER Business-Cycle Dating Committee. 2003. "The NBER's Business-Cycle Dating Procedure." National Bureau of Economic Research, Cambridge, Massachusetts.

———. 2010. "US Business Cycle Expansions and Contractions." National Bureau of Economic Research, Cambridge, Massachusetts.

———. 2011. "Determination of the December 2007 Peak in Economic Activity." National Bureau of Economic Research, Cambridge, Massachusetts.

———. 2013. "The NBER's Business-Cycle Dating Procedure: Frequently Asked Questions." National Bureau of Economic Research, Cambridge, Massachusetts.

Ncube, M., Z. Brixiova, and Q. Meng. 2014. "Can Intra-Regional Trade Act as a Global Shock Absorber in Africa?" African Development Bank Group Working Paper 198.

Neumeyer, P. A., and F. Perri. 2005. "Business Cycles in Emerging Economies: The Role of Interest Rates." *Journal of Monetary Economics* 52 (2): 345–80.

New York Times. 1987. "Arthur F. Burns Is Dead at 83; A Shaper of Economic Policy." June 27.

———. 1990. "Washington Considers a Clear Iraqi Defeat To Be Necessary to Bolster Its Arab Allies." August 22.

———. 2007. "BNP Paribas Suspends Funds because of Subprime Problems." August 9.

———. 2008. "As Goldman and Morgan Shift, a Wall St. Era Ends." September 21.

———. 2009. "Deal Reached in Congress on $789 Billion Stimulus Plan." February 11.

Norrbin, S. C., and D. E. Schlagenhauf. 1996. "The Role of International Factors in the Business Cycle: A Multi-Country Study." *Journal of International Economics* 40 (1–2): 85–104.

Nossiter, B. D. 1974. "Global Headache." *Washington Post*, September 22.

Obstfeld, M. 2012. "Financial Flows, Financial Crises, and Global Imbalances." *Journal of International Money and Finance* 31: 469–80.

———. 2013. "Crises and the International System." *International Economic Journal* 27 (2): 143–55.

Obstfeld, M., and K. Rogoff. 2002. "Global Implications of Self-Oriented National Monetary Rules." *Quarterly Journal of Economics* 117 (2): 503–35.

———. 2010. "Global Imbalances and the Financial Crisis: Products of Common Causes," in *Asia and the Global Financial Crisis*, edited by R. Glick and M. M. Spiegel. Federal Reserve Bank of San Francisco, 131–72.

Obstfeld, M., D. Cho, and A. Mason, eds. 2012. *Global Economic Crisis: Impacts, Transmission, and Recovery.* Edward Elgar.

Office of the Historian. 2013. "Milestones: 1989–1992," article published at history.state.gov /milestones/1989-1992/fall-of-communism.

Ohanian, L., J. Taylor, and I. J. Wright. 2012. *Government Policy and the Delayed Economic Recovery.* Stanford, California: Hoover Institution Press.

O'Neill, J. 2011. *The Growth Map: Economic Opportunity in the BRICs and Beyond.* Portfolio/Penguin.

———, and A. Terzi. 2014. "Changing Trade Patterns, Unchanging European and Global Governance." Bruegel Working Paper 2014/02.

Organisation for Economic Co-operation and Development (OECD). 2002. *Measuring the Information Economy.* Paris.

———. 2009. "The Jobs Crisis: What Are the Implications for Employment and Social Policy?" *OECD Employment Outlook.*

———. 2012a. *OECD Employment Outlook.*

———. 2012b. *OECD Internet Economy Outlook.*

———. 2014. *Economic Policy Reforms: Going for Growth.*

Orlowski, L. T. 2001. *Transition and Growth in Post-Communist Countries: The Ten-Year Experience.* Cheltenham, United Kingdom; Edward Elgar.

Osborne, G. 2014. "What the Economic Pessimists Are Missing." *Wall Street Journal*, April 10.

Otker-Robe, I., and A. M. Podpiera. 2013. "The Social Impact of Financial Crises: Evidence from the Global Financial Crisis." Policy Research Working Paper 6703, World Bank, Washington.

Otto, G., G. Voss, and L. Willard. 2001. "Understanding OECD Output Correlations." RBA Research Discussion Paper 2001–05, Reserve Bank of Australia, Sydney.

Oudiz, G., and J. Sachs. 1985. "International Policy Coordination in Dynamic Macroeconomic Models," in *International Economic Policy Coordination*, edited by W. H. Buiter and R. C. Marston, 274–330.

Pagan, A. R., and K. A. Sossounov. 2003. "A Simple Framework for Analyzing Bull and Bear Markets." *Journal of Applied Econometrics* 18 (1): 23–46.

Paletta, D., and M. Phillips. 2011. "S&P Strips U.S. of Top Credit Rating." *Wall Street Journal*, August 6.

Panizza, U., and F. Presbitero. 2013. "Public Debt and Economic Growth in Advanced Economies: A Survey." *Swiss Journal of Economics and Statistics* 149 (2): 175–204.

Papell, D. H., and R. Prodan. 2011. "The Statistical Behavior of GDP after Financial Crises and Severe Recessions." Working Paper, University of Houston, Houston, Texas.

Parikh, S. H. 2013. "A Secular View of Assets: Surfing the Wedge." *PIMCO Asset Allocation Focus*, June 11.

Paulson, H. M. 2011. *On the Brink: Inside the Race to Stop the Collapse of the Global Financial System*. New York: Business Plus.

Perotti, R. 2012. "The 'Austerity Myth': Gain without Pain?" in *Fiscal Policy after the Financial Crisis*. Cambridge, Massachusetts: National Bureau of Economic Research, 307–54.

Perri, F., and V. Quadrini. 2011. "International Recessions." NBER Working Paper 17201, National Bureau of Economic Research, Cambridge, Massachusetts.

Porter, E. 2013. "Economists Agree: Solutions are Elusive." Economic Scene, *New York Times*, April 23.

Prasad, E. 2014. "The Fed Is Not to Blame for Turmoil in Emerging Markets." *Financial Times*, February 12.

Queralto, A. 2013. "A Model of Slow Recoveries from Financial Crises." International Finance Discussion Paper 1097, Federal Reserve Board.

Rabobank. 2013. "The Mexican 1982 Debt Crisis." Economic Report.

Rajan, R. G. 2011. *Fault Lines: How Hidden Fractures Still Threaten the World Economy*. Princeton, New Jersey: Princeton University Press.

———. 2012. "The True Lessons of the Recession." *Foreign Affairs* 91 (3): 69–79.

———. 2014. "Competitive Monetary Easing: Is It Yesterday Once More?" Remarks at the Brookings Institution, April 10.

Ramey, G., and V. A. Ramey. 1995. "Cross-Country Evidence on the Link between Volatility and Growth." *American Economic Review* 85 (5): 1138–51.

Ramey, V. A. 2011. "Identifying Government Spending Shocks: It's All in the Timing." *Quarterly Journal of Economics* 126 (1): 1–50.

Ratha, D. 2005. "Remittances: A Lifeline for Development." *Finance and Development* 42 (4).

Reifschneider, D., W. Wascher, and D. Wilcox. 2013. "Aggregate Supply in the United States; Recent Developments and Implications for the Conduct of Monetary Policy." Federal Reserve Board Finance and Economics Discussion Series 77.

Reinhart, C. M., and K. S. Rogoff. 2008. "Is the 2007 U.S. Subprime Crisis So Different? An International Historical Comparison." *American Economic Review* 98 (2): 339–44.

———. 2009. *This Time Is Different: Eight Centuries of Financial Folly*. Princeton, New Jersey: Princeton University Press.

———. 2010a. "Growth in a Time of Debt." *American Economic Review: Papers & Proceedings* 100: 573–78.

———. 2010b. "Growth in a Time of Debt." NBER Working Paper 15639, National Bureau of Economic Research, Cambridge, Massachusetts.

————. 2011. "A Decade of Debt." NBER Working Paper 16827, National Bureau of Economic Research, Cambridge, Massachusetts.

————. 2012a. "This Time Is Different, Again? The US Five Years after the Onset of Subprime," *VoxEU*, October 22.

————. 2012b. "Five Years after Crisis, No Normal Recovery." *Bloomberg*, April 2.

————. 2012c. "Sorry, U.S. Recoveries Really Aren't Different." *Bloomberg*, October 15.

————. 2014. "Recovery from the Financial Crises: Evidence from 100 Episodes." NBER Working Paper 19823, National Bureau of Economic Research, Cambridge, Massachusetts.

Reinhart, C., and V. R. Reinhart. 2010. "After the Fall." *Proceedings—Economic Policy Symposium*, Jackson Hole, Federal Reserve Bank of Kansas City, 17–60.

Reuters. 2010. "S&P Downgrades Greece Ratings into Junk Status." April 27.

————. 2012. "Cyprus Seeks EU Bailout for Banks Budget." June 25.

Robinson, K. 2013. "Savings and Loan Crisis." federalreservehistory.org.

Rodrik, D. 2012. *The Globalization Paradox: Democracy and the Future of the World Economy.* New York: Norton.

————. 2013. "The Past, Present, and Future of Economic Growth." Global Citizen Foundation Working Paper 1.

————. 2014. "Death by Finance." *Project Syndicate*, February 10.

————. 2015. "Economists vs. Economics." *Project Syndicate*, September 10.

Rodrik, D., and A. Subramanian. 2014. "Emerging Markets' Victimhood Narrative." Bloomberg .com, January 31.

Rogoff, K. S. 2002a. "Press Conference on the *World Economic Outlook*." April 18. http://www.imf .org/external/index.htm.

————. 2002b. "The Recession That Almost Was." *Financial Times*, April 5.

————. 2008. "Inflation Is Now the Lesser Evil." *Project Syndicate*, December 2.

————. 2011. "The Second Great Contraction." *Project Syndicate*, August 2.

————. 2013. "What's the Problem with Advanced Economies?" *Project Syndicate*, December 4.

Rogoff, K. S., D. Robinson, and T. Bayoumi. 2002. "Was It a Global Recession?" *World Economic Outlook.* Washington: International Monetary Fund, April.

Romer, C. 2009a. "Lessons from the Great Depression for Economic Recovery in 2009." Presented at the Brookings Institution, Washington, March 9.

————. 2009b. "The Economic Crisis: Causes, Policies, and Outlook." Testimony before the Joint Economic Committee of the U.S. Congress, April 30.

————. 2013. "Lessons from the Great Depression for Policy Today." Teach-In on the Great Depression and World War II, University of Oklahoma.

Romer, C., and D. Romer. 2002. "The Evolution of Economic Understanding and Postwar Stabilization Policy." Federal Reserve Bank of Kansas City *Proceedings:* 11–78.

————. 2004. "A New Measure of Monetary Shocks: Derivation and Implications." *American Economic Review* 94 (4): 1055–84.

Rose, A. K., and M. M. Spiegel. 2010. "The Causes and Consequences of the 2008 Crisis: International Linkages and American Exposure." *Pacific Economic Review* 15: 340–63.

————. 2011. "Cross-Country Causes and Consequences of the Crisis: An Update." *European Economic Review* 55 (3): 309–24.

Rotemberg, J. J. 2013. "Patience after Accusations of Error: 100 Years of Monetary Policy at the U.S. Federal Reserve." Harvard Business School Working Paper, Cambridge, Massachusetts.

Rothstein, J. 2012. "The Labor Market Four Years into the Crisis: Assessing Structural Explanations." *ILR Review* 65 (3): 467–500.

Roubini, N. 2008. "The Perfect Storm of a Global Recession." *Project Syndicate*, August 13.

———. 2009. "Green Shoots or Yellow Weeds." *Forbes*, May 14.

———. 2011. "That Stalling Feeling." *Project Syndicate*, June 21.

Roubini, N., and S. Mihm. 2011. *Crisis Economics: A Crash Course in the Future of Finance.* New York: Penguin Books.

Rowen, H. 1974. "Experts Hedge on '74 Outlook: Oil Crisis May Trigger Worldwide Recession." *Washington Post*, January 13.

———. 1989. "Warning—Global Recession Ahead." *Washington Post*, April 6.

Sachs, J. D. 2008. "A Sustainable Recovery." *Project Syndicate*, November 30.

———. 2009. "The Economic Need for Stable Policies, Not a Stimulus." *Scientific American*, February 16.

———. 2015. "Paul Krugman and the Obama Recovery," Project Syndicate, January 5.

Sahadi, J. 2008. "Bailout Is Law." *CNN Money*, October 3.

Samuelson, R. J. 2012. "Why the Recovery Is Feeble," *Washington Post*, November 25.

———. 2013. "Times Have Changed, and Our Economic Vocabulary Can't Keep Up." *Washington Post*, December.

———. 2014. "The Recovery: Déjà Vu All Over?" *Washington Post*, February 26.

Sargent, T. J. 2002. "Commentary: The Evolution of Economic Understanding and Postwar Stabilization Policy." Federal Reserve Bank of Kansas City *Proceedings* 2002: 79–94.

———, and N. Wallace. 1975. "'Rational' Expectations, the Optimal Monetary Instrument, and the Optimal Money Supply Rule." *Journal of Political Economy* 83 (2): 241–54.

Sensier, M., D. R. Osborn, and N. Ocal. 2002. "Asymmetric Interest Rate Effects for the UK Economy." *Oxford Bulletin of Economics and Statistics* 64 (4): 315–39.

Shabecoff, P. 1975. "The Question in Capital: Recession or Depression?" *New York Times*, March 7.

Sharma, R. 2012. *Breakout Nations: In Pursuit of the Next Economic Miracles.* New York: Norton.

Sharma, R. 2015. A Global Recession May Be Brewing in China. *Wall Street Journal,* August 16.

Shiller, R. J. 2009. "The Ghost in the Recovery Machine." *Project Syndicate*, November 13.

Shin, H. S. 2009. "Reflections on Northern Rock: The Bank Run That Heralded the Global Financial Crisis." *Journal of Economic Perspectives* 23 (1): 101–19.

Sichel, D. E. 1994. "Inventories and the Three Phases of the Business Cycle." *Journal of Business & Economic Statistics* 12 (3): 269–77.

Sidel, R., D. Enrich, and D. Fitzpatrick. 2008. "WaMu Is Seized, Sold Off to J.P. Morgan, in Largest Failure in U.S. Banking History." *Wall Street Journal*, September 26.

Sims, J. 2013. "Latin American Debt Crisis of the 1980s." federalreservehistory.org.

Sinai, A. 1992 "Financial and Real Business Cycles." *Eastern Economic Journal* 18 (1): 1–54.

———. 2010. "The Business Cycle in a Changing Economy: Conceptualization, Measurement, Dating." *American Economic Review: Papers & Proceedings* 100: 25–29.

Solomou, S. 1998. *Economic Cycles since 1870: Long Cycles and Business Cycles since 1870.* Manchester University Press.

Sommerville, G. 2008. "U.S. Seizes Fannie, Freddie, Aims to Calm Markets." *Reuters*, September 7.

Sorkin, A. S. 2011. *Too Big to Fail: The Inside Story of How Wall Street and Washington Fought to Save the Financial System and Themselves.* New York: Penguin Group.

Spence, M. 2011. *The Next Convergence: The Future of Economic Growth in a Multispeed World.* New York: Farrar, Straus, and Giroux.

———. 2014. "Overshooting in Emerging Markets." *Project Syndicate*, February 20.

Spilimbergo A., S. Symansky, O. Blanchard, and C. Cottarelli. 2008. "Fiscal Policy for the Crisis." IMF Staff Position Note 08/01, International Monetary Fund, Washington.

Stein, J. C. 2013. "Yield-Oriented Investors and the Monetary Transmission Mechanism." Remarks presented at Banking, Liquidity, and Monetary Policy Symposium Sponsored by the Center for Financial Studies in Honor of Raghuram Rajan, September 26.

Stiglitz, J. E. 2009. "Developing Countries and the Global Crisis." *Project Syndicate*, April 6.

Stock, J. H., and M. W. Watson. 2005. "Understanding Changes In International Business Cycle Dynamics." *Journal of the European Economic Association* 3 (5): 968–1006.

———. 2012. "Disentangling the Channels of the 2007–09 Recession." *Brookings Papers on Economic Activity* (Spring): 81–156.

Stone, C. 2013. "Testimony of Chad Stone," Speech delivered at the Center on Budget and Policy Priorities, September 24.

Summers, L. 2009. "Remarks of L. H. Summers, Director of the National Economic Council Responding to an Historic Economic Crisis: The Obama Program." Brookings Institution, March 13.

———. 2013. "Why Stagnation Might Prove to Be the New Normal." *Financial Times*, December 15.

———. 2014. "What the World Must Do to Kickstart Growth." *Financial Times*, April 6.

Swagel, P. 2009. "The Financial Crisis: An Inside View," *Brookings Papers on Economic Activity* 40 (1): 1–78.

———. 2013. "Financial Crisis Reading List." *New York Times*, July 15.

Swanson, E., and J. C. Williams. 2013. "Measuring the Effect of the Zero Lower Bound on Medium- and Longer-Term Interest Rates." Federal Reserve Bank of San Francisco.

Tapsoba, S. J. A. 2009. "Trade Intensity and Business Synchronicity in Africa." *Journal of African Economics* 18 (2): 287–318.

Taylor, J. B. 2012. "An Unusually Weak Recovery as Usually Defined." *Economics One* (blog), October 26.

———. 2013a. "International Monetary Policy Coordination: Past, Present, and Future." BIS Working Paper 437, Bank for International Settlements, Basel.

———. 2013b. "With Better Policy, the Recovery Could Have Been V-Shaped." *Economics One* (blog), September 16.

———. 2013c. "Causes of the Financial Crisis and the Slow Recovery: A 10-Year Perspective." SIPR Discussion Paper 13-026.

———. 2014a. "The Role of Policy in the Great Recession and the Weak Recovery." *American Economic Review, Papers and Proceedings* 104 (5): 61–66.

———. 2014b. "The Economic Hokum of 'Secular Stagnation'," *Wall Street Journal*, January 1.

Temin, P. 1976. *Did Monetary Factors Cause the Great Depression?* New York: Norton.

———. 1991. *Lessons from the Great Depression*. Cambridge, Massachusetts: MIT Press.

Terrones, M. E., A. Scott, and P. Kannan. 2009. "From Recession to Recovery: How Soon and How Strong?" *World Economic Outlook*. Washington: International Monetary Fund, April.

Time Magazine. 1978. "Business: Yes, We Have No Bananas," December 11.

Totaro, L., and E. Ross-Thomas. 2011. "Italy, Spain Ratings Cut by Fitch; Belgium Is Put Under Review by Moody's." *Bloomberg*, October 7.

Turner, A. 2012. *Economics after the Crisis: Objectives and Means*. Lionel Robbins Lectures. Cambridge, Massachusetts: MIT Press.

Tylecote, A. 1992. "Why World Recession Has a Long Time to Run." *Guardian*, September 12.

Uchitelle, L. 1991. "Plea by U.S. on Rate Cut Is Rejected." *New York Times*, April 29.

United Nations. 1990. "United Nations Iraq-Kuwait Observation Mission." Resolution 678.

USA Today. 1996. "1991 Gulf War Chronology." September 3.

U.S. Department of the Treasury. 2013. "The Financial Crisis Five Years Later: Response, Reform, and Progress." Treasury Note, Washington.

van Dijk, M. 2013. "The Social Costs of Financial Crises." Working Paper, Erasmus University, Rotterdam.

Végh, C. A., and G. Vuletin. 2013. "The Road to Redemption: Policy Response to Crises in Latin America." Paper presented at the 14th Jacques Polak Annual Research Conference, November 7–8, Washington.

Voice of America. 2009. "Study: 2009 Likely to See Weakest Global Economy in Half-Century." November 1.

Volcker, P. A. 1978. *Rediscovery of the Business Cycle.* The Free Press.

Walker, A. 2009. "What Is a Global Recession?" BBC News, February 10.

Wallop, H. 2007. "Northern Rock Shares Crash as Customers Queue" *Telegraph*, September 14.

Walsh, C. E. 1993. "What Caused the 1990–1991 Recession?" Federal Reserve Bank of San Francisco *Economic Review* 2: 33–48.

Washington Post. 1994. "After the Worldwide Recession." Editorial, December 22.

Wearden, G. 2008. "British Government Unveils £37bn Banking Bail-out Plan." *Guardian*, October 13.

Weber, S. 1997. "The End of the Business Cycle?" *Foreign Affairs* 76 (4): 65–82.

Werning, I. 2012. "Managing a Liquidity Trap: Monetary and Fiscal Policy." Unpublished, Massachusetts Institute of Technology, Cambridge, Massachusetts.

Wessel, D. 2010. *In FED We Trust: Ben Bernanke's War on the Great Panic.* New York: Crown Publishers.

Wilkinson, M. 1982. "Prospects for Global Economic Revival Are Worsening." *Financial Times*, September 13.

Williamson, J. 2005. "The Potential of International Policy Coordination." Peterson Institute for International Economics.

Williamson, S. 2013. "The Balance Sheet and the Fed's Future." *New Monetarist Economics* (blog), March 10.

Wolf, M. 2009. "Why the G20 Must Focus on Sustaining Demand." *Financial Times*, March 10.

———. 2010a. "What We Can Learn from Japan's Decades of Trouble." *Financial Times*, January 12.

———. 2010b. "What the World Must Do to Sustain Its Convalescence." *Financial Times*, February 3.

———. 2010c. "Why Plans for Early Fiscal Tightening Carry Global Risks." *Financial Times*, June 17.

———. 2013a. "Austerity in the Eurozone and the UK: Kill or Cure?" *Financial Times*, May 23.

———. 2013b. "How Austerity Has Failed." Nybooks.com, July 11.

———. 2014. "We Are Trapped in a Cycle of Credit Booms, *Financial Times*, October 7.

Woodford, M. 2010. "Financial Intermediation and Macroeconomic Analysis." *Journal of Economic Perspectives* 24 (4): 21–44.

———. 2012. "Methods of Policy Accommodation at the Interest-Rate Lower Bound." 2012 Economic Policy Symposium, Jackson Hole, Wyoming.

World Bank. 2010. *The MDGs After the Crisis: Global Monitoring Report 2010.* Washington.

———. 2011. "Global Development Horizons 2011—Multipolarity: The New Global Economy." Washington.

———. 2013. "World Development Report on Jobs." Washington.

Wynne, M. A. 2011. "The Sluggish Recovery from the Great Recession: Why There Is No 'V' Rebound This Time." Federal Reserve Bank of Dallas *Economic Letter* 6 (9): 1–4.

Yellen, J. 2013a. "Panel Discussion on 'Monetary Policy: Many Targets, Many Instruments. Where Do We Stand?'" Remarks at International Monetary Fund Conference on Rethinking Macro Policy II, Washington.

———. 2013b. "Challenges Confronting Monetary Policy." Speech delivered at the 2013 National Association for Business Economics Conference.

Yilmaz, K. 2010. "International Business Cycle Spillovers." CEPR Working Paper 7966, Centre for Economic Policy Research, London.

Zandi, M. 2013. "The Impact of Political Uncertainty on Jobs and the Economy." Testimony before the U.S. Senate Budget Committee.

Zarnovitz, V. 1992. *Business Cycles: Theory, History, Indicators and Forecasting.* Chicago: University of Chicago Press for National Bureau of Economic Research.

Credits

Index

CPSIA information can be obtained
at www.ICGtesting.com
Printed in the USA
LVOW01*0709051215
464523LV00005BA/6/P